Writing for Academic Success

Gail Craswell
& Megan Poore

2nd Edition

SAGE

Los Angeles | London | New Delhi
Singapore | Washington DC

First published 2005

Reprinted 2015

SAGE Publications Ltd
1 Oliver's Yard
55 City Road
London EC1Y 1SP

SAGE Publications Inc.
2455 Teller Road
Thousand Oaks, California 91320

SAGE Publications India Pvt Ltd
B 1/I 1 Mohan Cooperative Industrial Area
Mathura Road
New Delhi 110 044

SAGE Publications Asia-Pacific Pte Ltd
3 Church Street
#10-04 Samsung Hub
Singapore 049483

Library of Congress Control Number: 2011923532

British Library Cataloguing in Publication data

A catalogue record for this book is available from the British Library

ISBN 978-0-85702-927-0
ISBN 978-0-85702-928-7 (pbk)

Typeset by C&M Digitals (P) Ltd, Chennai, India
Printed in Great Britain by CPI Group (UK) Ltd, Croydon, CR0 4YY
Printed on paper from sustainable resources

Contents

About the Authors

Gail Craswell was Senior Adviser to Graduate Students at the Australian National University. Gail developed, organised and taught on an extensive, academic and professional skills training program for research students, and did likewise with a preparatory program for international graduates. Her consultations with graduate students on their coursework genres, theses, presentations and publications afforded considerable insight into the complexity of graduates' communication challenges within and across disciplines. In 2008 she was funded to produce an online thesis-writing course for research students, and in 2010 received an Outstanding Service Award. She has published a number of papers on aspects of graduate study, research and academic writing. Gail holds a doctorate in English from the University of Queensland. She has recently retired.

Megan Poore is an Assistant Professor in Teacher Education at the University of Canberra where she works closely with graduate students in preparing them for teaching and learning in digital environments. She is known for championing best practice approaches to integrating digital technologies into the university and schools environments, and this includes developing both strong digital pedagogies as well as sound approaches to risk management. She has also worked as an academic skills adviser and an educational designer at the Australian National University, giving her a unique understanding of the issues that confront students and staff in the integration of digital technologies into their every day study and work practices. Megan holds a PhD in Social Anthropology from the Australian National University.

List of Figures

List of Tables

Introduction

Every new level of study is a new learning experience. This is self-evident as regards learning new content, but not so in terms of learning how to effectively communicate your research to lecturers, supervisors, examiners and publishers. The 2nd edition of *Writing for Academic Success*, which has been fully revised to accommodate a significant amount of new material about working effectively online in different contexts, and with digital technologies, is a comprehensive, practical guide designed to help you acquire the communicative rigour required of graduate-level writing. The intended audience is graduate students, either in taught courses and/or conducting research. Still, parts of this guide could be useful for later-year undergraduates, although challenges specific to undergraduate writing are not addressed. While the primary focus is on academic writing, issues unique to presenting, publishing and raising your profile online are given independent treatment in the final two chapters.

New learning takes place in a particular context, with all communication being influenced by that context. This context can be thought of as the academic social context in which you are writing, presenting or publishing – what may be thought of as your 'discipline'. As you may be engaged in cross-disciplinary or interdisciplinary study or research, we use the term 'disciplinary' broadly to refer to any academic social context.

Because disciplinary or course requirements exert considerable influence on the perceived appropriateness of end products (for example, submitted papers or theses), it is difficult to write or present well without understanding these requirements, including the variations of practice within disciplines or courses. We have consequently emphasized repeatedly the need to ground all advice in disciplinary/course contexts, to follow advice, written or otherwise, given by lecturers and supervisors on producing texts, and to consult with them frequently.

Nevertheless, not all academic writing practices seen to constitute good practice are disciplinary or course-dependent. Conciseness in writing is valued in general by the academic community, as is treating information critically, attending to audience needs, consistency in the mechanics of academic writing, careful referencing of sources, coherent development of texts, sound logic and evidential support in argument, and so forth. Material of this type is covered in Chapters 2, 3, 4 and 5.

Other aspects of context may also feature prominently in graduate communication. For example, disciplinary influences on style and language are much reduced where there is a broad audience for, say, a conference paper, or with publications in journals targeting a more general audience. While audience needs are a crucial consideration in all academic communication, at times they exert primary influence on both the treatment of information and the language, style and formatting of a paper or talk.

Aims, limitations and organization of the book

The overall aim of this book is to ease the path towards successful communication of your study and research. It is in this sense a practical, developmental guide. The usefulness of the book lies in your following through on suggestions and testing their appropriateness in the context of monitoring your own practices, attempting the exercises or following step-by-step procedures where relevant, applying strategies in practice, and opening up conversations with lecturers, supervisors, conference convenors and editors or publishers where uncertainties remain.

We make no claim to either comprehensive coverage of all types of graduate writing or detailed coverage of all the varied and complex communication challenges graduates encounter, both of which would be impossible. Nevertheless, much of the material covered in the first four chapters will apply in most writing situations, and the different types of self-help strategies presented throughout the book should prove useful if you encounter types of writing not covered here.

The book's underlying organization mirrors a developmental movement from consideration of general issues in academic writing and communication in the first four chapters, to coverage of issues specific to different types of writing, presentations and publications in subsequent chapters. In effect, the first four, foundation chapters engage a broad range of strategies that underpin all types of graduate writing and communication; hence the frequent references back to them in the chapters that follow.

Effective management of your writing environment will reduce stress and improve your confidence and efficiency. Chapter 1 explores multiple strategies towards this end, including strategies for networking, managing yourself and your writing in the context of life-commitments and goals, exploiting electronic tools to increase productivity, handling communication challenges (cross-cultural and digital), enabling positive communication with lecturers and supervisors, and developing capacity with mobile technologies.

No amount of effort during writing will result in well-written papers without careful preparation in the research and reading phases: you need to ensure your foundations are solid. This involves understanding the purposes of the type of writing (genre) you now have to produce, mastering disciplinary writing practices, defining task-specific goals before proceeding to reading and data-gathering, treating information critically, managing the reading load to cut down on unproductive reading, accessing quality sources, both print and electronic, and improving information retrieval to reduce frustration when writing, all of which Chapter 2 explores.

Chapter 3 provides an opportunity to review the essentials of academic writing with a view to improving or changing practice if needs be in a range of contexts including the mechanics of academic writing, referencing and plagiarism, and key aspects of academic style. As it is essential that readers do not become confused or lost, that they can follow development of your ideas and access your important insights, Chapter 4 explores principles of sound structure at different levels of the text to aid structural coherence. (Issues specific to structuring different types of writing are discussed at appropriate points in context.)

Chapters 5 and 6 discuss in detail prominent types of written assessment in many graduate courses: research essays, book or article reviews and online writing (blogs and wikis). Chapter 7 turns to coursework exams to consider effective revision and writing strategies for different types of exam papers. Chapter 8 enters the challenging terrain of the literature review and Chapter 9 continues with a detailed probing of other graduate writing genres: reports and research proposals.

Chapter 10 is devoted exclusively to thesis writing, both shorter and longer theses. Chapter 11 moves to full consideration of the topic of presenting. This chapter initially considers different types of presentations – tutorials, seminars, conferences and posters; it then engages a range of issues integral to the planning, formatting, rehearsal and delivery of a presentation. Chapter 12 takes up issues specific to publishing and raising your profile, which is particularly important if you wish to continue with a research career.

Terminology and other practices

We have tried to keep the terminology in the book as simple as possible. This means you may find it does not necessarily fit the understanding current in your institution (for example, under some systems, course = unit, or subject, and programme = course). Here, the term 'course' refers to the degree in which you are enrolled, and is sometimes used interchangeably with 'degree';

'subject' refers to a specific unit you are taking within, say, a taught course; and programme is used to refer to such as a 'doctoral programme'.

We make only three distinctions as regards graduate degree structures: degrees by coursework or taught courses (no research component), degrees by coursework and research, and degrees by research only. These distinctions do not allow for the wonderful array of titles given to different graduate degrees or the variable structures of degrees, but they are recognizable distinctions easy to apply to your own situation.

All identifying signifiers have been removed from illustrative materials taken from graduate student writing. To preserve students' anonymity, '[reference]' is substituted for actual details of source references, and [X,Y, Z and so forth] for countries, authors, etc. named in the writing.

1

Managing your Writing Environment

 developmental objectives

By applying the strategies, doing the exercises and following the procedural steps in this chapter, you should be able to:

- Take a proactive approach to reducing the stress that accompanies academic writing.
- Learn how to network for support.
- Identify strategies and online tools to increase productivity and manage more efficiently yourself and your writing.
- Ensure results-oriented communication with your lecturers and supervisors.
- Understand key cross-cultural challenges of writing and communication, why these exist and how to address them.
- Develop capacity with mobile technologies and make informed decisions about using commercially hosted web services.

It is common for graduates to experience ups and downs with academic writing and communication. Feelings of confidence, excitement, self-doubt, disinterest, frustration, lack of motivation, isolation and so forth may alternate, such mood swings being typical rather than unusual. This chapter covers a broad range of management strategies designed to reduce stress and improve the quality of your writing environment.

Effective self-management

Effective self-management for academic writing invites a variety of strategies. We begin with the importance of establishing networks.

Networking for support

While networking requires effort, it can be worth the investment of your valuable time, particularly if you are enrolled in a longer research degree. These networking strategies should help alleviate stress while contributing to a greater sense of integration in the academic community at large.

Generating peer support: local, national and international

Students in your course or research group can be an excellent support resource, so be proactive in making yourself known to them. Make contact too with the graduate student organization within your institution, if there is one. Such organizations usually provide a range of social and academic support, have useful online resources, are often advocates for resolution of issues of concern to graduates, and may represent graduates' interests on important institutional committees. It is similar with national sites, such as The National Postgraduate Committee (UK), the Council of Australian Postgraduate Associations or the National Association of Graduate-Professional Students (USA).

There are numbers of international graduate student and dissertation support sites on the Internet. Many enquiries about writing are posted on such sites, as is copious information about 'surviving' graduate studies. Even joining a chat group with other graduates sharing your interests can lend support – discuss this possibility with peers and academics in your area. Well-established and useful sites with an international reach include The Association for Support of Graduate Students, Graduate Junction: the worldwide community of graduate researchers and Vitae: Realising the potential of researchers.

If you do not know about it, check out Jorge Cham's 'Piled higher and deeper: a graduate student comic strip collection', which will afford light relief and a welcome sense of solidarity in knowing that, whatever your problem, others have been there before you!

Identifying institutional resources available for developmental assistance

Thoroughly explore your institution's website to find out what supplementary assistance is on offer for study, research and writing. Search across institutions too as you may locate the precise materials you need on another institution's site. Academic skills, learning or writing centres of different institutions in different countries often provide electronic resources specific to graduate writing and communication that could be useful. Check with your lecturer/supervisor that advice provided is sound in their view, if you are unsure.

6

Making use of visiting scholars and other disciplinary experts

Introduce yourself to visiting scholars and attend relevant conferences/seminars they give while at your institution. Where research interests coincide, a visiting scholar may be willing to give advice and even provide feedback on a draft. You could also benefit from contact with other disciplinary experts.

case study example

box 1.1 Other disciplinary experts can be a valuable resource

A doctoral student realized when writing up that there was a gap in her reading (not so unusual). She needed an overview of one aspect of a famous philosopher's work about which she knew little, as she was not a Philosophy student. A quick database search turned up literally hundreds of potential sources that left her, as she said, 'totally depressed'. So she searched for an expert in nineteenth-century philosophy, contacted him, explained her situation and asked him if he could refer her to an appropriate source for what she needed. This he did. In her own words: 'This saved me heaps of time – there were just so many sources – really put me on the right track with my reading.'

Cultivating understanding of close ones

Colleagues, friends and family can be excellent sources of support if you cultivate their understanding of your study commitments. Sometimes, however, it can be difficult for those closest to you to accept what appears to them to be inflexibility, or even selfishness on your part, when you are unavailable for a social invitation or a request for help. As this type of dilemma is not unusual, you may need to work at gaining more understanding from those close to you (see → the 'Balanced self-management exercise' below, which includes relationship goals in time management). Tell them well in advance that there will be times when you will not be available, and remind them of this when such occasions arise. Perhaps, too, keep reminding them, and yourself, that whatever the duration of your studies, the period will come to an end.

key points

By identifying peak writing periods in advance (see the next section), you will be able to give partners, family and friends ample warning.

Working on your inner resources

It is not easy to find the right words to express complex ideas, to structure or organize material on the scale of, say, a dissertation, a long report or essay, or to develop subtle arguments and discussions. Writing is an intellectually demanding task and one that rarely goes smoothly. As one student said: 'Writing is a matter of thinking writing, thinking writing, thinking writing – it is never just writing.'

There will be difficult spots. At such times there can be a tendency to be harshly self-critical, even to resurrect inner saboteurs ('I've always been hopeless at writing'), to use negative reinforcers that cement a sense of failure. It is then necessary to work on your own resources with a view to positively reinforcing your efforts, to recall past and present academic successes, to be patient with yourself, to remember that the act of writing is always about learning to write (it is little different with presenting), to genuinely value your own efforts and to visualize that degree certificate in your hand – it will happen.

Building your online networks

Having good relationships with your face-to-face research group or coursework colleagues is important, but so too is drawing support from online communities and contacts. Use Facebook and other social networking services not only for sharing experiences and keeping in regular touch with friends and family, but also for developing collegial and professional networks in your discipline area. These networks need not be limited by space and time and you could find some of the contacts you make extremely valuable later on. You might also consider starting up a Facebook group with your local 'study buddies' or one based on your field of research.

If Facebook does not appeal, then other social networking services can prove highly valuable. Ning.com is widely considered the standard for group social networking but it charges for most of its services. However, there are a number of free group services available, all with excellent functionality, including discussion forums, chat and instant messaging (IM), video and photosharing, blogs, event announcements, subgroups and more. Just Google 'free alternatives to Ning' and you will find a number of such services.

Pre-planning: maximizing effort

Maximizing effort entails effective self-management in all sectors of your life. It is near impossible to maximize effort in terms of communication activities in a course of study or research if other significant areas of your life are under strain.

exercise: balanced self-management

Step 1

Review closely the 'The self-management matrix' in Figure 1.1. Thinking about the implications of these four quadrants for your own situation can be illuminating, particularly if you are writing a thesis in a research-only degree where there are no course deadlines to meet.

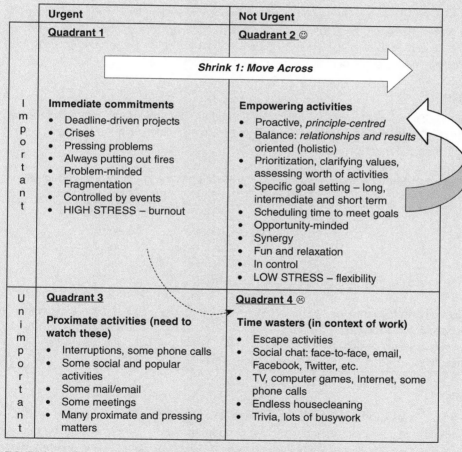

	Urgent	Not Urgent
Important	**Quadrant 1** *Shrink 1: Move Across* → **Immediate commitments** • Deadline-driven projects • Crises • Pressing problems • Always putting out fires • Problem-minded • Fragmentation • Controlled by events • HIGH STRESS – burnout	**Quadrant 2** ☺ **Empowering activities** • Proactive, *principle-centred* • Balance: *relationships and results* oriented (holistic) • Prioritization, clarifying values, assessing worth of activities • Specific goal setting – long, intermediate and short term • Scheduling time to meet goals • Opportunity-minded • Synergy • Fun and relaxation • In control • LOW STRESS – flexibility
Unimportant	**Quadrant 3** **Proximate activities (need to watch these)** • Interruptions, some phone calls • Some social and popular activities • Some mail/email • Some meetings • Many proximate and pressing matters	**Quadrant 4** ☹ **Time wasters (in context of work)** • Escape activities • Social chat: face-to-face, email, Facebook, Twitter, etc. • TV, computer games, Internet, some phone calls • Endless housecleaning • Trivia, lots of busywork

FIGURE 1.1   The self-management matrix (adapted from 'The time management matrix' Covey, 2004: 151)

(Continued)

Effective self-management means avoiding the trap of Quadrant 1 (all too easy for busy graduates), of being driven to the time-wasting distractions of Quadrant 4 because of Quadrant 1 pressures and stress, or of attributing undue importance to the activities of Quadrant 3, which need to be monitored closely. It means training yourself to reside comfortably in Quadrant 2 as much as possible, for as Covey says:

> The way you spend your time is a result of the way you see your time and the way you really see your priorities. If your priorities grow out of a principle centre and a personal mission, if they are deeply planted in your heart and in your mind, you will see Quadrant II as a natural exciting place to invest your time. (2004: 158)

Work towards embedding your study or research priorities as a set of balanced life activities. Generate expectations focused on preserving and enhancing relationships and on achieving results. Develop a clear idea of the results you desire in your life, and organize and execute priorities aimed at these results.

Step 2

Detail all regular commitments, and include prioritized weekly goals in terms of desired results. Do this for each of the four sectors tabulated below, with the aim of achieving balanced self-management:

Research/Study/Writing	Work/ Teaching	Relationships	Individual/Personal Development
		Partner? Children? Other family members? Friends?	Physical Mental Emotional Spiritual
(Detail priorities and specific goals for the week in terms of desired results)			(It is important not to exclude your private/ personal needs)

Step 3

Set up a **weekly timetable**. Build in flexibility – allow for (at least in your mind) the unanticipated 'urgent' of Quadrant 1. A scheduled activity might need to be passed over because of a higher value (for example, a sick child). Better still, is a **yearly diary or calendar** in which you can detail goals, and activities to meet those goals, week-by-week.

Step 4

Set up a timeline that gives you an overview of your whole course (whether a research or coursework degree):

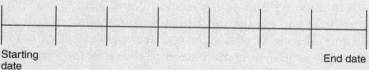

Starting
date

End date

Mark along the timeline **priority dates** (for example, due dates for items of coursework assessment, or dates for seminar/conference papers, progress review papers, thesis outlines or chapters, and so on). As these become known, include in your yearly calendar advance deadlines and dates for preparatory activities to meet those deadlines.

Exploit your natural biorhythms

On a more immediate level, individual circumstances, course requirements, personal preferences and personal peak energy flows can influence when you write and how you organize your writing time and other communication activities. Some students concentrate better in shorter periods, taking frequent short breaks. Others prefer longer writing periods with fewer but longer breaks. Some work a 9 to 5 day, or stay up half the night and sleep late. Some see no choice but to write at night after full-time employment and/or when the children have gone to bed. Maximize effort by harnessing your natural biorhythms to best effect, reserving peak energy periods for the harder intellectual tasks of writing.

Regularize your writing pattern

Whatever your circumstances, try to establish a regular writing pattern that is viable for you, allows you to write when you are likely to be most productive, given your various commitments, and that can be adjusted when necessary. Graduates have reported that regularizing the writing pattern helps in these ways:

- Reduces the anxiety often associated with the 'I'll write when I can' approach, an approach that easily leads to writing being delayed.
- Encourages thinking through the setting up of a detailed writing schedule.
- Provides a stronger sense of working steadily towards completion of the writing task.
- Increases confidence in completing the task given your many and varied commitments.
- Allows you to forewarn family and friends of your unavailability at certain times, which in turn reduces household stress.

Boost your motivation

Motivation is another issue frequently raised by graduates. Motivation levels will fluctuate. But your inner 'motivator' may at times need a full recharge. Perhaps your interest in your project is depleted – you feel bored, or your confidence has plunged and you seriously doubt your potential, or you are frustrated because you cannot get the help you need, or a troubled relationship is claiming all your attention, or you are oppressed by financial struggle and so forth. Any one, or a combination of these factors, can make you feel flat, not motivated at all.

At this point **STOP!** Try to recharge your motivation by employing the 'action before motivation' technique. The idea behind this method is that if you 'just do something, anything', then the motivation to continue will naturally follow. To help you get under way, begin with the 'principle of five': just do five pages, or five paragraphs, or five minutes, or five of anything you set yourself. If you can get through five of something, then you will probably find either that your motivation has returned, or that, because you have made a start, it is not worth stopping. If this does not work, then you might also try to pin down what is causing you to feel so unmotivated. Address the particular problems sapping your motivation, perhaps by talking these over with a professional counsellor, so as to take control of the situation.

Managing the hazards of computer work

Engaging in proactive strategies to manage physical stress is no less important than for psychological stressors. More attention is now being given to the health hazards accompanying long hours of sitting at a computer or desk. It is best to vary your activities as much as you can. Intersperse computer work with other tasks such as reading, monitoring experiments or tests, drafting ideas for the next chapter, outlining an essay or report and so forth, anything that you might be able to do *away from* the computer. Make your tasks multivarious, particularly when producing lengthy texts like theses and long reports. Also watch for web-based time-wasters – such as Facebook and YouTube – that drive you to spend lengthy periods at the computer screen.

Obtain advice or material from the occupational health and safety service in your institution on how best to avoid occupational overuse syndrome, which can lead to debilitating repetitive strain injuries. Ask if staff can review the set-up of your workstation and provide you with a range of simple flexing and stretching exercises to perform frequently.

Electronic tools for increasing productivity

Once you understand the principles of effective self-management you can begin to explore ways to support your planning activities through the use of productivity tools available both on the web and digitally. These tools can be downloaded and installed (for example, calendaring software such as iCal or Outlook) on your computer or smart device or accessed online by logging into an account (for example, Google Calendar).

Which tools you choose will depend on your needs and circumstances. For instance, if you work across a variety of digital devices – a computer in the office, a smartphone for when you are on the go, and a laptop at home – then you should choose tools that will synchronize across those devices or that are accessible anytime online. If you work primarily on one machine, for example, your home personal computer (PC), then installing locally hosted software might be your preferred option. Given the increasingly mobile nature of modern workplaces, however, finding tools that will synchronize across devices is probably the safest way to go.

Calendars and reminders

Calendar applications are available as software that you can install on your computer (for example, iCal or Outlook) or as applications that you can access anywhere online (for example, Google Calendar). Most digital calendaring systems allow you to set different 'views' – daily, weekly, monthly, yearly, and so on – and your activity can be made public or kept private.

If you work across several devices, then choose a calendar service that will synchronize. Calendars will also allow you to set 'reminders' for matters such as important meetings, events or due dates, but reminder applications are also available independent of calendar services, and can be downloaded for smartphones and tablet devices. Search your smartphone's app store for 'reminders' and you will pull up a number of useful applications.

To-do or task lists

Many people prefer writing their to-do lists on paper, but more and more are finding it convenient to keep such lists online or on their mobile devices. The more established calendaring systems will often support to-do or task lists, but smaller, more dedicated services such as Rememberthemilk.com or Toodledo.com provide more flexibility in how you set up your lists and have the added bonus of supporting apps that synchronize content across your devices.

Note-taking

Again, many students prefer to take notes on paper, but the advantages of taking notes electronically is that they become more accessible, can be archived more effectively, and are more easily searchable. The disadvantage is that you always need a digital device at hand for recording your notes! Online services such as Evernote.com and Zoho.com's Notebook allow you to include images, audio, hyperlinks, pdfs and other rich media in your notes. If you are fairly mobile, then a service that synchronizes across your devices is preferable. Many dedicated note-taking apps are available for smartphones and tablet devices – just do a search in your app store.

File storage

Because of problems with version control, it is not desirable to email documents to colleagues (or yourself!). At the same time, it is imprudent to keep all your important files on a flash drive. Having an online repository for your files is a smart way to manage your many documents and files, whether you are sharing them with others or simply accessing them yourself. Services such as Box.net and Dropbox.com permit you to organize your files and folders online and synchronize them to your local computer or device (including smartphone) for pick-up when you are offline. As with most such productivity tools mentioned here, you can choose to share materials with others or to keep them for your access only.

Online documents

Although most students are accustomed to using Microsoft Office products (that is, Word, PowerPoint, Excel, and so on), growing numbers of people are finding it convenient to use non-proprietary and freely available online document services such as Google Docs, Open Office and Zoho. These are online software suites that include word processing, spreadsheets, presentations (slideshows), forms, drawing, file storage, and more. They can be accessed anywhere online, meaning that you do not need to store your files separately or carry a flash drive around with you just so you can work on your thesis, report or essay. For most purposes, the basic functionality of these tools is comparable with that of Office products, but if you use more specialized tools, such as macros or labels, then you should stay with Microsoft Office.

Google

If you are looking for a 'one-stop-shop' that covers all of the above online productivity tools, then Google is probably your most efficient solution. A single Google account will give you access to dedicated calendar, file hosting and document services, and provide you with an array of 'gadgets' that you can add to your account settings to boost functionality. There are also smartphone apps available for many, but not yet all, Google services.

Managing multiple communication tasks

Managing multiple communication tasks can be complicated, particularly if you are a coursework student with several items of assessment for different courses due around the same time. This type of situation can cause course-work graduates much anxiety. As a research student, you may also have converging deadlines, and feel the resulting pressure. To improve your management of multiple communication tasks, consider these procedural steps well in advance.

 exercise: multiple communication task planning

Step 1

Count the number of days that remain to the due date of your final item of assessment. Now, decide how many days from your total number of days you wish to allot to each item of assessment. Consider the value of each item of assessment in doing this; an item worth 20 per cent does not warrant time equal to an item worth 80 per cent.

Step 2

Nominate an end-date for completion of all tasks for each item of assessment. Your end-dates will not be the same as actual submission dates or exam dates, as indicated below for three hypothetical items of assessment to take place in one week in June:

(Report due 16 June): end-date for completion 19 May
(Research essay due 18 June): end-date for completion 3 June
(Exam on 20 June): end-date for all revision 19 June

You may prefer to complete an item before moving to the next, or to work simultaneously on specific tasks associated with two or more items (for example, database searching for an essay while drafting a report).

Step 3

Discriminate tasks needing to be done to meet your end-date for each item of assessment. For example, for an essay (see → 'Research essays', Chapter 5), these tasks could be as follows:

- Search for appropriate source material after brainstorming the topic (see → 'Topics (or questions)' in Chapter 5).
- Read identified source material and take notes (see → 'Ensuring task-focused information' in Chapter 2).

(Continued)

- Produce an essay outline (see → 'Visual mapping of material' and 'Sequential outlining' in Chapter 4).
- Draft the essay (one, two or three drafts?).
- Proofread, check accuracy of references, figurative illustrations and their legends, and polish presentation.

Now, set up timelines for the different items of assessment. Include rough estimates of time to complete the specific tasks for each item of assessment, as indicated below by way of an essay example:

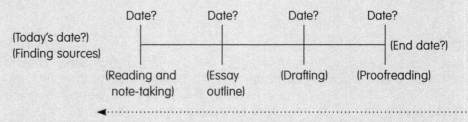

(Work backwards from the end-date in allotting time to completion of specific tasks)

Add your different timelines to your electronic calendar or pin them above your regular workstation so that you can monitor your progress in meeting deadlines.

Communicating with lecturers and supervisors

Good communication is the key to establishing positive working relationships with your lecturers and supervisors. Never think that you may be thought inadequate because of some question, however trivial, you want to ask: you are always learning and your lecturer/supervisor is there to help you progress. Also, never assume that your supervisor will recognize that you need help. Supervisors are busy, preoccupied people too, and may think that all is going well if you do not tell them otherwise.

key points

Ask questions – any questions you want to ask – and keep asking them until you understand, until the matter is clarified or resolved.

Resolving uncertainties

Simple communication queries may be quickly answered in class or even in casual conversation with your lecturer/supervisor at a chance meeting. If, however, you have more substantive enquiries, or indeed are having serious problems, you will need to take action to resolve these by arranging a meeting.

 exercise: resolution action planning

Step 1: clarify the nature of your uncertainties

Clarify the nature of your uncertainties before the meeting takes place by considering questions of this type:

- What precisely do I need to clarify or sort out (detail these)?
- Under what conditions do my uncertainties about writing/communication arise? Try to be specific.
- What outcomes do I hope for in a meeting with my lecturer/supervisor? Jot these down.

Step 2: set up a discussion agenda

Setting up a discussion agenda is a useful strategy when initiating meetings. When you have clarified precisely what you wish to discuss and reasons for doing so, (1) make a concise dot-point list for discussion (your agenda), and (2) give them a copy of your agenda before the meeting so that they have time to review your points.

Step 3: at the meeting

When you meet with your lecturer/supervisor, you want the discussion to remain focused on your concerns, not become sidetracked. These are strategies to help with this:

- If your lecturer/supervisor begins to digress (students do report this), try to refocus attention on your agenda, those points worked out during the clarification process.
- Keep an eye on time so that you will be able to get through all the points on your agenda.
- You want the meeting to be helpful to you, so do not hesitate to say so if you are still not clear about the advice being given.

Digital communication issues

Effective digital communication is key to dealing with your lecturer or supervisor. We cover some strategies for electronic communication below.

Email

Email communication between students and lecturers/supervisors is popular, convenient, easy, and may afford a welcome degree of anonymity not possible in face-to-face conversation. It can be an appropriate and effective medium of communication and is preferred in the workplace over forms of communication such as Facebook. Still, where there is a choice of communication media (for example, face-to-face talk, office telephone or email), it is worth considering whether email is the best option given the purpose of your communication and a possible need for privacy. Certainly, issues do arise in terms of the appropriateness and effectiveness of email as a medium of communication between graduates and their lecturers/supervisors.

Appropriateness   Most lecturers/supervisors will respond to emails, but do clarify with them the purposes for which email communication is to be used before dashing one off. Determine whether there are any restrictions on what types of emails they might welcome and when (for example, making an appointment might be welcomed whereas expecting written comments – let alone copious comments – on an attached draft might not).

Email communication may seem a less confrontational forum for discussing sensitive or difficult matters, but it may not be the most appropriate for resolution of these matters. It can be difficult to encode in written communication nuances of feeling, to achieve a fuller understanding without those non-verbal cues that can be so vital in resolution dialogue. Perhaps a telephone conversation or face-to-face talk might be a better option.

key points

It is most important to practise self-censoring.

Avoid sending an email that may antagonize or alienate the recipient if you are feeling angry or upset. Sit on the email for a day or night until you have calmed down, and, as a safeguard against accidentally hitting the 'send' button, do not write in the recipient's address in the address line until you are certain you want to proceed. Think further about the wording of your email before hitting the send button, or maybe you should not send it at all.

Privacy or confidentiality can never be assured with email, and deletion does not mean final erasure. Emails can go to the wrong address, others may have access to the recipient's computer, the recipient can pass emails on without a sender's permission, or they can be retrieved from servers after deletion. So think twice about using this medium if confidentiality is a high priority.

Effectiveness   The quality of the relations between you and your lecturer/ supervisor will influence the effectiveness of your email communications. Where there is trust and openness, these should work well. But where tensions exist, particularly in a context of unequal power relations, email might not be the best choice. At least think about it.

The desired timescale of the communication can also affect effectiveness. Many students report frustration at delayed responses, or no response at all. This might mean that the lecturer/supervisor is away, that the email is not welcomed, that it has been accidentally overlooked in a hundred other unread emails (a big problem) or that the pressure of overall responsibilities has prevented the lecturer/supervisor from providing a timely response. A follow-up email may help, but not necessarily; you may still need to telephone or make a face-to-face appointment if possible.

Clarity of communication is also important. As with any written text, it is important to think carefully about readers' needs and overall text quality to ensure a message will be clearly understood by the recipient. It is easy for misunderstandings to arise with hastily put together emails, and so invite an unhelpful or negative response. Be aware that the online medium itself constrains development of the more task-sensitive dialogue developed in face-to-face communication, which is so valuable in negotiating understanding about textual production and settling on strategies for improvement. So bear this in mind if the email feedback seems somewhat brusque or even insensitive.

As a final point, where sensitive issues are being dealt with via email over time, keep hard-copy records in case there is a future need to review this 'conversation' as, for example, in resolving differences of opinion about what transpired in the course of events.

Facebook

Social networking services such as Facebook today provide many people with their primary means of online personal communication. Although your lecturer or supervisor may have a Facebook profile, they may prefer to receive 'work' communications in the form of emails. Similarly, you may not wish your lecturer or supervisor to have access to your private profile. Discuss with them whether or not Facebook (or similar) is an appropriate means of communication in your situation.

Mobile phones and texting

Just as social networking is popular as a means for personal communication, so too is communication via mobile phones, and similar questions apply as to their appropriateness or otherwise as a means of contact between teacher and student. Some lecturers or supervisors will prefer that you call their mobile phone, others will not. There may be limits around texting or the hours between which to call; of course, the same applies for you and your own preferences. Again, discuss the matter early on, so that there are no misunderstandings about what constitutes a fitting method of contact.

Issues in cross-cultural writing and communication

Many of the writing and communication challenges experienced by international students are similar to those experienced by other graduates; so do review the previous sections. Nonetheless, it is unwise to assume that what has previously worked for you will do so now, and equally unwise to attribute all communication difficulties to a problem with English if English is a second language, perhaps even a third.

Cross-cultural issues of the following type can arise because of embedded expectations about teaching and learning and the conduct of relations between students and academic staff.

Being critical

It will be expected that you take a fully critical approach to all materials being discussed in your writing and communication. If the need for analysis, critical appraisal and argument in writing is proving difficult and challenging, the section on 'Treating information critically' in Chapter 2 will help; also review → 'Building an argument' in Chapter 5.

Developing independence

If you come from a culture where the teacher/supervisor is viewed as the authority from whom the student is to learn, you may expect your supervisor to direct every stage of your studies or research. A major expectation in Western universities is that students be self-directed, with *guidance* from a lecturer/supervisor. This is a crucial reason to talk through a supervisory relationship early, so that you are clear about what will be expected of you and what you can expect from your supervisor. Expectations can vary across supervisors.

Accepting guidance

If you are returning to study from a position of authority and respect in your home country, perhaps as a senior public servant or academic, you may find it difficult to accept student status. Your adjustment in this case will invite strategies the opposite of those just mentioned. You might need to work at not being too independent, at accepting an appropriate level of *guidance* from your supervisor. Supervisory input is vitally important to ensure that the thesis meets the standards appropriate for the level of the degree, of which supervisors will certainly have the best understanding.

Entering tutorial 'conversations'

You may find the tutorial meeting a somewhat strange affair, with everyone talking at once. Students may be perceived as disrespectful to the lecturer, and the tutorial unhelpful in providing instruction. But this is a matter of different cultural behaviour. Because of the emphasis on critical engagement, lecturers mostly choose not to provide answers, preferring instead to stimulate students to think for themselves by asking questions of them, allowing them to discuss issues as a group, to challenge each other's viewpoints and the lecturer's own, and to argue and debate at will.

Some international students can find it difficult to join in, being too polite to interrupt others. If you have this problem, ask for your lecturer's help. Try at every tutorial meeting to have at least one point from your reading you want to introduce into the discussion, and ask your lecturer if he or she could invite you to speak at an agreed-on signal. You will gradually become confident enough to enter 'noisy' tutorial conversations.

Using the English language

Most graduates worry about giving tutorials, seminars or conference presentations (see → 'The nature of oral presentations', Chapter 11), though not all have the added burden of speaking in a language not native to them, so that pronunciation becomes a concern. Or it may be that English language/expression is preventing you from communicating clearly in writing. Explore these avenues of assistance to determine what help is available:

- Find out what writing assistance your lecturer/supervisor is prepared to provide.
- Investigate assistance provided by academic skills, learning or writing services within your institution.

- Ask an English-speaking friend, or some other appropriate person to run through your paper with you to practise pronouncing words about which you are uncertain.
- Search for helpful web materials or online services that focus on English grammar/expression/pronunciation (Purdue OWL is very good – Google it).
- Download pronunciation, grammar and dictionary apps to your smartphone or other digital device. Pronunciation apps, and some dictionary apps, will provide audio examples of correct pronunciation. When choosing a pronunciation app, try to find one that displays visual examples.
- Identify whether there are courses for credit in English for Academic Purposes that you may be able to take that fit with your schedule.

Most useful is to practise your English in context, meaning in situations where you are actually in the process of producing the various texts required in your degree, or preparing your presentations. While this type of developmental assistance will help you to improve your control of English, it will not necessarily extend to a full editing service – that is to say, fixing the grammar. Other second-language issues appropriate to context are discussed throughout this book.

Using the disciplinary language

Effectively using the disciplinary language (as distinct from English) may also cause concern when writing and presenting, in which case visit the exercise under → 'Mastering disciplinary writing practices' in Chapter 2.

Conducting interpersonal relations

In conducting interpersonal relations with lecturers and supervisors, you may find marked differences. You may need to be more proactive in asking questions, in negotiating the terms of, say, a relationship with your supervisor, in adjusting to different forms of address (for example, using first names), or in setting discussion agendas for meetings with your supervisor. If you are asked to do the latter, between meetings with your supervisor keep notes on the following:

- Interesting ideas about or interpretations of your readings and data.
- Ideas you have about your overall research plan.
- Suggestions for changes in focus or direction of your research.
- Any uncertainties about or difficulties with content or research procedures that need discussing.
- Anything else you consider important to discuss.

Researching on the move

Mobile technologies are becoming increasingly central to everyday communication practices. Such technologies present students with new, more flexible ways of accessing learning content, increased opportunities for contributing to real-time debates in the field, and improved methods for data recording and distributing research.

Advantages of using mobile technologies

Mobile phones

You do not need to own the latest smartphone to have access to a powerful mobile learning and research tool. The most simple of mobile phones today is equipped with robust data recording and playback functions, including a camera and voice and video recording; still others have the ability to record text notes. You can use these functions to record data *in situ* and to access it later at a more convenient time. Some institutions will send you important communiqués via text message to your mobile, such as emergency alerts or automated course information, so make sure you keep your contact details up to date on the student administration system.

Smartphone applications

If you own a smartphone, such as an iPhone, Blackberry or Android phone, then you have access to a myriad of 'apps' that can extend your study or research. Productivity apps can be accessed regardless of location to allow you to schedule events or tasks, retrieve documents or files and take notes. If you are an international student for whom English is a second language, then having instant access to applications for grammar, spelling and punctuation can be especially useful. Other apps that you might find useful include calculators, unit and currency converters, clocks and stopwatches, compasses, protractors and rulers and sound level indicators – just about anything that you might need in your particular discipline area.

Tablet devices

These touchscreen devices are finding a niche among students and academics who want an 'always on' computing appliance that is both portable and versatile. Tablet devices allow you to download and read 'e-books' and course texts, access files, write notes either by hand or via keyboard, and make use of many apps similar to those provided for smartphones. The advantage of a tablet device over a laptop is that it is considerably smaller and lighter in weight, making it perfect for on-the-go Internet access, data recording and travel.

However, its small size can also be a drawback: if you need a more powerful device, then you should invest in a laptop computer.

Laptops

For many students, a laptop is their main personal computing device. As opposed to a tablet device, a laptop will do everything that a normal computer will do and thus provides a sensible middle ground for mobile study and research if you cannot afford a device for all occasions.

Voice recording

Graduate students do not typically exploit the benefits of voice recording even though it is simple enough and you can probably do it with a device you have either on your person or in your bag right now, that is, your mobile phone or laptop. Voice recording can be used to make a note of ideas that suddenly pop into your head while you are walking to the bus, or to document conversations about course or research topics with fellow students. It can even be used to record lectures or seminars – with permission, of course. You can then listen to the recording in your own time and at your own pace, which can be particularly effective if you are a second-language speaker.

Some students use voice recordings as part of their everyday research activities, such as when they record interviews with study participants who are in their own environments or workplaces. In such cases, you will require a dedicated digital voice recorder, which typically has more storage space for voice files than, say, a mobile phone. Such recorders are small and unobtrusive and essential for certain types of fieldwork and research, but they come with varying degrees of quality: in general, you get what you pay for. Your laptop may also have the ability to record, but it might be too cumbersome to carry around and too intimidating to place in front of an interviewee.

Do remember that you will likely be in breach of privacy laws if you record someone without their permission, and/or if you upload a digital recording to a third party website – even if you keep the file 'private' (see → section 'Keeping safe online' later in this chapter).

Video recordings and photographs

Quick video recordings or photographs can be taken on just about any mobile phone and can be effective if you need to chronicle more visual proceedings, such as performances, certain laboratory experiments, or any other phenomena that you encounter in your studies or research. The same principles apply for video recordings and photographs as for voice recordings: if you need a dedicated video set up, then be prepared to pay for quality, and do not post anything online containing someone's image unless you have their express permission to do so.

Podcasts and digital audios

A limitless supply of podcasts and audios can be found online, and many of these will be relevant to your study or discipline area. Take the time to search iTunes, iTunes U or other podcast directories such as Podbean.com, PodcastDirectory.com or PodcastAlley.com to find material to subscribe to or to download onto your MP3 player. Being able to listen to such material at your convenience can greatly enhance your comprehension of study topics and may give you ideas that you can follow up on later.

Keeping safe online

As you make your way through this text, you will see that we advise you to use commercial online digital tools or services to support your writing and planning. Finding the right digital tools can greatly help you in your studies and research: they can increase your productivity, help you to visualize an argument, organize your research materials and streamline the writing process. However, it is important that you do not sign up for, or download from, sites and services indiscriminately. Here are some points for consideration before you sign up for anything online.

 **key points**

Exercise caution whenever you create an account with an Internet-based service.

Copyright and intellectual property, including university regulations

When you sign up for an Internet-based service, you should be especially aware of the implications for copyright and intellectual property (IP), as you may be inadvertently giving away rights to material that you do not technically own.

Copyright   Copyright laws vary greatly from country to country and are very complicated, but in general copyright automatically reserves to you all rights in any creative work you produce, such as research essays, theses and slide-shows. Reputable services will not ask for any control over your copyright, and any work or data you post to the service will remain yours, assuming that you are, indeed, the copyright holder to begin with.

As a student, you are likely to own copyright in any material you produce during the course of your degree, but this is not always so, as might be the case if you have, for example, an industry scholarship. You should be clear about what you do and do not own in terms of copyright – it can be easy to assume that once you have created a work it is yours, even though someone else may actually own its copyright.

key points

You need to check your university's copyright and IP policies to clarify what rights you have – and what rights your institution has – to your work.

Intellectual property (IP)   Services are also likely to ask for a sub-licence to your IP (so that they can display your work). Both staff and students typically retain their intellectual property rights, but this varies from institution to institution, and some institutions will require an exclusive licence to any IP you produce under their auspices, regardless of whether you are staff or student, as might an industry scholarship provider.

Terms of Service

Many of us create accounts with websites and Internet services without reading the Terms of Service (aka Terms and Conditions), even though we are asked to agree to those terms before signing up. It can seem tedious to have to read a lengthy screen of legal jargon, but there are a few things you should look for and understand before clicking the 'submit' button. Do remember, of course, that the Terms of Service can change at any time. Copyright issues have been covered above, but here are some further issues under the Terms of Service that you should be familiar with.

key points

Make sure you understand, and are comfortable with, the privacy policy of the service you wish to sign up for.

Privacy   You should be aware of how much personal information the service stores and to whom this information is made available. Many services allow you to keep some or all parts of your site 'private', but in effect this only means 'not publicly viewable', which may be perfectly acceptable to you in your situation. You need to ensure that you, yourself, comply with the privacy legislation of your jurisdiction. In many countries, you are not allowed to give away other people's personal information without their permission, so if you upload a database of contacts to a third party you could be breaking the law.

Data security How will the service store and secure your data? Some services allow third parties to access your data, but only for the purposes of maintaining the service and only after those parties have signed confidentiality agreements. Other services are less scrupulous and will allow anyone who pays them (such as advertisers) to view your details. You should also see if the Terms of Service outlines how the service secures your data against unauthorized access or attack.

Deleting information Some services will delete data that have remained idle for a certain period of time. For example, if you have not accessed your account for six months, the service might automatically shut down your account or remove your material as a matter of course.

Providing information to a service You should only be required to provide a username, email address and password to create an account with any given service (some services do request a date of birth if there are minimum age restrictions on users). Even though there may be signup fields that ask for your address, ethnicity, hobbies, religious affiliation, or political beliefs, these should not be required fields and you should be circumspect about providing such details.

Controlling email notifications Better services will allow you to control the notifications or advertising emails they send you. If there is no way in your profile settings to turn off these messages, then you probably should not sign up for the service. In many countries, such messages are counted as 'spam' and are illegal if you cannot control receipt.

Pricing Many tools and services available on the web are supplied free of charge, even though they are provided by a commercial company. These companies often make their money through contextual advertising and by offering 'premium upgrades' to their basic services. If you do not want to have to pay for a service, then only select services that provide for free the baseline functionality you need. But, even then, be aware that some services may choose to start charging for their product at any time they like.

Considerations regarding the service itself
The Terms of Service will lay out many of the conditions under which you agree to use a service, but that is not all you need to know about a company when signing up. If you think that you will be using a service in the longer term, then it useful to know a little bit about the business and its business

model. Technology industry websites such as Mashable.com and Techcrunch.com can be excellent sources of information in this regard, and they frequently comment on the remaining points now discussed.

Business robustness and longevity   In the modern web environment, a company that is five years old is often regarded as well established and successful, but it should also have a sound business model behind it. For example, how does the company make its money? Who are its investors? What other sources of capital does it draw on? How many people does it employ? You do not have to become a business guru to understand these things, but you should have some knowledge about the company that is hosting your data.

Reliability   All online services will have periods of time when users cannot access them, whether it is because the company needs to make upgrades to their software or hardware, or because a technical glitch has entered the system. Having said this, some services are more reliable than others. Visit the service's discussion forum (it should have a forum or similar) to see if there are complaints about the service's dependability. You can also gauge from these forums how satisfied users are with the service overall.

Data lock-in   Regardless of how reliable or otherwise a service is, you do not want to sign up with a company that locks your data into it, and it alone. To this end, you should choose a service that allows you to export your data in a common format (for example, XML, OPML, RSS, depending on the type of data you are working with) so that you can transfer that data to another place if you wish.

Practicalities

Finally, there are some practical considerations to take into account when using a commercial online service. These are items that are largely within your control and include the following:

Public versus private sites   Many commercial services allow you control over who can and cannot view your material. You need to decide upon the level of visibility you want for your data. For instance, if you were seeking to raise your profile amongst the research community (see → 'Raising your profile: setting up an eportfolio' in Chapter 12), then obviously you would want your work to be public. If, however, you are using an online service to host confidential or sensitive research findings, then choosing a service that allows you to keep your work 'private' is essential.

Backups   If a company were to disappear overnight, would you lose all the data or work you had stored there? This is a frightening scenario for any graduate student, but it is one that can be mitigated quite easily by choosing a service that (1) allows you to export your work so that you can keep a local backup, and that (2) exports that backup in a common format (see the earlier point about data lock-in). Even better is to find a service that synchronizes your data to your local hard-drive automatically, in which case you will not have to think about taking regular, manual backups (see → the next section, 'Backing up your work').

Help and support   Free web services are designed so that you do not need an instruction manual in order to use them as the instructions are typically built into the very design of the site. This is why there is usually no 'helpdesk' to call when you have an account with an online service. However, there may be times when you simply cannot figure out how to use a certain feature, or why your file did not upload as you anticipated it should. In these situations, you are expected to help yourself by searching the site's FAQs (frequently asked questions) or forum, or by 'Googling' the problem and finding an answer elsewhere on the web.

Bandwidth, Internet access and student quotas   The amount of bandwidth needed to support your online activities will vary, depending on the type of service you are using. If you are uploading large files (for example, video, audio or image-intensive slideshows) to a site, then you need a fast Internet connection — otherwise it could take hours. The same applies for downloading. You should also bear in mind whether or not you have Internet access all the time. This may seem an obvious point, but if you are conducting fieldwork in an area without Internet or wireless coverage, then you will not be able to access your online data (yet another reason for finding services that synchronize your data to your local device/s). And, finally, there is no point in using a suite of online services and tools if there are quotas on your Internet usage at your institution and you are likely to exceed those quotas regularly.

In the end, it is up to you as to what you sign up for or even if you sign up. The key point is to be aware of the issues and implications involved and to account for them whenever you are online. Digital data are different from physical data and having your work in digital environments exposes you to both risks and rewards — you need to be able to manage both safely. It is useful to keep in mind, here, what danah boyd [sic] (2011) identifies as being the four main characteristics of what she calls 'networked publics':

- **Replicability.** What you put online can be copied, forwarded, repurposed and reused in ways that you have no control over — but also in ways that might delight you!
- **Searchability.** Anything online can be sought and found, regardless of whether or not you have your site set to 'private' — there are always people who can find their ways around your privacy settings.

- **Persistence.** What you post online will be there forever. Even if you think that you have removed something from public view, a search engine is likely to have found and cached (archived) your material.
- **Invisible audiences.** You cannot be sure who is watching. Indiscreet comments or poor quality work may be read by unknown spectators – always be professional, just in case.

Backing up your work

A final consideration in managing the modern graduate writing environment is that of backing up your work in electronic format. Much of your work, whether essays, notes, photographs, databases, or the like, will be in digital format and you must create backups so that you can continue to access your material in the event of a computer crash or any similar incident that prevents you from retrieving your originals. Backing up, however, is not the same as simply 'saving' your work: backing up means taking a whole copy of a digital asset and placing it in, ideally, two different digital places, whereas saving your work means only that you have a single local copy of the latest version of the file you are working on.

 **key points**

Remember: backing up your work is your responsibility.

Backing up the less obvious

Most students habitually backup thesis chapters or coursework essays but neglect to backup less obvious items such as photographs, databases, video collections, diagrams, lists of websites, electronic notebooks and, even, software packages. Anything that goes into the production of a piece of writing or research should be backed up. You should also keep copies of important emails and communications from your supervisor, lecturer or institution, as you never know if they may be needed. 'Tag' everything using keywords so that you can easily search for and find them later, or use a well-organized folder system to arrange your digital materials.

Backing up online assignments

If you are required to complete an assignment online (such as via a wiki, blog or discussion forum), then it is your responsibility to have a backup of the submitted version of your work, just as you would if you were handing in a paper assignment. If your lecturer has chosen wisely, then the service you are using for your assignment will allow you to export your material in a standard file format and keep a copy of it wherever you want (thumb drive, local hard drive, and so on). If being able to export your material direct from the service is not an option, then take an html copy of your work via your Internet browser. Simply go to File > Save As and save your work locally that way, and then create an external backup, just to be sure. You will be able to open and read a local copy of the page you have saved by opening it in your browser software.

Backing up regularly

You should backup your work at least weekly as a matter of course. Set aside a regular time for backing up your work, for example Fridays at 5 p.m. However, you should backup more frequently if you have made significant or important additions to your materials: this might mean you are taking a backup once a day or even every few hours. Let common sense dictate when you need to take a backup, but remember that it is better to have a backup and to not need it than it is to not have a backup and to lose an entire month's work through poor backup practices.

Creating external backups

Having an extra copy of a file on the hard drive you are currently working from is not a backup; it is just an extra copy of a file on your hard drive. A proper backup exists on a different system or device altogether from the one on which the file normally resides. The most obvious and common way of creating this type of 'external' backup is to save your materials to a 'thumb' drive. These small drives are perfect for keeping files and folders that do not take up much disc space. However, if your work consists of larger files (for example, specialist three-dimensional design records or high-resolution images or video), then thumb drives are unlikely to hold everything you need. Invest in a large-capacity (that is, 500 GB, 1 TB or larger) external hard drive so that if or when your computer crashes you have a full backup of all your hard work.

Keeping your work online or, 'in the cloud' as it is also known, is a further way of creating an external backup; as long as you have Internet access, you have access to your work. It can also be prudent to burn your most precious work to CD or DVD, as this means you have yet another way of accessing lost work in a worst-case scenario. And do not forget that hard copies of your work also count as external backups. Drafts of thesis chapters, for instance, can be printed out and kept in a filing cabinet just in case your digital data are corrupted. However you choose to keep your external backups – and we recommend that you use a variety of formats – you should have at least two external backups to have a proper redundancy in your backup procedures.

Having backups in different locations

There is no point in having two external backups in the one physical location if that location becomes unviable due to fire, flood or other catastrophic event. Keep a backup of your work at home and in the office, or in another secure location, or make sure that your online backup is up to date.

Using automatic backups

As an adjunct to backing up your work yourself manually, you should also consider finding ways of creating backups automatically. Numerous online providers provide this service at a cost (search for 'automatic data backup' or 'automated backup service' or similar), so do some investigating before choosing this option. Having said this, however, the advantage of using such a service is that an external backup on the Internet is created at the same time as your work is automatically backedup. If you have a Macintosh computer with 'Time Machine' facility, then make sure you have it activated with an external hard drive and schedule it to take hourly backups. Time Machine automatically backs up not only your documents and files but your entire system, including applications and settings, allowing a crashed Mac to be completely rebooted from scratch and re-set to the latest saved version on your computer (or even to an earlier version, if you prefer). A final way of creating an automatic backup is to use an online folder or notebook service such as Evernote.com, Dropbox.com or Box.net that automatically synchronizes your local materials to an online environment, as well as across multiple devices if you so choose.

 **further resources**

Fowler, H.R. and Aaron, J.E. (2001) *The Little, Brown Handbook*. 9th edn. New York: Longman. Anything but little, but rather a valuable reference book that works hard to live up to its claim: 'answers all your questions about writing'.

Mainhard, T., van der Rijst, R., van Tartwijk, J. and Wubbels, T. (2009) 'A model for the supervisor–doctoral student relationship', *Higher Education*, 58(3): 359–73. An article describing the problems that can arise in a supervisory relationship, and presenting both a model for interpersonal supervisory behaviour and a questionnaire on supervisor–doctoral student interaction.

Swales, J. and Feak, C. (2004) *Academic Writing for Graduate Students: Essential Tasks and Skills*. 2nd edn. Ann Arbor, MI: University of Michigan Press. An excellent resource for dedicated students for whom English is not a first language who are willing to invest time in exploring the intricacies of cross-cultural writing differences and learning how to overcome these to produce solid academic papers.

2

Fundamentals of Solid Preparation

 developmental objectives

By applying the strategies, doing the exercises and following the procedural steps in this chapter, you should be able to:

- Understand the influence of genre (type of writing) and disciplinary practices on academic writing, and build on your current skills by studying practices suited to the types of writing you now have to produce.
- Develop competence in treating information critically so that you do have the right types of information for your writing tasks.
- Appreciate that having the best information means accessing quality academic sources.
- Realize the importance of clearly defining research goals/aims, before reading or data-gathering, to ensure task-focused information.
- Identify strategies to manage the reading load, cut down on unproductive reading, and improve information retrieval.
- Manage concerns relating to the efficiency of your approach to writing, handling feedback from lecturers/supervisors, and dealing with 'writing blocks'.

Effective academic writing is seeded in solid preparation. Understanding the shaping influence of genre and disciplinary practices on all academic writing is an essential step in that preparation. Most importantly, you will need to embed sound information management practices that will issue in the best and right information to successfully complete a specific writing task, whether that task involves writing a report, a blog entry, a research essay, a thesis, or any other type of writing.

Understanding the graduate writing culture

The graduate writing culture is indeed complex. You are likely to be producing genres as different as, for example, a blog entry, a report, an essay, a substantial thesis, a conference paper or a journal article. Because different academic genres have distinctive purposes, they can have different underlying conventions that affect the language, style, structure and treatment of information, all of which are further influenced by preferred disciplinary practices.

Because of this complexity, you could find yourself confronting unanticipated challenges: doing types of writing with which you are unfamiliar; or finding your understanding of a particular type of writing is now insufficient (for example, you have experience of writing reports in the workplace or for an undergraduate degree, but find you need to change/adapt your practices to meet specific requirements of report writing in your present course); or discovering that the *types* of questions raised in treating familiar concepts/information are now different in your present course.

 **key points**

Take time to orient yourself to specific requirements of course genres if you are transferring disciplines at a graduate level, returning to study or research after many years in the workforce, or have not previously studied in Western universities. Enlist the help of your lecturer/supervisor.

Or perhaps you are grappling with a new disciplinary language because you are transferring disciplines or, even, cultures where you now have to develop proficiency in using the disciplinary language in academic texts written in English. Disciplinary language refers to distinctive language of the type emphasized in these extracts from students in different disciplines:

Law:

In ACTV and Nationwide, a majority of the Justices **drew the implication** of a freedom of speech from the overall structure or fabric of ... X argued that freedom of speech regarding political matters is required for the proper working of government and as such **ruled the relevant sections** of the Political Disclosures Act 1991 (ACTV) and the Industrial Relations Act 1988 (Nationwide) as invalid [reference].

Systems Engineering:

Reports from the sonar sensor were combined until **the belief** converged to be equal to or greater than 0.99.

You will see that it is not just the nature of the subject matter (the content) that is different in each case, as expected. In the Law example, the phrases emphasized are distinctly legal; we would not normally talk about drawing the implication of 'a freedom', or ruling 'relevant sections'. Equally distinctive is the unusual use of the word 'belief' – meaning 'probability distribution' – in the Systems Engineering example.

Mastering disciplinary writing practices

By studying models of the types of writing you now have to do, you can gain insight into composition processes: how a text is put together in terms of focus, structure and disciplinary writing practices, including the disciplinary language.

The next exercise, which is designed to help you to gain control of genre and disciplinary writing practices, is potentially very beneficial if you invest time in it.

 case study example

box 2.1 Students report significant benefits from studying disciplinary writing practices

A second-language student experiencing difficulty in using English verb tenses gathered an impressive set of examples on their complex usage in thesis writing in her discipline of Archaeology, which helped her to overcome the problem. Another graduate reported that he felt he had 'learnt' the art of argument by studying, as he said, 'how they put their arguments together and what evidence means'. Yet another student having difficulty writing strong discussion sections studied organizational strategies of 'discussions' in published articles and said he felt 'much more confident about how to do it'.

exercise: mastering disciplinary writing practices

You are already highly trained to read for content, what an author is saying. It is also possible to train yourself to focus systematically on how a text is put together, what it does rather than what it says: the composition processes and language choices. When doing this exercise, you can build up sets of notes relating to disciplinary practices, either online or in a notebook, for easy future reference.

Step 1

Select a sample of the type of writing you now have to do (for example, an essay, report, proposal or thesis) – ask your lecturer/supervisor to provide you with a good model (not always possible) or to refer you to well-written theses. If working from a published article, select one that you find enjoyable and easy to read regardless of the difficulty of the content, as not all publications are equally well written.

Step 2

Set aside regular time for this exercise – perhaps an hour or two twice a week. Now select which aspects you need to focus on from the categories below – focus on only one thing at a time:

Treatment of information

- Think about the types of information the author includes in different sections of the text.
- Consider how the author treats information: the questions raised, the issues thought important, the theories, models, methodologies, procedures applied, and so forth (important in contexts of disciplinary transfer).
- Explore how the author handles theory in discussions, utilizes models or applies methodology, whatever is specifically relevant for you.
- Trace the development of an argument, and look closely at how the author provides supporting evidence to secure that argument.
- Focus on how the author presents and discusses results or data. For example, what differences in practice do you notice between presentation of findings and discussion of these?
- Scrutinize referencing practices in a section or two: when and where referencing occurs; style practices in terms of the use of direct quotes, paraphrased material, additional footnotes, or listed references to studies or groups of studies.
- Investigate the amount of detail used in different contexts of the writing as, for example, in detailing procedures and methods.

Linguistic features

- Look closely at the typical terminology or phraseology being used by the author.
- Consider the language/phraseology used to describe specific procedures or methods or other processes.
- Check whether first person 'I' is used in some parts of the text, or not at all.
- Think about the verb tenses chosen to report on other scholars' work, or verb tenses preferred in different parts of a text, or the range and type of reporting verbs used.
- Review language choices. Think about how obvious, predictable, unusual, striking, effective the language is, and also the range of the vocabulary, which may become a way of extending your own vocabulary.

Organizational features (see also → 'Principles of sound structure', Chapter 4)

- Spend time on how authors divide up the overall text by way of parts, chapters and/or subdivisions. Scrutinize the actual headings. Think about whether these provide a sense of how the whole text fits together.
- Consider how effective titles of sub-headings are in focusing the main theme of the text beneath, how much text appears under sub-headings, whether these sub-headings are numbered and/or titled, and whether there are explicit or implicit attempts to link the different subdivisions.
- Examine how an introduction, a conclusion, a literature review, a results, a discussion, a theory or methodology section, or any other part of the writing is organized. Look at what the author is actually doing, the step-by-step moves, and give some thought to why this organization suits that author's purposes.
- Scrutinize the structure of a paragraph, the implicit or explicit strategies used to ensure the logical flow of ideas within the paragraph and linkages across paragraphs, the actual words or phrases employed (see → 'Developing texts' in Chapter 4).
- Look at the layout of illustrations, the positioning of legends, and how tables, figures, graphs, charts, plots, and so on are integrated into the text for discussion.

Audience features

- Isolate examples of 'signalling' in the document where the author is assisting you to follow the line of discussion. How much of this signalling is there? Where does it take place in the text? How subtle or obvious is it?
- Look at how the author moves into different subsections of the writing. How much context (if any) is provided to ensure readers are kept in the picture?
- Identify strategies the author uses to position the reader to respond positively to discussions. Are there any points where you can see the author making an effort to get readers onside or to offset potential criticisms?
- Is there anything else that strikes you about the author's relationship to you as a reader of this text?

Treating information critically

In extracting factual information from source materials, your focus will be on the details of what is being said: you will need to know the facts, a fact being information that is accepted as true and is not contested in the literature as some so-called facts are. Questions in the order of what? when? where? and who? tend to stimulate the recall of information for the purpose of reproducing knowledge. This is a legitimate and important purpose in writing, which may at times dominate the process and at other times may complement critical appraisal, which is fundamental to all academic writing and communication.

Critically appraising source materials

Critical appraisal involves evaluating strengths and weaknesses of discussions/arguments across a range of authors or sources, bearing in mind that the generation of knowledge turns on the clash of ideas emanating from the community of world scholars.

It is indeed vital to realize that, however well intentioned they may be, authors do have 'prejudices, assumptions and beliefs' (Wallace and Wray, 2006: 26) just as we all do. You will therefore need to exercise your critical intelligence when reading: question the underlying assumptions, consider the possibility of theoretical, methodological and other biases, assess the soundness of the data or evidence presented, the rigour of authors' analyses, the logic of their arguments and so forth. In short, you will need to extend your range of questions when dealing with source materials to engage questions to do with the why? and the how? of the research: to hold your sources in relation, to compare and contrast the positions of different authors, to draw out the issues being debated and so on. If you are unpractised in critical appraisal, refer to the next exercise (see also → 'Critical appraisal of the literature' in Chapter 8).

 exercise: critical appraisal

The scenario

Imagine you are required to read reports, articles and other studies about the topic 'Greenhouse effects on the global environment' in order to produce a report advocating measures to reduce greenhouse emissions. On reading, you discover that there is considerable disagreement among scholars about which measures should be introduced, and why.

The challenge

How then do you begin to evaluate the experts? If your previous tertiary experience was one in which critiquing was not common, this could prove challenging. But the challenge will seem less if you recognize that where there is difference of opinion in scholarship the different viewpoints themselves will provide material for your critique. It is often explicit or implicit in one author's discussion what is problematic in another's.

The critique (question-raising)

In conducting the critique, you would be drawing on your knowledge of the subject, which may include valuable general, specialist, experiential and/or cultural knowledge that you have.

At the same time, you would be raising questions of this type in order to map central issues in the arguments and debates surrounding the subject:

What is the full range of measures identified by the different authors? List these as you read, and perhaps categorize them too in a way that seems useful. To what extent do the authors agree or disagree about which measures should be implemented: is there considerable agreement? A reasonable amount? Hardly any? Draw up a list of measures commonly agreed on, another where there seems to be a reasonable amount of agreement, and another where there seems to be strong disagreement, presuming this sort of division applies.

In the process of clarifying what is being said, think about why authors take the positions they do. The first question to ask yourself is: what are the issues here? What are the points on which authors disagree and why? Identify and consider these carefully: list points and reasons. One issue on which authors might disagree could be the division of costs across state boundaries; another, whether or not there should be compulsory reduction targets for all nations.

Continue your questioning like so:

What reasons do authors give for the measures they prefer? Is there any overlap here? How do these measures line up in terms of advantages and disadvantages, and for whom? From where do these authors draw their evidence? Are their sources reliable? What types of evidence do they present in advocating different measures? Do they use statistics, examples from scientific reports, or what, as evidence? Are the statistics sound? Do the examples make sense to you: why? Why not? Could a discussion be too narrow (or too broad) because important information

(Continued)

is left out? Perhaps you can recognize this from reading other authors. Can you see any biased assumptions behind the evidence, perhaps because of the methodology or theory framing their discussions, or cultural biases (for example, the East/West divide)? In short, how convincing are the reasons they give for the measures they advocate?

During reading, you will generate further questions as you refine your understanding of the subject.

The outcome

By the end of the critique a transformation will have taken place in your knowledge base, as you will have used a range of authors to deepen and clarify your thinking about the subject. The intelligence and creativity with which you handle source materials, and the subtlety of your insights, are matters of individual judgement that will influence the position or point of view you take on any topic. You have to decide which authors or aspects of their studies convince you and why they do, and which do not and why they do not. In rearranging all that you have taken apart in the analysis of a subject or topic – any topic – when you write your paper you will be making a new synthesis, with your own position at the centre of that synthesis.

Critically evaluating theory

If theory does feature in your writing, you will need to critically engage with it. Reading and critically evaluating theory, or philosophical works applied in analysis, can be particularly challenging, as can the appraisal of models or methodologies. It could be that your course includes much new theory so that you do not feel you have a sound knowledge base from which to exercise your critical judgement. Or you may be unpractised in critiquing theory, having never before done this in an academic context.

The term 'theory' is often used loosely in the academic community. The meaning followed here is: 'The formulation of abstract knowledge or speculative thought; systematic conception of something' (*New Shorter Oxford English Dictionary*). Theory then, is a clearly identifiable, abstract body of knowledge that has been conceived systematically.

Theories are abstract systems in which certain aspects (the key ideas or principles of a theory) are privileged by an author over other possibilities. Theorists abstract from the chaotic, actual world of everyday events and activities that which they consider most significant to explain that world, or some aspect of it. Theories are useful for their explanatory value, and sometimes their predictive value. They can open up different possibilities in ways of perceiving and understanding complex events and happenings important in your context of academic enquiry, and so prove to be valuable tools of analysis. But they do have their limitations.

Before conducting your critical appraisal, you will first need to have a sound overview of the theory. All established disciplines have specialist dictionaries or reference works, many of which are also available as e-books, as applications for smartphones, or tablet devices such as the iPad. Making use of these is a useful orientation strategy to gain a clear overview before you read more deeply and comprehensively in the theoretical literature.

You will then need to critically evaluate how well the particular theory does in fact explain what it sets out to explain – its strengths and weaknesses. Critiques by other scholars or schools of scholars, and those of your lecturers/supervisors, can provide a sound starting point for your own critical appraisal of a particular body of theory.

As you read, probe the assumptions about the nature of the world that underpin the key ideas or principles of the body of theory you are studying. Think about whether these assumptions are biased or not (see Figure 2.1). Cultural bias, for example, would be evident if the assumptions underlying a theory of human behaviour proved to be strongly Western-centric and not inclusive of other cultures.

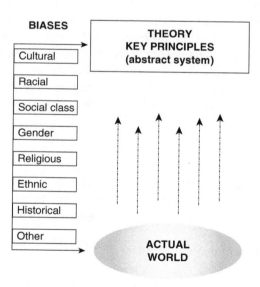

FIGURE 2.1   How theories work

Furthermore, if you are asked to develop a theoretical framework, an analytical framework or a conceptual framework for your thesis or other writing, confusion can arise, as students have noted. Figure 2.2 distinguishes these frameworks by how they might function in academic writing, though do confirm with your lecturer/supervisor that these understandings will apply.

Analytical framework	Conceptual framework	Theoretical framework
Explain and perhaps justify the choice of an existing body of theory being applied by you. Or set up and expound on a framework you are constructing from a range of different theories.	Detail and expound on the parts of the analysis as well as the logical relations among those parts. Or propose a model for analysis of data, which may involve addressing theoretical issues.	Outline the general notions or themes being engaged in the research and expound on the logical relations among those. This too may involve dealing with theory.

FIGURE 2.2   Different types of frameworks

Critical enquiry and the status of existing knowledge

Recognizing the status of existing knowledge on a subject can also be important when exercising your critical judgement: the extent to which that knowledge is strongly evidence-based or, at the other end of the scale, whether that knowledge is necessarily speculative because of the scant evidence available to scholars.

Figure 2.3 is a vocabulary aid both to identifying the status of existing knowledge about a subject and to finding language for your own discussions that reflects that status. Do take a little time to study it.

Working with different types of information

Like other graduates, you may also have concerns about the best critical approach to working with different types of source material, that is, primary and secondary information, although the meanings of these types is not uniform in academia.

Here, primary information refers to:

Raw data generated by you through, for example, tests, experiments or field research; data sets from pre-existing databases generated by others; archival materials (for example, journals, diaries or letters written by, say, historical figures, or original historical documents); policy documents generated by, say, governments and other organizations; state and international legal legislation – also court judgements; literary, art or religious works; and so forth.

Guide	Quantity	Frequency	Probability Adverbs/adjectives	Verbs
100%	all/every/each most	always	certain(ly) definite(ly) undoubtedly probably/probable likely	will is/are must/have to should ought to
	a majority (of) many/much a lot (of) enough some a number (of) several a minority (of)	usual(ly) normal(ly) general(ly) regular(ly) often frequent(ly) sometimes occasional(ly)	perhaps possibly/possible maybe	may might can
	a few/a little few/little	rare(ly) seldom hardly ever scarcely ever	unlikely	could
0%	no/none/not any	never		will is/are + not can could

FIGURE 2.3   Scale of qualification (Jordan, 1980: 60)

Secondary information is understood as:

> Any texts that provide critical commentary of whatever sort on texts categorized under primary information above, such as journal publications, books or chapters in scholarly books, blog posts, book reviews, and so on.

Adopt a circular approach when working across primary and secondary sources: read the primary source first, move to secondary sources, return to the primary source and continue to move between the two types as you refine your critical judgement.

Following your hunches

Your greatest asset is your own critical intelligence. You will have hunches as you read: something does not seem right, or the argument does not convince you, or you sense that some approach or procedure is problematic, or you think perhaps there is a better way, or the data appear dubious, or the underlying assumptions just do not seem to add up, or you suspect the theory being used has skewed the interpretation, or the questions being asked do not seem to be the right ones, or something mentioned in passing strikes you as important but has not been recognized as such. These hunches may be vague and imprecise: half-formed ideas, questions marked by uncertainty, sceptical or doubtful responses or passing intuitions about other possibilities.

It is easy to let these hunches, these instinctive responses, slip away as you push on with the reading. But try not to do this. Stop and ask yourself why you might be responding as you are. It may be that your hunch arose spontaneously from the fact that your general life or work experience suggested something different from what was being reported, or that other disciplinary knowledge you have was pushing you to respond sceptically. Make a record of your hunches, either electronically or in a notebook. While it may take time and further reading to clarify the reason for your response, having such hunches come to fruition in a reasoned argument is the peak of treating information critically.

 **key points**

Hunches can be the seeds of the best critical insights, the subtlest ideas, the very ideas you want to bring to your research and writing.

Ensuring task-focused information

It is possible to have masses of data and source material but still to lack the information you need to successfully complete your writing task. There are different reasons why this occurs, four major ones being:

1. Uncertainty about how to proceed with a particular type of writing, or parts of the writing, as perhaps with what to cover in a specialized report and how to structure it, or what to include in an introduction as opposed to a discussion section of a paper, and how each part might be focused and developed. Uncertainty about how to proceed with a specific writing task inhibits prediction of information needs. This is a matter given considerable attention in Chapters 5–12, which look closely at different types of writing and presentations.
2. Uncertainty about how to pin down the best information when searching large databases or conducting general Internet searches. This type of uncertainty often leads to information overload as well as inadequate information for the task in hand.

3. Insufficient attention to assessing the academic merit of potential source material. This can especially be a problem if you rely too heavily on material you find in the top several hits of a Google search; such material is often not peer-reviewed.

4. Gathering information without first defining your precise goals as these relate to the writing task in hand.

Points 3 and 4 are now discussed, the latter from two angles: generating data and reading the literature.

Assessing the academic merit of source materials

key points

To refine search techniques, find out what information literacy training programmes are available in your institution.

To produce a quality paper you will need the best information possible, so think carefully about the academic merit of all potential source materials, both print and electronic. A definite danger in this regard is relying on general Internet searching for source materials.

Evaluating sources on the Internet

Although there is copious information on the Internet, which can be accessed quickly, much of it has not been through the traditional reviewing processes in place for scholarly print sources. There are informative and valuable web resources with solid, reliable publications (for example, government, industry or organization sites, or reputable electronic journals). There is also a lot of junk, which, however interesting to read, is worthless for your academic research.

key points

Ensure that your online sources have equal academic merit with your print sources.

Take care, just as you do with traditional print sources. Maintain a healthy scepticism. The following are a few questions and points for you to keep in mind:

- Is the purpose of the site or resource clearly evident? Can you identify any particular agenda (political, ideological, religious, and so on) behind the site's formation? If yes, the information presented might be biased rather than balanced, and therefore unsuitable for academic research.
- Who is the author of the site or resource? Is it an individual, organization or institution that has some credibility and authority? If so, how is this demonstrated? Does the site allow for multiple contributions and what appears to be the status of the contributors; is there any evidence of scholarly credentials?
- What does the site or resource contain? How comprehensive is it? Is there enough information? Is there too much information? How will the information gathered complement other sources you are using?
- How up to date is the site or resource? When was it created? When was the last time it was updated and how often is it updated?
- Will the site or resource still be traceable, at least in some form, in the future – in a week? A month? A year? Longer?
- What particular benefit does the site or resource offer? How does the content compare with that of other sites you have accessed, or to related print-based materials? How confident are you that the content is scholarly, accurate and reliable? Is there equivalent or better information readily obtainable from more stable and verifiable sources?
- Is the site or resource presented so that the content is easily accessible, and the access path clear? This is important because your assessors may wish to follow up sources you have used.

Just as you need quality academic source materials to ensure the best information, you also need the right types of information to successfully complete writing tasks.

Avoiding the urge to rush into data-gathering

The intricacies of data-gathering, collation, analysis and writing up are complex across disciplines and beyond the scope of this book. The details you record when collecting data and how you go about recording them will of course depend on the nature of your research and discipline (for example, details of: design of questionnaires, conduct of interviews, selection of informants, transcriptions, participant observation, and so forth; equipment or materials used; experimental or test procedures; instrument calibration; measurements; seasonal/weather/date/time information; or anything else). Nevertheless, be aware that problems of relevance may arise if you rush into data gathering of any type.

key points

Clarify precisely which details you should be recording (and why), and be rigorously consistent in your recording methods.

For example, using surveys and/or interviews attracts many researchers across a range of disciplines as a primary method of data collection. But, as suggested by Preece: 'Many students make the mistake of rushing out to do premature and ill-prepared surveys before the research question ... and the concepts involved have been properly defined' (1994: 97). Preece further notes that '*surveys do require careful thought, advice, discussion with more experienced researchers and time for preparation, and ... the role of surveys within the organization of the research needs to be clearly defined*' (1994: 97; emphasis in original). Linguistic traps plague the design both of surveys and interviews, particularly across cultures. In choosing the interview option other matters arise, such as 'a clear vision of the issues to be discussed', appropriateness of type, access to informants, funding, building in time for transcription and data analysis, and much more (Denscombe, 1998: 121).

It is necessary to carefully discriminate information needs in the process of designing data-gathering instruments, whatever these happen to be. In deciding which details to record, return to your research goals, to the issues you are engaging with in your research, and talk further with your supervisor and others in your test or research group before final decision-making. Insufficient or incorrectly recorded details are time-consuming to redress later, and cause considerable stress when writing: keep a research diary, a notebook or an online site for this. It can be easy to forget precisely what transpired and sometimes difficult to know what details you will need until you write your paper or thesis.

It could also be instructive to compare your chosen method of recording data with those of other practitioners. There may be better ways of organizing the information, and it is useful to realize this at the outset. If you are keeping a paper-copy laboratory book, for example, you might consider recording your data electronically via online notes, wikis or shared folders.

Discriminating information needs

As with data-gathering, your objective when reading is to ensure that the information you gather into notes is best suited to the specific writing task in hand. It is all too easy to rush into reading without discriminating clearly the information you will need to complete a specific writing task, a task that will have clearly defined research goals/aims, or specific topic or project objectives.

Think carefully about why you are reading a source and what you hope to gain from reading it: not the details but the *types* of information. Initially, review your information needs in terms of whether you are (1) attempting a broad understanding of the literature, as when trying to get on top of the current status of the relevant literature for a big research project, or (2) searching for more focused information to meet already defined research goals of a specific writing or presentation task in your course, as with an essay or report. In the latter case, the more time you put into brainstorming and thinking about your topic or project (see → 'Topics (or questions)' in Chapter 5), the more likely it is that the information you gather will issue in a solid piece of work.

Ensuring task-focused information is no less important in the following learning contexts.

Student laboratories, clinicals and practicals

The common component of student laboratories, clinicals and practicals (as distinct from tutorials) is that you learn by doing in a context of practical training suited to future employment. Such learning usually takes place in a structured environment under the guidance of a demonstrator, instructor or lecturer, which puts considerable pressure on your listening, note-taking and questioning skills.

 **key points**

It is vital to clarify the precise objectives and procedures for assessment. If the instructor delivers these verbally at the beginning of a practical, take careful notes.

Clarify the precise practitioner knowledge, skills and competencies you are required to develop before the start of a practical, and what communication tasks will be expected of you in assessment. For example:

- Will you have oral and/or demonstration and/or written tests (for example, a laboratory report, an essay or an exam)?
- Will you, for example, be tested on your ability to describe accurately particular apparatus or equipment, or procedures for using these, including how to adjust, say, the tension on a piece of equipment?
- Will you be tested on your knowledge of requisite safety procedures in using particular materials or equipment?

- Will you be expected to detail the nature of responses taking place under certain stimuli or to codify the underlying principles of such responses (not the same thing)?
- Will you be tested on the effectiveness of your communication skills, say, with patients, including your understanding of cross-cultural communication needs?

Managing your reading load

You will also need to vary your reading strategies to improve efficiency, as much time can be lost to unproductive reading in both coursework and research degrees.

Reading intensively and skimming

At times you will need to read intensively: read every word of a text from the first to the last word. This is most likely in these contexts:

- There is a set text for a course, perhaps to be read gradually throughout a semester.
- You are trying to build up basic but in-depth knowledge about some area of research or a new discipline.
- You are conducting archival research or need to read primary texts in detail (for example, literary texts, legal or historical documents).
- You have to read difficult, dense texts (for example, legal, scientific or philosophical texts or those that are highly theoretical). Such texts or parts of them may even need re-reading to improve understanding.

Quick review of a source will not necessarily confirm its appropriateness for your writing task information needs. This is when you should activate **skimming**. Skimming is appropriate in situations of this type:

- When you are conducting a broad survey of the literature to determine what has been done generally, perhaps with a view to identifying a suitable topic for research.
- When you are trying to extract only key points or general information from a text. In this case, you would be trying to by-pass the multitude of detail typically embedded in academic analyses and arguments – keyword skimming can be useful with online texts.
- When you have set up your own topic of investigation, having thought through the precise type of information you will need to meet the research goals/objectives of that topic.
- When you have been given a set assignment or project in which the research goals/ objectives and scope have been explicitly laid out.

The last two points are particularly relevant if you are a coursework student.

Unproductive reading leads to the information gathered being insufficient to the task, only marginally relevant or even irrelevant. Although it might seem unnatural at first not to read every word, skimming can cut through unproductive reading, thus giving you time to search out more useful source materials.

key points

The time constraints on completing writing and presentation tasks in taught courses mean it is imperative not to lose time to unproductive reading.

First, consider these questions preparatory to skimming:

- In setting up my own topic or project, have I defined my goals/aims/objectives and scope clearly enough to begin, or to refine, information-gathering?
- In addressing a topic set by the lecturer, have I brainstormed the topic to ensure I can deal fully with the central concerns of the topic – all of them? (See → 'Topics (or questions)' in Chapter 5).
- Am I clear about the type and extent of information I will need to write the different parts of my text? For example, in the discussion section of a report you will need to situate your findings in relation to those of other scholars, and so will need to have this information to hand when writing.
- Will the information I am gathering allow me to answer the research questions or meet the research goals of my paper, and meet expectations of the type of writing I am doing? Check during the process of reading that you are on target with relevant information, including critical information.

A major objective of skimming is to determine what *precisely* the author is discussing or talking about at different points in the text. This will help you to decide whether to read the whole text intensively, or only parts of it because only those parts will meet your present information needs.

Skimming can work because of the way academic texts are organized (see → 'Effective paragraph development' in Chapter 4). To recap briefly, in academic writing academic paragraphs are built around main ideas that are often placed in the first or last sentence of the paragraph, so making it easy to identify the precise subject being discussed.

Strategies for information storage

You will also want to retrieve information efficiently so as to reduce the frustration of time wasted when writing. Options may include local computer folders or index cards, but, where possible, you should use an online research or note management tool such as Evernote.com, Mendeley.com or Zotero.org. Such tools are easy to use, customizable and improve retrieval efficiency through the use of **tags** (keywords) and advanced search functions; some will even search photographs of handwritten notes. Evernote, Mendeley and Zotero all have the capability to synchronize your notes across the various computers and mobile devices that you might be using, so you can always access the latest version of your data, and even work offline. They also allow you to take a local backup of your data, and, in some instances, to annotate pdfs.

These further strategies can be used in tandem with an online research management tool or independently of such usage:

- When you have a rough idea of how you might divide up, say, your thesis chapters (for example, theory or methodology chapters), set up separate folders or notebooks for each chapter. Many students find it useful to set these up quite early in the research. With these folders or notebooks in place, you can add source materials plus ideas, thoughts, notes and hunches – anything that might be at all relevant – as they occur to you along the way (keep paper and pen beside your bed for those brilliant 3 a.m. insights!). If your chapter organization subsequently changes, then you can re-sort the material into new locations, discarding what you no longer want.
- Categorize information and notes in ways that make sense to you. For example, you might have a folder or notebook that contains all your reading materials and annotations, with each item given tags or keywords. Other sets of notes might be categorized as, say, key concepts, themes, issues, theories or methodologies, or perhaps subject categories.
- Keep everything in Evernote.com. An all-purpose, electronic note-taking system, Evernote allows you to save various file formats, including image formats; record voice memos; email or Tweet notes directly to your collection; clip web pages; synchronize your notes across digital devices; search handwriting in photonotes; import and synchronize from other reference managers; and create manual backups. Storage upgrades are available.
- Use Mendeley.com to store research papers. Mendeley's homepage describes the service as being 'Like iTunes™ for research papers'. With Mendeley, you can automatically extract citations from pdfs; synchronize your work across digital devices; import and synchronize from other reference managers; create pdf sticky notes and annotations; and create manual backups. Storage upgrades are available.
- Create a library with Zotero.com. This is a simple Firefox extension that creates a library for you to store, manage and share your materials. Zotero allows you to archive web pages; install plugins for Word and OpenOffice; take notes next to the source; synchronize across digital devices; and create manual backups. Storage upgrades are available.

Managing common writing concerns

Some common concerns that students frequently raise when producing their texts are now discussed.

Monitoring your approach

One concern centres on the time and effort it takes to write, which often ties in with the approach taken to writing.

> It has been suggested that there are two distinct types of academic writers: 'Serialists' … see writing as a sequential process in which the words are corrected as they are written and who plan their writing in detail before beginning to write. 'Holists' … can only think as they write and compose a succession of complete drafts. (Lowenthal and Wason, cited in Phillips and Pugh, 1994: 65)

You may shift between these approaches depending on the difficulty of your text, or parts of the text you are producing. Another notable approach is the **layered approach to writing**, where authors start with a reasonably structured, but basic first draft that is repeatedly expanded on – filled in, so to speak – as research continues and understanding of the subject is progressively refined.

The important issue in all this is the efficiency of your approach in terms of the time and effort it takes to produce your texts. Serialists may well see their approach as efficient, though a few suffer from over-perfectionism, correcting every little detail over and over again, so that progress is exceptionally slow. Holists (sometimes called 'get-em-all-outers') often hold the preconception that their approach is indeed inefficient. As a holist, you will prefer to go straight to the computer and start writing. Little thought will be given to structure, the idea being to work out what you want to focus on and to generate ideas about your topic. Rough writing of this type serves a useful function for the holist and is not in itself necessarily problematic.

Following through on solid preparation, as discussed throughout this chapter, may be the key to reducing the time invested in producing your texts, rather than changing your approach. If your approach works for you, stay with it, as there is no one 'right' way. If you are uncertain about the efficiency of your approach, or feel that you struggle with writing, try this self-monitoring exercise from which interesting patterns and insights can emerge.

 exercise: self-monitoring when writing

Step 1

On the next occasion of writing, monitor the conditions under which you struggle (for example, generating ideas about your topic; uncertainty about how to proceed with the type of writing you are doing; organizing your paragraphs or linking parts of your discussion; marshalling evidence in an argument and ensuring logical development of your ideas; or writing up a theory section or chapter). Take concise notes about these instances. Note what is actually happening, why you think it is happening (if you can), and how long it takes you to overcome the difficulty: A matter of hours? Days? Or what? Also monitor how many days/weeks it takes you from the first phase of writing to completion of a draft, along with how many drafts you write.

Step 2

Make an appointment with a lecturer, supervisor, or a language, learning or writing adviser to discuss your notes, and gain advice on how to improve the situation.

Confronting the 'writing block'

Many students phrase their concern in terms of a 'writing block'. This is a fuzzy concept that generally translates as 'I just can't write'. But do take heart. Writing blocks can usually be traced to quite identifiable factors, often interrelated, of the following type:

- Confusion about specific task requirements, such as uncertainty about how to proceed with a particular type of writing or part of it, or not having to hand the type of information needed to complete the task (see → 'Ensuring task-focused information' earlier in this chapter).
- Uncertainty about expectations of academic writing practices and how to take control of specific situations, like avoiding plagiarism (see → 'Referencing and plagiarism' in Chapter 3).
- Insufficient control of strategies for structuring and developing texts (see → 'Principles of sound structure', Chapter 4).
- Lack of subject matter comprehension, perhaps because time pressures have thwarted attempts to build up a thorough understanding of your material, in which case review your time management strategies (see → 'Effective self-management' in Chapter 1).

Word processing too can feature in writing blocks. Word processing provides many advantages when writing, for example, shifting chunks of material within and across documents. But doing this can contribute to incoherence in the writing. Print out texts that you have altered by shifting material around. It is easier to identify disruptions to the flow of a discussion, and other substantive problems, by reading a printout than it is by moving down a screen.

Nevertheless, deeply rooted psychological problems (for example, a fear of writing or obsessive over-perfectionism) can cause severe blockages, which may need to be worked through with a professional counsellor at your institution.

Ensure that you allow sufficient time to complete your writing tasks. Sometimes the stress occasioned by having to rush the writing to meet deadlines itself becomes a block, so adopt these strategies:

- Write early and write often. To begin writing a first draft of a thesis or long report without having produced writing along the way that will feed into it is not a good idea.
- Access the writing at a point at which it seems least difficult, if you are struggling to start. Usually some parts are easier to write than others. Do not concern yourself initially with issues of focus and structure – just get ideas down.
- Try not to leave off writing at a point at which you feel blocked. This makes it harder to return to the writing. Knowing where you are going in your writing provides incentive to return to it.

Handling critical feedback

Another important concern relates to critical feedback from lecturers and supervisors. Criticism is a valuable feedback mechanism. Understandably though, students can be sensitive to criticism of their drafts and presentations. Where the criticism is perceived as unduly harsh, some become so upset their confidence plunges and they are left feeling vulnerable. If this should happen, it is important to remember that it is your writing that is being criticized (or it should be), not you.

Consider these strategies:

- Seek immediate support from your institution's counselling centre if you are very upset.
- Put aside your draft for a few days until you can assess the criticisms with more detachment.
- Think carefully about the usefulness of the criticisms in terms of your research focus and objectives, your arguments, structure and so forth.
- Discuss the criticisms further with your lecturer/supervisor, if you feel this is warranted.
- Use your online networks for support.
- Seek assistance from an academic skills, learning or writing adviser when redrafting.

Sometimes though, it is not the criticism itself but the tone of the criticism that upsets. You may perceive comments as overly aggressive or condescending. Take this up with your supervisor/lecturer if you feel able to. Let them know that, while you value their critical feedback, you were upset by the way this was given; have an example or two to show if they ask: 'What do you mean?'

Many students also mention the unbalanced nature of critical feedback on their writing, noting that lecturers and supervisors seem to view useful feedback as consisting solely in negative comments. They may well perceive such comments as being the most useful, and they will be as long as you understand how to apply advice to improve your work.

key points

Try to extract value from *all* criticism, however negative – make it work for you by not taking it too personally.

further resources

Denscombe, M. (2007) *The Good Research Guide: For Small-scale Social Research Projects*. 3rd edn. Buckingham: Open University Press. An easy to read but thorough introductory exploration of the purposes, functions, advantages and disadvantages of a range of qualitative data-gathering methods.

Sage Research Methods Online (SRMO). An excellent research tool for students in the social and behavioural sciences, which not only contains a comprehensive list of leading book and reference materials on research methods, but also editorially selected material from Sage journals. http://srmo.sagepub.com

Wallace, M. and Wray, A. (2006) *Critical Reading and Writing for Postgraduates*. London: Sage Publications. A systematic, in-depth analysis of the dynamic relation between evaluative reading, argument development and writing in different contexts, with careful scaffolding of advice and tasks.

3

Essentials of Academic Writing

developmental objectives

By applying the strategies, doing the exercises and following the procedural steps in this chapter, you should be able to:

- Understand whether or not you need to modify, adapt or develop new practices to meet the communicative demands of your current situation.
- Renew your acquaintance with standard academic writing practices that contribute to the overall quality of writing.
- Realize the usefulness of style manuals, when to reference sources and how to avoid plagiarism.
- Appreciate the complex role of the reader and identify strategies for accommodating the reader when you write.
- Identify strategies to ensure clarity in writing, conciseness, and appropriate use of voice and tone.

You will already possess a bank of general ideas about writing, along with specific textual knowledge, skills and strategies built up from previous tertiary study and/or work experience. While these are indeed valuable, this chapter provides an opportunity for reflection on your current practices.

The mechanics of academic writing

Good practice involves close attention to academic standards of consistency and accuracy in terms of writing practices, formatting, spelling and punctuation.

The discussions that follow in this chapter draw attention to some standard practices with which you may wish to reacquaint yourself.

Ensuring consistency of practice

Consistency is expected of all academic writing. Consistency refers to just about everything: the way you write dates, numbers, percentages, foreign words (non-English), refer to other scholars and set up bibliographies, hyphenation and capitalization practices, typography and so forth. Decide how you will write something and stay with that practice throughout your text – take notes if need be. Work out which fonts (italics, bold, underline, plain) and font sizes (9, 10, 12, 14, and so on) and combinations of these you want to use for specific purposes, and follow these rigorously. It can be time-consuming to alter formatting and typography later if you are not using an electronic reference or style manager. Even then, inconsistencies might need to be addressed manually as, for example, if italics, bold type and underlining have been used inconsistently throughout a thesis for emphasis.

key points

Finalize formatting and typography decisions *before* writing a first full draft.

The best method of ensuring consistency is to follow a discipline-appropriate style manual or to review author practices in relevant refereed journals and follow those. While certain practices may vary from article to article or journal to journal, you should find internal consistency in a published text. More is said about this matter of consistency in ensuing sections.

Spelling, grammar and proofreading

key points

There are many excellent grammar and spelling applications available for smartphones and tablet devices.

Many graduates now report sole reliance on spelling- and grammar-checkers. A computer spell-checker can help standardize your spelling, and it will pick up many errors. But it will not pick up everything, including incorrect substitutions (for example, 'an' when you mean 'and', or 'form' when you mean 'from'). Grammar-checkers also serve their purpose but they are more intuitive than logical, so that suggestions given are sometimes dubious, and even wrong. Applying grammar-checkers can aggravate rather than alleviate second-language error if you do not have the confidence to assess the validity of suggestions. Nor will they help you to identify more substantive textual problems, such as flow problems due to shifting material around on the computer, missing or incorrect references or illogical arguments, and so forth. In many instances it is preferable to turn off spelling- and grammar-checkers altogether.

You should proofread your work, preferably in hard copy, as it is easier to detect errors/textual problems in this way. Even better, organize exchange proofreading with a fellow student if possible, as it is less taxing to proofread another's work than your own.

Professionalism means proofreading your texts carefully before submitting them.

Punctuation

Punctuation is part of the *meaning* of a text.

You will need to know how to punctuate correctly, whether you incline to minimal or heavy punctuation. Preferred disciplinary practices, the complexity of sentence structure and personal preference can all influence the extent of punctuation. If punctuation practices trouble you, then refer to one of the many excellent punctuation guides available on the Internet, the best of which are published on library and university websites. Alternatively, you might want to download a punctuation and/or grammar app for your smartphone or tablet device, or subscribe to a regular grammar podcast such as 'Grammar Girl'.

Referencing and plagiarism

In producing your texts, you will also need to apply rigorous academic standards when acknowledging and referencing source material.

Choosing a referencing style

As referencing practices are bound to disciplinary cultures, there are many different style manuals. Some of the better known are Vancouver style, which follows rules established by the International Committee of Medical Journal Editors; *The Publication Manual of the American Psychological Association (APA)* (popular in the social sciences and some sciences); *The MLA Handbook for Writers of Research Papers (MLA)* (popular in the arts and humanities); *The Chicago Manual of Style* (used across research areas); and the *Australian Guide to Legal Citation* (Law).

Style manuals provide information on how to reference, or cite, in the body of a text, and how to write the 'bibliography', which usually includes all sources consulted in producing a text. A 'references list' or a 'list of works cited' usually includes only those sources to which you actually refer in the body of your text. Such manuals also illustrate the differences in style for citing sources in your text and putting these in a bibliography. They further illustrate how to cite a range of different items, for example, an article, a book by several authors, a television documentary, a play, a blog entry, an unauthored document, a podcast, a multi-volume reference work, a Facebook comment, different types of Internet sites, and many more. Regardless of what you are referencing, you will need to include sufficient detail to allow readers to *easily* access that source if they so wish.

Online reference managers

If you are using an electronic or online reference manager (for example, Mendeley or Zotero), selecting a referencing style is as simple as clicking a button, with standardization being automatic; styles can also be switched at any point to accommodate course/disciplinary or publisher preferences. But note that automatic style generators are no substitute either for proper proofreading or for an understanding of correct referencing and citation practices in the first place.

Offline strategies

If you are not using such software, consider these strategies:

- Ask your lecturer/supervisor to refer you to an acceptable style manual. Many can be found online, but paper copies are also located in the reference sections of libraries; there are even style apps available for smartphones and tablet devices.
- Follow the journal house style used by authors who have published in a quality, refereed journal in your area.
- Listen to a podcast or view a presentation about referencing on iTunes U.

Be rigorously consistent in using the referencing style you do adopt. Such consistency extends to types and placement of punctuation marks, the use of capitalization, whether titles or works published independently are underlined or italicized, whether an item published within another publication (for example, journal articles or chapters in a multi-authored edited volume) is in inverted commas or not, and so forth.

In preparing a bibliography, some basic considerations are:

- Arrange items in alphabetical order of authors' names.
- Insert an unauthored source alphabetically by way of the document's title.
- Make sure your bibliographic style is rigorously consistent in every respect.

Avoiding plagiarism

Universities treat cases of plagiarism very seriously, and lecturers and supervisors are skilled in detecting plagiarized work. You should therefore take time to familiarize yourself with your institution's various policies, guidelines and codes of conduct relating to plagiarism and research integrity, and read carefully any departmental handouts on the subject, as ignorance is no excuse when it comes to plagiarism.

key points

Honesty is crucial in study and research.

Deliberate plagiarism is viewed as outright cheating (for example, downloading or copying-and-pasting unsourced material – sometimes whole essays – from the Internet, or copying another student's work), and penalties can be harsh, and even include dismissal from an institution.

The causes of plagiarism, however, can be complex. As examples, each of the following is discussed in turn:

1. Insufficient understanding of conventional practices governing the use of source material in academic writing.
2. Insufficient understanding of the task-specific uses to which source material will be put.
3. Failing to distinguish when you are drawing on source material and when you are interpolating your own comments.
4. Poor time management.

Practices governing the use of source material

When you write, you need to acknowledge the hard work (including mental work) of those scholars on whose work you draw. Disciplinary practices can vary, which is why it is vitally important to follow an appropriate style manual. Still, in general, you will need to cite your sources, including sources from the Internet, in situations such as the following:

60

key points

If English is a second language, do take care. It is all too easy to introduce second-language errors into direct quotations and can be time-consuming to check the correct wording of the flawed quotations.

When you quote directly from another author   This means when you reproduce the *exact* words of the author in your own text, and do make sure they are exact. Signal direct quoting by using double ("....") or single ('....') quote marks around the extract. Or indent longer quotes (usually over four lines) about five spaces from the margin.

If you insert anything into a direct quotation or change anything in that quotation, it is usual to indicate this by placing square brackets [...] around the word/s you have inserted or changed. If something unusual appears in the original quotation (for example, a misspelling), place [*sic*] meaning 'thus' after the misspelt or otherwise seemingly incorrect word or expression. '*Sic*' communicates 'this is how it appeared in the original source'.

When you paraphrase what another author has said   This means when you put what another has said into your own words. Make sure you do use your own words. Paraphrase proves challenging for some students. If you are uncertain about this, Google OWL Purdue, which has a good discussion of 'Quoting, paraphrasing, and summarizing'.

When you summarize, refer to or use another author's ideas, theories, methodologies, models, procedures, arguments, results, insights, interpretations, information or data   All these require intellectual, and sometimes manual, effort on the part of another and you need to acknowledge this.

When you use distinctive language or phrases from another author, including those phrases that have been coined by an author to denote a concept or specific meaning.

When taking notes from reading, work out a system (use colour-coding if that works for you) that clearly distinguishes the following:

- Direct quotations from other sources, that is, where you are reproducing the *exact* wording of an author (note page number/s).
- Material from other sources that you are paraphrasing: putting into your own words. No page numbers will be needed if you are referring to a source in general, but these will be needed when citing specific information from some part of a source in your discussions.
- Your own observations, views or comments that you wish to document.

61

Task-specific uses of source material

The second point above is now addressed by way of a case study example.

 case study example

box 3.1 Plagiarism can arise from the misunderstanding of task-specific objectives

Three graduates for whom English is a second language were advised to seek help because they were not using their 'own' words when paraphrasing source material; in effect they were plagiarizing. In discussing the problem with each of them in separate consultations, it soon became clear that their real difficulty lay elsewhere. Their writing task involved critically evaluating a published article. But the students had not understood that their lecturer did not want them to report on, or simply repeat, what the author was saying, but rather to assess the strengths and weaknesses of the paper. With this new understanding in place, the students were encouraged to concentrate on formulating the key points they wanted to make in developing their critical review, to think about why they were taking that position, how they would develop their key points, and to use material from the paper to backup these points (by way of summary comment, by incorporating key words or phrases as direct quotations, and by using only page references). As all three students were able to verbalize their critical insights, it was clear that they had already thought deeply about the article. The true cause of their apparent plagiarism was a misunderstanding of writing task objectives.

Distinguishing source material and comment

Plagiarism may also be suspected if you do not make clear whether the ideas being discussed belong to another or are your own comment. Take the text below, where in the original version it is impossible to determine which ideas belong to X (the source) and which to the writer:

Original text:

X's critique of truth [reference] is based on his analysis of discursive procedures. The relation between truth and power is one between truth and discursive practice. Truth is not a stable and independent entity.

Amended text:

X's critique of truth [reference] is based on his analysis of discursive procedures. The relation between truth and power is **[seen by him as]** one between truth and discursive practice. **[This suggests]** that truth is not a stable and independent entity.

It is clear from the inserted material shown in bold type in the amended text that the ideas in the first two sentences belong to the source (X), on whom the writer is drawing, and that the writer herself is interpolating her own comment in the third sentence.

Nor is placing a reference at the end of a succession of paragraphs a sound practice. If all the ideas in a paragraph are being taken from a single source and you are not interpolating any comments of your own, then simply phrase your lead sentences to indicate that this will be so, as in these hypothetical examples:

1. The following discussion draws on an empirical study undertaken by X (2009).
2. Further support for this type of intervention is found in X's argument (2006), as now discussed.
3. The extent of military interference in the political process is attested to in an extensive study undertaken by X, Y and Z (2000).

As lead sentences in paragraphs, sentences of this type would set up reader-expectation that all that follows in that paragraph is taken from the nominated source.

Poor time management

Many students find themselves under pressures of time when it comes to submitting work for graduate studies. In such situations, it can be easy to cut-and-paste sections of work without due acknowledgement simply in order to meet a deadline. It is always better to ask for an extension in such instances – or even to hand in your work late – rather than risk plagiarizing. It will surely help to revisit your time management, as discussed under → 'Effective self-management' in Chapter 1.

Attending to readers' needs

When immersed in complex trains of thought while writing, it is easy to forget that you are always writing *for* someone. It is vitally important to understand and take into account the needs of your readers on every occasion of writing. No matter how impressive your ideas and insights, these will be lost if your readers cannot understand what you are doing and why, or follow where you are going.

Just who your readers will be depends on the type of communication task in which you are engaged, which is why this subject is taken up in different contexts throughout this book. Still, in many cases your readers will be your lecturers/supervisors, who may also be your examiners, and, in the case of some dissertations, your external examiners. This is the group now considered, with initial emphasis on the all-important matter of disciplinary practices from the angle of the reader.

key points

Always take full account of readers' needs to ensure effective communication with them.

The reader as disciplinary practitioner

Academics will bring to the reading of your text the expectation that it will evidence appropriateness, that is to say, what they 'judge' to be appropriate (see Fairclough, 1992). Reader expectations of the style and structure of, say, an engineering report, an engineering essay involving sustained argument, or an engineering research proposal, will be different. Academic readers will also expect appropriate treatment of subject matter, which is important to recognize when transferring disciplines. For example, an anthropologist, a sociologist, a political scientist or an art historian will engage different questions and issues when treating the same subject of 'identity'.

As another example, if your writing task were a 'briefing paper' intended to address, say, a particular group of farmers, then your lecturer would expect you to take full account of the nature, make-up and interests of that audience – the group of farmers. In reading your paper, your lecturer would assess how effectively you had managed to address that particular audience.

In making these observations about appropriateness, we do not intend to imply that academic readers will not allow for and welcome creativity in your writing. There is much room for you to manoeuvre creatively within the framework of genre and disciplinary writing practices, just as the experts do. Still, as Mikhail Bakhtin observes: 'genres must be fully mastered to be used creatively' (1986: 80).

The reader as subject specialist

Your lecturers and supervisors are subject specialists. It is not, however, a good idea to fix on the fact that you are writing for experts in the content when you write. Doing this can lead to insufficient textual explanation, underdeveloped ideas, definitional and other problems because you assume that your lecturers/supervisors, as experts, will know what you mean. They may well do, but they want to know what *you* know.

key points

Readers who critically appraise your texts will be authorities on the subject, but you are the communicative authority who can help ensure a positive appraisement.

It is more important then, not to focus on what your reader knows, but to direct your efforts to demonstrating that *you* have a thorough critical understanding of all materials being worked in your text, that you do know what you are talking about. In this way, you are more likely to forestall criticism from your readers, those subject specialists your lecturers and supervisors.

Signposting: signalling your intentions

Regardless of their being subject specialists, your readers will expect you to recognize that they are certainly not experts in the decisions *you* make (for example, the meanings *you* give to terms, phrases, and so on, what *you* choose to focus on, why *you* take the approach you do, how *you* organize and develop discussions, and so on). You will need to signal your intentions, which is sometimes called 'signposting'.

You are the tour guide on this journey through your research, and like any thoughtful guide, you need to work out a coherent tour of your (intellectual) journey, and anticipate where, what and how much contextual information might be needed to keep readers in the picture before moving on to the next spot in your writing. Provide sufficient information, particularly as you lead into new subdivisions, to ensure readers are kept in the picture, that they understand what you will be doing and why. Mark the stages of your writing by signalling or signposting your intentions: where you are going, why you are doing what you are doing, what you want to show or demonstrate, reasons for departures from main lines of discussion, and so forth.

The extent of signalling can vary because of preferred disciplinary or individual practices. Still, however subtle signposting may be, it does need to be there, so respect the intelligence of your readers by not clotting the text with too many such signals.

Clarity: the first rule of style

Clarity of course encompasses much more than style (for example, the whole of the next chapter on structure might be invoked), but it is also the first rule of style. It is a rule that will serve you well in all your communication activities.

In 1985, US economist Donald McCloskey wrote a substantial article entitled 'Economical writing'. His is a lively, rich probing of the bad 'habits of style' of economists. It is an impassioned plea for stylistic reform and the ways to reform. Essentially, McCloskey's article is a eulogy to clarity that has generic value. He belongs with a host of writers similarly concerned, including George Orwell, more famous for his novel *1984* than his spirited essay of 1946 'Politics and the English language', which continues to be resurrected and can be accessed on the Internet.

One topic McCloskey alludes to is the 'affliction' of abstraction, a disease that obscures rather than clarifies meaning. It *is* possible for you to deal with complex theory, ideas, abstract concepts and the like in a way that makes meaning easily accessible for your reader, and that should be your goal.

Good writers do not rely on highly inflated abstract language to impress. Good writers impress with the quality of their research, the complexity of their thinking, the soundness of their reasoning, the subtlety of their insights, the rigour and crispness of their prose, the sophistication with which they use the disciplinary language and engage the theory. Good writers prefer language that is 'definite, specific, concrete' (Strunk Jr and White, 2000: 21). They care about readers and readability. They can be found everywhere, in all disciplines, across the entire academic community of writers. And you can be one of them.

key points

Good writers are as concerned not to be misunderstood as they are to be understood.

You will quickly recognize these writers when you come across them. Take a close look at the stylistic features of their texts (see → 'Mastering disciplinary writing practices' in Chapter 2) and you will see why you have so enjoyed the reading, regardless of the difficulty of the content.

Other style issues

Style is not merely decorative but part of the meaning of a text. Improving aspects of style can increase the overall effectiveness of your communication.

An incisive, vigorous prose style contributes to the communicative rigour and precision of academic writing, thus ensuring a more positive appraisal of your work and increased reader enjoyment.

The strategies now suggested may require vocabulary extension if you wish to apply them; but, then, extending vocabulary is important for effective communication. Try for language that invigorates the prose, adds some zest. An excellent starting point is scrutiny of verb choices, as the English verb is a singular carrier of energy. Not only do active verbs enliven prose, so too do more striking verbs and other diction.

Pause to consider the energizing effects of these replacement verbs, which also aid conciseness:

1. These reforms *led to more* **[accelerated]** interest in conservation programmes.
2. We examined the factors that *were responsible for* **[governed]** the stability of the regulating system.
3. A route selection process was *put into operation* **[invoked]** to determine which was preferable.

Try also to avoid clichés, worn-out words and phrases that will depress your writing, drain it of energy. One prominent example is the repeated use in a text of the tired media phrase 'has played a role in' (and its variations). The writing could be energized by selecting a variety of simple replacements, for example: has *influenced, affected, shaped, contributed to*, or whatever seems appropriate in context, as illustrated below by way of three examples taken from a page and a half of writing:

1. The organization *played a leading role* **[was instrumental]** in stopping …
2. The organization has *played a disproportionately large role* **[been pivotal]** in moving …
3. The organization *played an important role in* **[helped shape]** …

On this issue of variation, do take care though. It is helpful to vary language for reader interest, but not just for the sake of variation itself so that the reader becomes confused:

> Elegant Variation uses many words to mean one thing, with the result that in the end no one, not even the writer, really knows what the thing is. A paper on economic development used in two pages all these: 'industrialization,' 'growing structural differentiation,' 'economic and social development,' 'social and economic development,' 'development,' 'economic growth,' 'growth' and 'revolutionized means of production.' With some effort one can see in context that they all meant about the same thing. (McCloskey, 1985: 210)

This is another illustration of the same problem from a student text:

> *As I do not speak Mandarin, I had to use **interpreters** with newly immigrated Chinese. **Translators**, however, create a screen between researcher and informants. The researcher has to rely on the accuracy of **interviewers** in translating both questions and responses.*

While all three emphasized words actually meant the 'interpreters', a reader will struggle to recognize this because of unhelpful variation.

It is also important to respect the meanings of words. Words such as *aspects, features, issues, elements, factors, parts, concepts* and *ideas* are sometimes used interchangeably to have the same meaning when they have distinctive meanings. *Issue*, meaning 'the point or matter in contention', is repeatedly misused in writing. Issue is selected when not really discussing an issue at all, but rather a subject or topic, a particular fact, an idea or notion. You should clarify the meanings of even commonly used words of this type if you are uncertain – use a good dictionary or a thesaurus. A dictionary of synonyms and antonyms can also be a useful resource.

Avoid, too, practices certain to cause vagueness in writing. A typical example is use of the old media favourite 'dramatic': 'a dramatic increase', 'a dramatic turnaround', 'a dramatic slump or fall or drop', 'dramatic changes'. A word such as dramatic does not convey the type of rigour expected of graduate writing. Instead of the vague 'dramatic increase' be more precise: 'exports rose by 89%', or 'exports doubled in 1993', or 'exports increased from around $US1.5m to $US2.3m'.

Conciseness

Conciseness aids clarity. But do not confuse conciseness with density. Whereas conciseness is a positive attribute of writing, density is not. If your text is dense, a reader will find it difficult to follow your line of discussion because of cognitive leaps, insufficient detail, marginal signalling, under-developed ideas, missing links and so forth.

Conciseness is the opposite of wordiness, that is, taking too many words to say what you have to say, a practice that pads the writing, sometimes so much so as to obscure main points. Excess wording is a major cause of over-writing, and takes up valuable space that can be put to better use, such as bringing in more points to support a position you are developing.

key points

Google 'The Wasteline Test' to see how your writing is travelling – it can be very illuminating.

exercise: developing conciseness

Step 1

Select a wordy paragraph from your own writing, preferably a long one. Your objective is to reduce the number of words by about one-third while conveying the same information.

Step 2

Scrutinize each sentence carefully. Be ruthless: remove unnecessary words and repetitious material. Substitute one word for several, for example, 'now' for 'at this point in time', or 'yearly' for 'on a yearly basis'; cross out adjectives/adverbs (often superfluous); rework sentences to convey information more concisely (see → 'Manipulating sentence structure' in Chapter 4). Exclude details that add nothing to your discussion; but do not exclude important details needed to support ideas you are developing, which is unfortunately often a first choice for students wanting to cut back on length. This is an example of tightening at the sentence level, which illustrates just how wordy even sentences can be:

Original text

Initially, they test the impact of growth in the working population and growth in the total population on economic growth, and find that an increase in the former will improve economic growth, but an increase in the latter will depress economic growth. (42 words)

Tightened text (two options)

a) Their initial test shows that economic growth is improved by growth in the working population but depressed by growth in the total population. (23 words)
b) They find that while growth in the working population improves economic growth, growth in the total population does not. (19 words)

Here is another example:

Original text

RRV is the etiological agent of epidemic polyarthritis, a disease which was first described in 1928 [reference]. Epidemic polyarthritis has a wide geographic distribution in X [country named], occurring regularly as epidemics in eastern X and as sporadic outbreaks in other parts of X [references]. (45 words)

(Continued)

> **Tightened text**
>
> RRV is the etiological agent of epidemic polyarthritis, first described in 1928 [reference]. This disease occurs regularly as epidemics in eastern X, and as sporadic outbreaks elsewhere in X [references]. (30 words)
>
> Perhaps this author wished to emphasize the point about 'wide geographic distribution', in which case the revision might not be acceptable as it merely implies this point. That is another consideration to keep in mind when you are doing this exercise: what ideas do you want to profile? (See → 'Effective paragraph development' in Chapter 4.)

Aspects of voice and tone

Voice in writing is shaped by individual style, including tonal qualities of your text or presentation and diction choices, as well as how you manipulate academic and disciplinary writing practices. Two issues of voice are often raised, and sometimes confused, by students:

Impersonal versus personal mode

Some disciplines favour sole use of the first person 'I', considering such usage a matter of principle that authors accept full responsibility in their writing for their ideas and research. Other disciplines reject this usage altogether, as deflecting attention away from a true focus on discussions and arguments and towards the writer. Many authors from a wide range of disciplines, including the sciences, now use a mix of impersonal (for example, in the body of the writing) and personal (for example, in introductory sections).

Active versus passive voice

As with personal or impersonal mode, lecturers/supervisors often express a preference in terms of active and passive voice, which can mean changes to your practice.

When the active voice is used, the agent/producer/instrument of the action expressed in the verb is foregrounded. The reverse is true of the passive construction. Take the following examples:

Active construction:

Management **introduced** new measures to address output problems. (Foregrounding the agent of change, 'management'.)

Passive constructions:

(a) New measures **were introduced** by management to address output problems. (Foregrounding the 'new measures', while acknowledging the agent of change, 'management'.)

(b) New measures **were introduced** to address output problems. (Foregrounding 'new measures', while obscuring the agent of change, 'management'.)

The active construction, which is more direct and energetic, need not involve use of the personal mode, as seen in these examples:

Active constructions:

(a) Results **confirm** an increase in the incidence of this type of crime. (Passive would be: An increase in the incidence of this type of crime **is confirmed** by the results.)

(b) Interventionist policies of the British colonial government **aggravated** tensions among ethnic minorities. (Passive would be: Tensions among ethnic minorities **were aggravated** by the interventionist policies of the British colonial government.)

It is not unusual to see a mix of active and passive voice in a single text, because authors may wish to apportion emphasis in a sentence differently at different times.

Strategic use of tone

Tone is a device that can be manipulated in writing to achieve desired effects. Whether you recognize it or not, the tonal qualities of your writing will convey emotional and/or mental attitudes that are influential in shaping audience responses to your text.

Tone can be approached on three levels, as follows:

1. Your attitude towards yourself as the writer (aim to be confident).
2. Your attitude towards the subject matter you are discussing (aim to show interest in and commitment to your ideas).
3. Your attitude towards your readers and/or listeners (aim to be respectful).

Confidence can be an issue for some students. Tentative language (for example, perhaps, it appears, it seems, it could be) is appropriate to use when commenting on possibilities, as when speculating. But too much of such language may trigger the reader-response that you lack confidence, as illustrated:

More confident writer:

This study **shows** that ... or This study **suggests** that ... In section 2, I **assess** the reasons for ...

Less confident writer:

This study **might mean that** ... or It **seems that the author is saying** ... In section 2, I **will try to assess** the reasons for ...

Neutral, impartial or judicious tones, with varying degrees of engagement, tend to characterize formal academic writing.

 exercise: voice and tone

It can be informative to interrogate the use of voice and tone by scholars you are reading by considering these questions:

- Are the best writers using personal or impersonal voice, and in what situations of writing if there is a mix?
- Do they favour the active or passive voice, or is there a mix and in what situations of writing?
- What is the writer's attitude towards herself/himself, towards the subject matter, and towards readers? How do these encoded attitudes influence your response to the text?

 further resources

Alley, M. (2000) *The Craft of Editing: A Guide for Managers, Scientists, and Engineers.* New York: Springer. Provides an abundance of useful information and strategies for *any* academic writer wishing to take full control of the editing process.

Gilmore, J., Strickland, D., Timmerman, B., Maher, M. and Feldon, D. (2010). 'Weeds in the flower garden: an exploration of plagiarism in graduate students' research proposals and its connection to enculturation, ESL, and contextual factors', *International Journal for Educational Integrity*, 6(1): 13–28.

Strunk, W. Jr and White, E.Bs (2000). *The Elements of Style.* 4th edn. Boston, MA: Pearson Education. An all-time favourite in the academic community (in print since 1918), this compact little book covers basic rules of grammar, misused words and phrases and aspects of style and presentation, all with straightforward practical illustrations.

4

Principles of Sound Structure

developmental objectives

By applying the strategies, doing the exercises and following the procedural steps in this chapter, you should be able to:

- Comprehend key principles of structure to avoid practices that lead to common academic writing problems.
- Identify strategies to gain control of coverage through brainstorming or mind mapping, and sequentially outlining a text.
- Realize how to use sub-headings as an effective structuring device: contributing to argument development and overall coherence.
- Develop paragraphs logically around main ideas that contribute to the development of a unifying point of view or thesis (as in argument).
- Access strategies for linking paragraphs to ensure the logical or coherent development of ideas.
- Learn how to manipulate sentence structures to give focus to important ideas and avoid monotony in the writing.
- Appreciate the necessity of discarding material that does not fit the context.
- Improve the overall structure of your writing.

Structure is the coherent ordering of your thinking about a subject in such a way as to make your ideas, discussions and arguments easily accessible and convincing to readers and examiners. Insufficient attention to matters discussed in this chapter accounts for many (but not all) problems evident in graduate writing: fragmented text, disruptions to flow, repetition, labouring the point, underdeveloped ideas, cognitive leaps, irrelevant material, and so forth. The focus here on principles of sound structure is supplemented by discussions in subsequent chapters that address structural issues specific to different types of writing.

Visual mapping of material

Visual mapping of material is a useful way to begin to gain textual control. The idea here is to mine the extensive knowledge you have on emerging from reading or other information gathering, knowledge that often goes unrecognized by students themselves.

Brainstorming and mind-mapping

A brainstorming plan can take any shape you wish. One student favoured the image of an upside-down tree; another liked to work with free-floating and intersecting boxes. You might need more than one of these plans: for a whole thesis, for each chapter, or for each subdivision.

First write your topic – a working title of, say, a chapter or section, or your research question – in the centre of a large piece of paper, then branch out from there. The idea is to brainstorm *coverage* so as to work out what you need to cover, to identify issues and to generate ideas that you want to develop. Jot down quickly anything at all that springs to mind. It does not matter how disorganized or messy your brainstorming plan is, just let your imagination float free. Get as much information into your plan as possible, and ignore structural issues at this point. You can use different coloured highlighter pens for different purposes. To give you an idea if you have not used this method before, Figure 4.1 shows a partially complete plan, but yours could be quite different depending on your visual design inclinations.

To extend this illustration, if this were a brainstorming plan for a chapter, then the different topics could be used to generate subdivision headings in terms of what is being covered; the sub-topics could be a means of focusing more precisely what needs to be covered in each subdivision; and the issues could be a means of focusing more precisely the subdivision headings in terms of *why* the topic is being covered (see → 'Using sub-headings effectively' later on in this chapter). But do not be constrained by this illustration; your needs might be different.

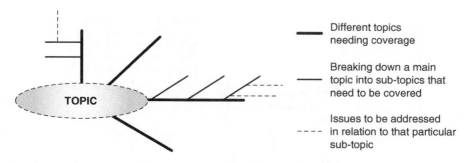

Different topics
needing coverage

Breaking down a main
topic into sub-topics that
need to be covered

Issues to be addressed
in relation to that particular
sub-topic

FIGURE 4.1   Simple brainstorming plan

Rather than brainstorming on paper, you may prefer to mind map with an online mapping application such as Bubbl.us, Cacoo.com or Mindmeister. com. If you would prefer a desktop (rather than web-based) application, then Freemind or CmapTools have proven popular. There are other, proprietary softwares available, but most come with a cost attached, as do those available for smartphones and tablets. Still, these tools generally offer a very simple 'click-drag-drop' interface, enabling you to move text, ideas and images around the 'page', and to create linkages between concepts. They also allow you to use different colours to highlight various sections of your mind map- ping plan, and to export your mind maps as images (for example, jpeg or png), or to embed your mind map in your blog, wiki or other website using an embed code.

To choose a tool or service that suits you, conduct a Google or Wikipedia search for 'mind mapping software comparison' to find a number of useful sites that will take you through the features, similarities and differences of the various mind-mapping tools and services available.

A mind map of a 30,000-word thesis is illustrated in Figure 4.2.

Sequential outlining

Brainstorming plans and mind maps can be as simple or as complex as you choose. They are particularly useful in gaining control of coverage, and they can be further developed to show a host of textual relations. Sequential out- lining is more useful for determining the logic of relations among parts of a discussion, that is, the order in which topics and sub-topics are to be covered – your overall textual design.

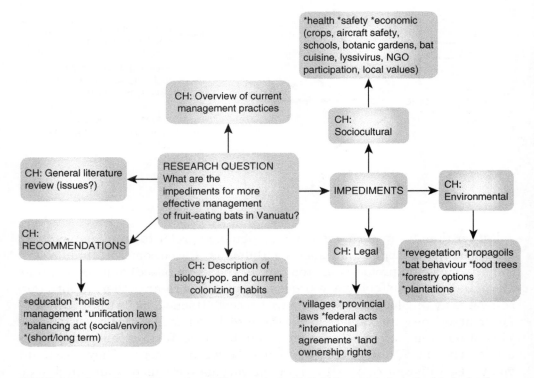

FIGURE 4.2   Sample mind-mapping outline created with Bubbl.us. (Note how the big topic of 'impediments' was broken down into three chapters.)

key points

It is not just a matter of sequencing what to cover, but sequencing stages in a discussion or argument in a coherent and logical manner.

Bear in mind these simple, but important, principles when generating sequential outlines:

- Take account of word length where there is a designated word length.
- Consider the appropriateness of information for the different parts, chapters, subdivisions, and so on.
- Determine the logical relations between parts, chapters, and so on in order to ensure coherent sequencing. The idea is to experiment with different sequential arrangements until you come up with one that seems to have a strong flow-on effect in terms of the *point of view* you are developing.

- Ensure that, in the ordering of material, the reader will have sufficient information, at each point, to follow the sequential arrangement you settle on. In particular, ensure that key concepts, terms, theories, and so on are defined, or signal where they will be defined, *before* using them throughout discussions in, say, your paper, report, or thesis chapter.

In short, think carefully about whether the sequencing you are contemplating will allow readers to follow easily your overall line of discussion.

As a next step towards further refinement of this level of outline, consider these points:

- Include working titles for chapters and/or subdivision headings.
- Designate material to be covered in the different chapters under the newly set up subdivision headings. Be as precise as possible (you may already have done this on a mind map).
- Jot down any *main ideas/points* you have in relation to material to be discussed in the different subdivisions of the different chapters – ideas around which your discussions will be built.
- Note any data/evidence you will be using to develop the main ideas you wish to bring forward.

Using sub-headings effectively

Subdivision headings, which are commonly used to divide up texts, are an important structuring device. Used properly, sub-headings can help you avoid full rewrites because of problems of textual incoherence and assist the reader to follow your lines of discussion/argument.

Some authors prefer to use different fonts to differentiate sub-headings; others favour numbering (for example, 1.1, 1.2, 1.3 and then further breakdown, for example 1.3 into 1.3.1, 1.3.2, and so on); and some use a combination of the two. Also, the extent to which sub-headings are used tends to vary, with some subject areas approving greater frequency and others insisting on substantial discussion following a sub-heading. Regardless of such differences, sub-headings cannot perform the hard work of structuring – only you can. (The sole exception here is where there is a formulaic use of sub-headings, which you will surely know about.)

 **key points**

Avoid using sub-headings as a substitute for careful structuring. This practice can lead to textual incoherence.

case study example

box 4.1 Textual incoherence due to excessive use of sub-headings

A supervisor requested that a chapter be completely reworked because it was 'incoherent'. The chapter had 29 sub-headings in 34 pages of writing. The separate bits of discussion were disconnected, and the overall composition of the chapter was fragmented. As there appeared to be no underlying logic in the selection and arrangement of sub-headings, it was impossible to identify a coherent line of discussion throughout the chapter, to detect a unifying point of view. In other words, the sub-headings were distracting rather than helpful to a reader. To address this problem, it was necessary to go back to the planning stage: to rethink the whole structure, to reduce greatly the number of sub-headings, to generate new sub-headings that accurately reflected the true focus of the discussion beneath and to review the logical flow of these newly created subdivisions to ensure they would allow development of a coherent line of discussion. Then came the rewrite.

Do ensure that your sub-headings are not merely decorative, but meaningful, as now illustrated.

Illustration   Where the topic of 'development schemes' is only one of many topics being covered in, say, a research essay on 'environmental degradation', it is not helpful to use this type of sub-heading:

Development schemes

Certain questions immediately arise:

- What is the writer's interest in development schemes as regards the topic of 'environmental degradation'?
- Why is the writer discussing these schemes at all?
- What does the writer hope to demonstrate, show or establish in discussing these schemes?

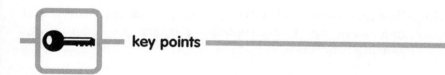

key points

In generating sub-headings, you need to consider *what* you want to cover, *why* you want to cover that subject matter and *what you want to show, demonstrate, establish or prove*.

By indicating the connection between environmental degradation and development schemes, a more precise and informative sub-heading of this type becomes possible:

Increased pesticide usage in development schemes

A reader can now easily identify from the lead-words that the writer's interest lies in 'increased pesticide usage' in development schemes, can see how this focus ties in with the theme of environmental degradation and can deduce that part of the argument will turn on this matter of increased pesticide usage.

In undertaking a lengthy discussion of the topic 'development schemes', say, in a chapter, a more general sub-heading would suffice, before breaking this down further:

1 Development schemes

    1.1 The variety and nature of existing schemes
    1.2 The effects of government policy on implementation
    1.3 The issue of 'local' knowledge
    1.4 Improving overall effectiveness

The lead-words in these headings convey the true focus of each section of the subdivision, and it is those lead-words that will guide a reader.

Developing texts

Once sub-headings are in place, the next step is the development of text. This brings us to the academic paragraph, which is the basic unit of structure in academic writing. (See also → 'Words and phrases for developing discussions' in the Appendix.) As a graduate, you are likely to have reasonable control of the academic paragraph, perhaps even fine control of it. Still, many writing problems can be traced to inadequate paragraph control, perhaps because paragraph development is intuited rather than based on clear understanding of the academic paragraph's function and significance in ensuring coherence.

Effective paragraph development

To arrive at effective paragraph development, it is necessary to fully understand the basics of how the academic paragraph functions, as is now discussed.

Capturing your main ideas

Typically, the academic paragraph is organized around a *main idea* that takes the form of a general assertion or statement that is then subsequently developed. These main ideas capture your evolving understanding of the subject you are discussing.

key points

Ensure that you do have main ideas around which to organize your paragraphs by clearly identifying these in your text.

Main ideas usually, but not necessarily, appear in the first sentence of a paragraph called the **topic sentence**, which Popken (1987) showed was a 'standard feature in academic articles' (and not only articles), with some variation in usage across disciplines. By skimming through these topic sentences, readers are able to chart the progression of your thinking.

Using main ideas to push along your thesis

Each main idea is used to advance your overall point of view, your position, or your thesis. This tight interlocking relationship is illustrated in Figure 4.3.

Your research theses and essays, or any other type of academic writing, should be organized around an identifiable point of view that you are developing. The main ideas you bring forward in your paragraphs should support your point of view – push it along, just as the details you include in developing your paragraphs should support your main ideas.

Determining paragraph length

There is no set length for a paragraph. They are, however, often long because of the amplifying detail needed to completely develop ideas within

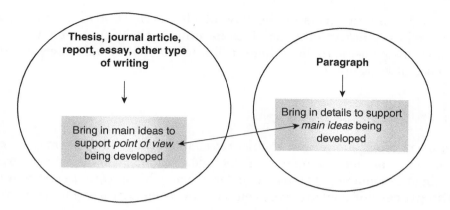

FIGURE 4.3 The structural relationship between point of view and paragraph development

the paragraph. Prominent 'organizing' ideas, as in this example, can take many paragraphs to develop:

Significant changes had taken place in the geographical landscape during this period.

Where a paragraph is used as a structural or organizational device, it may be very short, and effectively so, as in this example, where the author proceeded to discuss his results over several pages:

Previous research has relied on a recessive model that limits available options [references]. The results of this study, however, suggest that there are sound reasons to re-define the accepted boundaries.

Ensuring internal paragraph coherence

Sentences within a paragraph need to hang together, to cohere, so that they evidence a logical flow. Consider what happens in this example, where coherence breaks down:

Recall bias has been a problem in this investigation. Despite the inconclusive results, the investigation has identified the need for a review of food preparation techniques at this venue. It was not possible to identify clearly the source of contamination.

As you see, the expected paragraph focus in the first sentence is 'recall bias'. However, the next sentence ruptures this expectation by directing attention to another topic, review of 'food preparation techniques'. There is a further rupture in the third sentence as the reader is directed to yet another topic, the impossibility of identifying the 'source of contamination'. The paragraph is not coherent in terms of the flow of ideas. There are too many ideas presented too quickly, with each idea needing further development.

There also needs to be coherent linking of paragraphs across longer stretches of writing.

Strategies for linking paragraphs

Linking is often subtle and sophisticated in writing. Linking may even be unnecessary as, for example, in a methods section, where logic inheres in detailing the sequence of steps taken. Or you may be **mapping the structure in the process of writing** (very common) by using organizing topic sentences or short, sharp paragraphs that signal subsequent structure of the writing.

In situations where you will be discussing points at length, take care in using the **technique of First(ly), Second(ly), Third(ly)** to introduce paragraphs, because a reader will have forgotten what you are talking about by the time she/he gets to the fourth point on the third page of writing. Linking phrases of this type would be better:

> One strategy involved ... Another strategy ... A third strategy brought into effect because of spiralling costs was ... [reminding the reader of what you are discussing] Finally, senior management found it necessary to ...

Try to use a range of linking or transition strategies of the type now discussed, rather than rely on a standard few.

Repeating words/phrases

One of the simplest, most common and subtle transitions is the repeated word, phrase or idea:

Last sentence of a paragraph:

The nature of the ceremonial **rites** performed at this initiation ceremony is particularly important.

First sentence of the next paragraph:

These **rites** are organized around three basic activities, each with its own religious significance.

Last sentence of a paragraph:

Here X postulates two general linguistic notions: the **notion of polarities** and the notion of equivalence.

First sentence of the next paragraph:

The **notion of polarities** derives from X's insight concerning ...

The question-and-answer transition

While this type of transition can be effective, use the rhetorical question with caution, as clumsy overuse tends to produce a forced stylistic effect:

Last sentence of a paragraph:

Why did the plan fail?

First sentence of next paragraph:

X, in his analysis, suggests three major reasons.

The summarizing transition

This technique can be illustrated by this example, where, say, a writer has just completed a lengthy comparison of high school and university teaching methods and now wants to move to a new, but related, topic of 'personal responsibility' in learning. The first sentence of the next paragraph is:

Because of **these differences in teaching methods**, universities throw more responsibility on the student.

The transition is marked by using a summary phrase – 'differences in teaching methods' – to refer to the lengthy discussion just finished.

The summarizing transition may take even briefer form, with pronouns like *this, that, these, those* or *such* being used to sum up a topic discussed in the preceding paragraph/s. Such pronouns though, like all English pronouns ('it' can be a real problem), carry with them the danger of the unclear referent. It is not altogether clear in the following example whether 'these' refers back to 'policies' or 'fiscal arrangements':

Last sentence of a paragraph:

The different institutions have produced incoherent policies in terms of the tight fiscal arrangements proposed on introducing the scheme in 1992.

First sentence of the next paragraph:

These have been the subject of vigorous debate in the literature.

This problem is easily overcome by naming the referent: 'these policies' or 'these fiscal arrangements'.

 **key points**

If English pronouns give you trouble, name the referent rather than let a pronoun stand alone.

Using logical connectives

Paragraphs can also be linked by words showing logical relationship: *therefore, however, but, consequently, thus, even so, conversely, nevertheless, moreover, in addition*, and many more. Usually, though, logical connectives are used to move from one sentence to the next within paragraphs, that is, as internal paragraph transitions.

To illustrate, say a writer has just completed a paragraph summarizing an author's analysis of a documented riot and now wants to move the discussion along. Here are three different logical connectives:

Last sentence of a paragraph:

Brown's analysis provides useful insights into the existing power relations between the army and the government at that time.

Possible first sentences of the next paragraph:

(a) **However**, the power relations embedded in the social structure may be more important in explaining the causes of the riot.
(b) **Even so**, there is no real attempt to grapple with the issue of the government's role in the army's attack on unarmed men, women and children.
(c) **Consequently**, Smith's much quoted analysis of this same event needs to be reconsidered in view of Brown's findings.

Whatever its form, an inter-paragraph transition should be unobtrusive, shifting readers easily from one topic to the next.

Manipulating sentence structure

Understanding how to manipulate English sentence structures will allow you to emphasize important ideas, give focus to your writing and avoid alienating or boring readers.

These basic English sentence structures provide for very sophisticated combinations of simple, compound and complex sentences:

Simple sentence (one main idea):

Trade figures have improved.

Compound sentence (two ideas of equal weight):

Trade figures have improved and so has the economy.

Complex sentence (two ideas of unequal weight):
Although trade figures have improved, the economy remains slow.

Or:

Although the economy remains slow, trade figures have improved.

Note the shift in emphasis in the turn-around here. In the first sentence the main idea is the 'slow economy'; in the second it is the 'improved trade figures'.

Do vary your sentence structure. If writing consists of a series of simple short sentences strung together it will be monotonous and lack focus. It will be difficult for a reader to discern what *you* consider more or less important about what you are saying. An excess of long sentences can be equally troublesome. Overloaded sentences that are not well constructed can also cause reader confusion, making it difficult, even impossible, to understand the intended meaning. So do take care, particularly if English is a second language.

key points

Short, sharp, emphatic sentences (simple sentence structure) draw readers' attention to your important ideas or points and ensure they are not overlooked.

exercise: improving sentence structure

Review sentence structure in several paragraphs of your own writing and compare what you do with the practice of a disciplinary writer you admire. Could you improve?

The 'discards' file

When developing texts, you need to ensure that all ideas you bring forward are directly relevant to the topic under discussion. It is certain that at times you will need to discard material because it just does not fit the context of discussion. This can indeed be hard when it comes to being ruthless about insights and ideas you have developed as beautifully constructed sentences, paragraphs, even longer stretches of writing – pieces of writing to which you remain doggedly attached even though you sense they do not fit. Every academic writer knows about this dilemma.

Resistant though you may be, force yourself to discard such material. But never delete it. Cut it and transfer it to a special 'discards' file; give each piece of writing a summary title designating its central import. It is likely that discarded material of this type will slot perfectly into another context of writing at another time.

Improving overall structure

If you think you have structural problems in a draft you have written, the procedural steps in this exercise should help you to improve it

exercise: the coherence test

Step 1

It is now time to become your own critical reader. Print out a stretch of your writing: either a short text, or a subdivision or two of at least six to seven pages of a longer text. Skim quickly through your text with a view to identifying the main ideas around which you are building your paragraphs.

Summarize your main ideas concisely in the margin of your text. As you do this note whether:

- Each main idea is being fully developed, or only partially developed so that you seem to be picking up on it in different parts of your text.
- You are repeating yourself (mark 'repeat' on the page), or labouring the point, saying the same thing over and over again in much the same way (note this too).
- You are presenting too many ideas too quickly so that some main ideas are not being developed at all, or seem to be underdeveloped.

Step 2

Create a sequential list of your main ideas, as noted in the margin of your text. Print this out and put it aside.

Step 3

Now consider the overall coherence of your piece of writing. Take a highlighter pen and run quickly through your text, looking for evidence of linking – mark any sentences, phrases or words that indicate linking within and across paragraphs.

Step 4

With your printout of main ideas and other findings, consider these questions:

- Do you think you already have the best order for your main ideas? Or would over-all coherence be improved by rearranging them into a new order?

- Do you think there is sufficient linking to ensure the logical flow of your ideas?
- Can you see how your main ideas contribute to the development of a unifying point of view or a thesis, as in argument?

Now you can redraft or simply attend to the parts of the text that need improvement.

further resources

The University of Huddersfield has produced an excellent guide to visual mapping of material. It is available for download in pdf format from http://eprints.hud.ac.uk/7843/. The full reference is Burton, R., Barlow, N., and Barker, C. (2010) *Using Visual Tools for Analysis and Learning.* University of Huddersfield.

Gillett, A. (2011) *Using English for Academic Purposes: A Guide for Students in Higher Education.* http://www.uefap.com/ (accessed 8 November 2010). Provides useful exercises and feedback on paragraph control and development, if you wish to pursue this matter further. Check also Purdue OWL, one of the best, all-round online sites.

'Improving your sentence structure', Writing Services, The Learning Commons, University of Guelph. http://www.lib.uoguelph.ca/assistance/writing_services/components/documents/sentence.pdf (accessed 12 October 2010). An expanded discussion of material above on sentence structures that probes problematic sentences and provides alternative, good practice examples.

5

Research Essays

developmental objectives

By applying the strategies, doing the exercises and following the procedural steps in this chapter, you should be able to:

- Recognize the unsettled meanings attached to the term 'essay'.
- Appreciate the meaning of academic argument in the context of research essay writing, and be able to distinguish ideas from opinions.
- Identify strategies for dealing with topics, compiling an introduction, building an argument, marshalling evidence, avoiding faulty reasoning and strengthening argument, working up a conclusion, and ensuring unity and coherence in your research essay.

This chapter provides a detailed focus on the research essay, which is a common form of assessment in taught classes, as well as notoriously challenging to do well.

'Essays' and their synonyms

It is helpful to be aware of the unsettled meanings surrounding the term 'essay'. Sometimes a **literature review** – reviewing the literature and developing an argument in the process of the review – is referred to as a research essay.

Or, alternatively, a 'literature review' can take the form of a research essay – the development of a line of argument strongly supported by reference to the literature.

A **position paper** usually takes the form of a research essay in that a position is adopted and developed by way of argument. However, with a position paper the argument often turns on what *should* be done, so that the argument itself becomes an instrument of change in some context or other (for example, government policy, legal or education reform). But this type of 'should' argument also frequently occurs in what is termed a research essay. It may be that there is no difference between a position paper and a research essay in graduate study, but do clarify this if needs be.

The **exploratory essay** is similar to a problem-solving exercise in that the approach tends to conform more to the type of approach laid out under → 'Business reports' in Chapter 9 than to development of a formal argument. Some shorter essays, though, explore a topic as an analytical exercise in which no firm conclusion need be reached. Or you may be asked to produce a **synoptic essay**, which usually involves providing a comprehensive overview of a subject or topic, drawing attention to key problems, concerns or issues, and, perhaps, assessing these before presenting a conclusion.

Essays can also be structured along various lines, such as the following, which may or may not be acceptable (you would need to ask):

1. Introduction.
2. Discussion of the 'pros' – points in favour of a question.
3. Discussion of the 'cons' – points that can be marshalled against a question.
4. A summary of the writer's own conclusions with supporting evidence (the most demanding part to write).

Given the variable understandings of the term 'essay' you may need to clarify expectations with your lecturer. Strategies for dealing with a short essay are now discussed before proceeding to full discussion of the research essay as formal argument.

The short essay

Short essays, of say from 600 to 1,500 words, can be difficult, particularly if you are expected to read widely in the literature. This puts great pressure on you in terms of selection – what to include for discussion and what to leave out. First, confirm: (1) whether you are expected to deal with the topic precisely as set; or (2) whether it is permissible to narrow the topic in some way as, for example, if you were to address topic concerns in the context of a particular country, event or situation, or even focus in greater depth on some aspect of the topic.

In the case of (1), it is likely that a broad topic has been designed to test your understanding of what might be significant to discuss and in how much detail (perhaps, for example, certain key issues), with what you select to discuss being a consideration during assessment. Having identified what you want to cover in the essay, then think about the following:

- Main ideas you want to bring forward to develop your discussion.
- The best order in which to arrange these ideas.
- Building paragraphs around these main ideas (see → 'Effective paragraph development' in Chapter 4).

Perhaps you will do the above after writing a first, rough draft.

If (2) applies, you will need to confirm with your lecturer that your revised topic will be acceptable.

Short essays do evidence argument, as do theses, reports, other types of academic writing, and what is often called the 'research essay', as now discussed.

The research essay as formal argument

The research essay is characteristically an *argument*, a term that has a special meaning in the academic context.

Decoding the meaning of 'argument'

Argument is a type of academic writing, and, while argument will be the dominant discourse when you write your research essay, this does not mean that you will not be engaged in other discourse activities. Describing, explaining and informing will all have a place in the process of developing your argument.

 **key points**

The amount of description or explaining you do, the amount of detail you include, should be controlled by what is needed to ensure your argument is strong.

An argument can be thought of as an **appeal to reason** in which you develop a position, sometimes called a point of view or thesis, on a topic or question. Taking a position involves the exploration of *issues*, though there can be confusion as to what is meant by this term 'issue':

An *issue* is a topic that sparks controversy within a community of speakers, readers, and writers. More specifically, an issue is a topic that creates a tension in the community, a discontent or dissatisfaction with the status quo. (Kaufer et al., 1989: 3, original emphasis)

Formal argument, then, is concerned with seminal issues, or sets of related issues, to do with the what, why and how of your research.

Your objective will be to convince your reader, even one unsympathetic to your position, that the position you develop in your essay is indeed **reasonable**. For your argument to be reasonable it needs to be a strong argument. A strong argument depends on the **quality of your ideas**, which, in turn, depends on the **quality of the evidence** you include to support those ideas, and the quality of your reasoning. Note that it is not necessarily a matter of whether the argument is true or false, right or wrong (the exception is the use of formal proofs), but whether it is strong or weak. All these observations are expanded on in the following discussions.

Distinguishing ideas from opinions

Lecturers do want to know what you think, but they do not want your opinions. We all have opinions about a multitude of things, and, in expressing them in everyday conversation, we do not need to substantiate these opinions. Unlike an opinion, an idea does need to be backed up by solid evidence, and that is the essential difference between the two.

Basic criteria applied in assessing essays

When assessing essays, lecturers will apply at least these basic criteria, and possibly others (Clanchy and Ballard, 1997: 4–8). It is expected that your essay:

- Will be clearly focused on the set topic and will deal fully with its central concerns.
- Will be the result of wide and critical reading.
- Will present a reasoned argument.
- Will be competently presented.

Each of these criteria is now explored in turn.

Topics (or questions)

You may be setting up your own topic or question, have been given a specific topic or question to work on, or have selected one from a list provided by your lecturer.

Setting up a topic

If you have been given explicit instructions on how to focus and develop a topic or question of your choice, follow these. Otherwise, consider these questions, because you need to be realistic in setting up a topic, presumably in an area that genuinely interests you:

- What is the word length of your essay?
- How much time do you have available for the essay?
- What is the scope of the literature in the topic area that interests you (too little or too much literature may leave you struggling in different ways)?

The real danger is in setting up a topic that is over-ambitious. A topic that is too broad will mean sacrificing in-depth analysis to mere coverage, allowing little opportunity for interesting and subtle insights to emerge.

key points

Consider whether your topic will allow you to engage in in-depth analysis for a longer essay.

A useful starting point is to reflect on the nature of topics as set up by your lecturers. Such topics are usually designed to throw you into controversy, to force you to engage the issues with a view to taking a position and developing it into an argument. You are likely to be addressing a range of issues in your essay, although a single major issue is also a possibility. Take care to consider whether the issues or controversies that interest you relate back to course objectives by revisiting your 'Course Guide' (if you have been given one). Browse through lecture and tutorial notes to determine the types of issues being raised by lecturers. Consider also, for example, whether your topic is expected to engage theory, if theory is an important focus of your particular course.

As a last piece of advice: write out your topic in some detail so that you can have it approved by your lecturer before you begin your research. The more refined it is the more able your lecturer will be to assess its viability in terms of length and time available for research and writing.

Analysing a given topic

Recall the above criterion for assessment: that your essay 'will be clearly focused on the set topic and will deal fully with its central concerns'. Interpretation of the topic is the first point at which the writing of an essay can go wrong, as it is all too easy to rush into the reading (see also → 'Ensuring task-focused information' in Chapter 2). If you do not gather the best information to fully address your topic, then it will be impossible to write a great essay.

exercise: analysing topics

As already mentioned, most essay topics are designed to force you to engage the issues as you read, and to evaluate different points of view presented in the literature (see → 'Treating information critically' in Chapter 2). So bear this in mind as you apply the following Subject/Angle/Process (SAP) method to analysis of your topic. A sample topic is used to illustrate how to go about analysing your own:

Sample topic

If the arms control enterprise is a child of the Cold War, what use is it now? Should it give way to more radical disarmament efforts or is the arms control disarmament enterprise now irrelevant? Your discussion should take account of theoretical debates of current interest.

Step 1: the subject

Ask yourself: *what* am I being asked to investigate?

With the sample topic it is simple: 'arms control'. But identifying the true subject of a topic is not always easy, as topics can be complex and have several parts to them. If you are uncertain about precisely what you should be investigating, get together with fellow students and brainstorm the topic and/or consult your lecturer – do not proceed to research if you are uncertain.

Step 2: the angle

Now ask yourself: *why* am I being asked to investigate this subject matter?

At this point you want to ensure that you will deal *fully* with the central concerns of the topic, all of them. If you were a student in this discipline, you would be able to produce a more refined set of questions than that now offered, though this set adequately illustrates the all-important brainstorming process:

What is meant by arms control? Does it need to be defined or not? (Definitely yes, if there is no settled agreement on its meaning in your discipline.) Is arms control a child of the Cold War – yes or no? Now move to the central concerns of the topic:

(Continued)

What does the 'disarmament enterprise' consist in? (Do you know precisely what is meant by this phrase?) To what extent does arms control remain relevant – a lot, reasonably so, only minimally or what? In what precise ways does it remain relevant, or not? Are there security measures other than arms control that need to be taken into account post Cold War? What are these?

Evaluate the literature and ask yourself: what is my position on all this? (Take care to identify the **issues**, the points debated by scholars, and to gather evidence to support the position you will be taking in building your argument.)

Information providing answers to questions of this type would need to be gathered to deal effectively with the sample topic. By skimming (see → 'Managing your reading load' in Chapter 2), you should be able to avoid wasting time on reading material not directly relevant to your topic.

 **key points**

Brainstorm your topic to generate a set of questions that can be used to control your reading and ensure you acquire the best and right information.

Step 3: the process

Ask yourself: *how* should I conduct my investigation?

The sample topic contains a clear directive on process: 'Your discussion should take account of theoretical debates of current interest', meaning whatever else you do, you *must* apply the theory in your research essay. Apart from specific process directions of this type, other commonly used directional words and phrases are: 'Discuss', 'Explore this comment', 'Analyse ...', 'Examine carefully', 'Evaluate this claim', 'To what extent ...', 'Critically review ...', 'Compare and contrast ...', or 'Do you agree?'. Directions of this type always imply the need for argument. Engage the issues, and develop your own position using solid evidence as support when building your argument.

Compiling an introduction

As the introduction serves only to orient your reader to your discussion, keep it short and to the point, something in the order of a page or so for a 3,000-word essay. Short it may be, but the introduction does have an important function in the research essay, as with all academic genres.

Establishing the context

Provide *relevant* information to establish the context of your discussion. Note how this extract from the introduction to an essay on the sample topic in the previous section is indeed relevant to that topic. It does not stray from the central concerns of the topic, which is a danger when providing contextual information:

> The Cold War and nuclear age were born at about the same time. Seen strictly in this context, the Cold War merely added the nuclear dimension to the arms control enterprise. However, the concern about the devastating nature of nuclear weapons resulted in the greatest media emphasis being placed on nuclear arms control efforts, particularly on the arms race between the two nuclear hegemons, the US and the USSR [reference]. Nevertheless, in the same Cold War period, much effort was put into conventional arms control such as Mutual Balance Force Reduction (MBFR) [reference], and areas of chemical and biological weapons as well as confidence building measures (CBMs).

Defining important terms, phrases or concepts

Communication with readers can go seriously awry because of failure to define. If there is no settled agreement on the meaning of a word, term, phrase or concept appearing in your essay topic, acknowledge this, find the common factor, and give a working definition for your essay. Referring to a specialist dictionary or reference work in your discipline is a useful starting point. You can then build a working definition from other scholars' attempts at definition (see → the example later on in this chapter under 'Strategies that strengthen argument').

Laying out a position

Provide a summary statement of the argument (your position on topic) that you intend to develop in the body of your essay.

Rather than lay out a position, you may be expected to *state the main conclusions* reached in your essay. Or rather than state a position (although it is a good idea to do so), or detail your main conclusions, you will provide *a statement of purposes*, as this writer did after establishing context by way of a brief review of a major debate in the literature:

> The main purpose of this essay is to provide a critical evaluation of the different positions as outlined above.

It could be that you find yourself making several of these moves in your introduction.

Making a procedural statement

Orient your reader to the structure of your essay, the way in which you intend to organize your discussion in general. Phrases signalling procedure may be of this type:

Initially, I examine ... This is followed by a review of ... A discussion of the theoretical underpinnings of X is then presented. The fourth section provides a comparative analysis of ... Finally, I draw out recommendations for ...

In many cases though, the procedure is indicated in a more subtle way in the process of laying out the parts of the argument, as in the hypothetical example given in Box 5.1:

---

box 5.1 An introduction should fulfil its reader-orientation function while being tightly focused on the topic

Topic

'Economic rationalist policies are responsible for the declining economy.' Discuss.

Factors identified as important from the reading parts of the position

- Policy-making areas: car manufacturing, technology, primary exports – foodstuffs
- Industrial action (national transport and miners' strikes).
- Natural disaster: widespread flooding.
- Factors in the international political economy.

Steps in compiling the introduction

Step 1: provision of background information relevant to the topic (three paragraphs of summary comments (with references) on the economy's decline over the period of interest)

Step 2: definition from the literature of what 'economic rationalist' means

Step 3: laying out the position and procedure in a single move as follows (the four-part ordering of the position as expressed below reflected the overall structure of the essay):

(lst part) Economic rationalist policies of the present government have had a slow-growth effect on three major export industries: car manufacturing, technology and primary exports. Such policies do not, however, account fully for the evident economic decline.

> **(2nd part)** Industrial strife during the past two years has been particularly disruptive to growth in some sectors. **(3rd part)** The economy has also had to contend with extensive flooding in parts of the country. **(4th part)** As well, there have been specific developments in the world political economy, which need to be addressed in discussing reasons for the economic decline.

This level of generality is usual when laying out an argument and signalling procedure. At this stage you are just orienting your reader to the discussion to follow in the body of your essay.

Building an argument

Building the foundation and scaffolding of an argument does not occur during the writing of your essay, but rather during the process of gathering the information required to fulfil topic aims (see → 'Topics (or questions)' earlier in this chapter and 'Ensuring task-focused information' in Chapter 2). It is during the reading process that you should be identifying: (1) where you stand on the topic – your **position** (the foundation), (2) what **ideas** you will bring forward to develop that position into an argument (the scaffolding), and (3) what **evidence** you will use to support your ideas, ensure that your argument is a strong one. The details of what you want to say will emerge when you write, but no amount of effort will ensure a strong argument if you have not already put in place a solid foundation and scaffolding before you begin to write.

Building a 'position' as you read

A 'position' can be defined as follows:

> The position is the point of view arrived at on completion of critically assessing the relevant literature. The position you take on your topic of research captures your thesis (as in argument).

As you build your position through the process of reading, think about these questions:

- Does the position you are leaning towards address *all* parts of the topic?
- Are you likely to adopt a unified position, or is the argument such that you will have a more complex position with several parts to it?

Although your topic may appear to be straightforward, topics in graduate study are rarely so. Consequently, the position taken will often be complex, with several parts (see → the example in Box 5.1 above).

Your primary evidence supporting your position will come from sources in the literature which, again, you need to document during reading, as direct quotes, paraphrase, or general references, and perhaps too from raw data that you have generated.

Arguing from sources

Arguing from sources means using references, such as direct quotations or paraphrases, book, chapter or page references to marshal support for your position. (See → 'Referencing and plagiarism' in Chapter 3). (See also Kaufer et al., 1989; Davis and McKay, 1996: Ch. 5 'Cause and effect' and Ch. 6 'Argument'.)

Your essay should reflect familiarity with and understanding of the ideas of other scholars; it should be the result of wide and critical reading (see → 'Treating information critically' in Chapter 2). This does not mean merely describing what others have thought and said. Rather, use source material to advance *your* position, or, if you prefer, build your argument. During reading, take careful notes on ideas you incline towards in terms of the argument you will develop in your essay, and evidence from other scholars that you can use to develop those ideas.

You could, of course, be challenging other scholars in the process of building your argument, that is, **neutralizing opposing arguments**, as this student did:

> *X [reference] offers sound reasons for the continuing centralisation of services in terms of the economic benefits to government. However, he does not take account of the high costs of maintaining centralisation when determining these benefits.*

In developing a position favouring the cost–benefit effects of 'decentralising' government services, the student recognized that X's argument could be used to challenge her own, so she had to neutralize it by showing there was a flaw in that argument: it was too narrow.

Unless you are working with primary source materials (for example, literary texts, archival documents such as letters, diaries, or legal documents), where it might be appropriate, you should avoid overlong direct quotations. The idea is to *process* the source materials you are reading, so a paraphrase of two or three key points in a long discussion may be sufficient for your purposes. Effective paraphrase demonstrates thorough critical understanding of source materials.

Avoiding faulty reasoning

Solid evidence is a necessary but not a sufficient condition for strong argument. There also needs to be sound reasoning. Take care with fallacies of the following type, which signal incorrect or faulty reasoning. (For a more comprehensive overview of logical fallacies in argument, see Downes, 1995–2000.)

Circular reasoning or arguing in a circle: For example: 'Penal reform is necessary because of prison corruption, which shows the need for prison reform.'

Reasoning that does not follow: This means that the conclusion does not follow from the premises of the argument you have set up.

Black and white thinking: The tendency here is to go from one extreme to another. For example: 'If teachers cannot fix the problems in schools they should stay out of the debate altogether.' That fact that teachers cannot 'fix' the problem does not mean that they could not contribute to the debate.

Assuming that what is true of the part is true of the whole (or vice versa): For example: making the assumption that drugs are a big problem among 13–16-year-old school students when this age group has been surveyed in only a small sampling of schools.

Begging the question: This occurs when you ask a question that wrongly assumes something to be true. For example: 'Why are men more aggressive than women?' This 'begs the question' of whether men are in fact more aggressive. You must prove that men are more aggressive than women, not assume that this is so.

Assuming the conclusion: For example: 'This action is wrong because it is immoral.' You must prove that the action is wrong because it is opposed to moral principles, not assume that this is so.

Appealing to an unsuitable authority: This will occur if you draw on an authority who may be a recognized expert in one field, but is not an authority in the subject matter you are discussing.

Attributing causality: It is important to distinguish cause–effect relationships from statistical correlations or coincidences. The data may show a strong correlation between two events, X and Y, but this does not then mean that X (or X alone) caused Y.

Drawing inferences/conclusions: Before drawing an inference/conclusion ensure that there is actual 'evidence' to support it. For example, detailing problems in higher education would be an insufficient basis for concluding that policy reform is needed. Such a conclusion could only be drawn from a careful (and convincing) demonstration of the actual link between those problems and current government policy.

Strategies that strengthen argument

Arguments can be severely weakened by a lack of detail. For your argument to be *reasonable*, you will need to include sufficient detail to secure it, and you can do this by way of a range of discourse or writing strategies that you will already be using (see also → 'Effective paragraph development' in Chapter 4).

exercise: strengthening argument

Look closely at the nature of the detail in the following paragraphs and the effects achieved by the different writing strategies used to advance the arguments. Consider too the quality of the reasoning in these paragraphs. Note as well how these writers integrate academic source materials in the process of arguing.

Definition is used in this introductory paragraph to establish clear communication with readers as to how a problematic term will be understood during argument development. The writer provides a working definition of 'public law' by comparing it with constitutional law, while drawing support from scholarly sources in the process:

> *Constitutional law is concerned with the ways in which public power is institutionally organised and applied, with the relations between the institutions which exercise public power, and with the relations between these institutions and other social interests [reference]. Public law is a more ambiguous term that refers to the principles governing disputes between the State and its subjects as determined by the courts [reference]. It has been argued [reference] that public law has come to include administrative law, criminal law and even environmental law depending on how the State is conceptualised as a legal actor. For the purposes of this essay, if government action can be defined as the regulation of individual liberty, public law can be defined as the regulation of the government's ability to regulate individual liberty* [our emphasis]. [Further explanatory information was included in a footnote.]

Comparison is favoured below to demonstrate the difficulties of determining the origins of rugs from their representation in paintings. Note the use of **comparative illustration** at the end, where the writer picks up on details mentioned in the first sentence to strengthen her position:

> *In trying to identify the origin of a rug, we can use as guiding principles the elements of design, the decorative style and patterning, colours and their combinations, as well as known geographical connections [references]. It may also be possible to physically examine the rug itself – the thickness of the warp and the weft, the types of dyes used, the techniques of application, and so forth. With a rug in a painting, however, these tools of analysis are either unavailable or less reliable.*

The medium of painting is an illusion of reality, even if it pretends to be a depiction of the fine details of reality. The rug plays a part in that illusion, and is likely to be shaped by the artist to fit the desired overall composition. A rug in a painting may have its pattern altered by the angle of perspective, or a fold in the material may distort the appearance of the pattern; the colours may have been changed for artistic effect, as might the ornamental design and other features [our emphasis].

Causal analysis characterizes the development of the next paragraph. Note how the writer develops his general assertion in the first sentence by analysing the causes of technological development in Japan, and strengthens his analysis by drawing on other scholars as support:

Technological development is not a natural process. Social forces lie behind the development of any given technology. In Japan's case, 'economic and technological development have been enshrined as Japanese social goals since the Meiji restoration of 1868' [reference]. It has even been suggested that the 'military class, the samurai, [were] by their own life experience … able to recognise the benefits and "rationality" of Western technology' [reference]. Be that as it may, the more immediate forces leading to the development of microelectronics and IT in Japan derived from the changes and crises facing Japanese capitalism from the late 1960s onwards [explanatory footnote added]. These included a recognisable slow down in economic growth, and demographic changes causing labour shortages, followed by more recent concerns with an aging population.

Restatement means saying the same thing in a different way, but it is not merely repetition. Restatement is a useful strategy to clarify difficult ideas and/or reinforce their importance. Restatement is sometimes signalled by such phrases as 'That is … ', 'By this I mean … ', 'In other words … ', and often by nothing at all. In the following example, ideas in the restatement, the material emphasized, are much the same as those expressed in sentence 2. The restatement both clarifies the writer's initial statement on orthodox historians, and strengthens it by drawing support from the literature. Comparison is again a favoured method of developing the paragraph as the writer distinguishes the approach of orthodox historians and that of the more radical X:

*X's approach to history is considered radical by orthodox historians. Conventional historiographers presuppose that history is a record of 'facts' that, with careful investigation, can be objectively verified. **As Y argues, 'orthodox historians adhere to a "discovery" view of the past, holding that the past is there, a field of real entities and forces waiting for the historians to find' [reference].** They also view history as a linear sequence of events that is characterized by continuity. X, however, takes an 'archaeological' approach. He is concerned with the discontinuity of events, with 'analogies and differences, hierarchies, complementarities, coincidences, and shifts' [reference], with uncovering the discontinuities themselves in the interstices of time* [our emphasis].

(Continued)

Specification means saying precisely what is meant by a more abstract phrase; in this case, 'the great reform measures'. Failure to specify can weaken your argument because there is no way for a reader to tell if *you* know what you are talking about, as would occur if specification were omitted below:

*The great reform measures – **the reorganisation of parliament, the revision of the penal code and the poor laws, the restrictions placed on child labour, and other industrial reforms** – were important factors in establishing English society on a more democratic basis* [our emphasis].

Qualification is needed in this next example, which highlights the problem of using generalizations in argument, something we all need to watch:

The racist attitudes of opponents of increased immigration are cause for concern.

It is a poor argument because of oversimplification. The writer implies that all opponents of increased immigration have 'racist attitudes', which would be impossible to establish, though this may be true of some opponents. Even then, such 'attitudes' cannot be assumed. There would need to be detailed evidence as support, perhaps extracted from the language and rhetoric used by some opponents in their publications or in excerpts from public speeches.

Developing an argument

Your essay will need to evidence a coherent line of argument throughout. For this, a coherent structure is essential and the ideas you bring forward must be directly relevant to the topic.

Ensuring structural coherence

Structural coherence refers to the logic of the organization of the parts of your discussion, the interconnectedness of ideas, how it hangs together, coheres, as discussed in → 'Principles of sound structure', Chapter 4. Refer also to 'Words and phrases for developing discussions' in the Appendix.

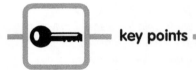 **key points**

When structuring a research essay remember: you are not carving up information to cover but sequencing information in an argument.

Note the following points also. When using subdivisions to section your essay, work on the premise that you are not merely working out what to cover, but building an argument. So:

- Why have you arranged your subdivisions in the order in which you have? Is it the best arrangement?
- What are you trying to show/demonstrate/establish in each subdivision in relation to your overall argument? How will each subdivision serve to advance your argument – what will each contribute to the development of your position/thesis?

In every instance of structuring – whether the whole essay or the subdivisions – consider this set of key questions:

- What am I focusing on here? What am I covering?
- Why am I focusing on this? What are my reasons for covering this subject?
- How do I want to develop this discussion? What do I want to discuss and in what order do I want to discuss these topics?
- What/so what? What are the main ideas I want to bring forward in developing my argument and what are the implications of my discussions? Build your paragraphs around these main ideas. Make sure your reader is not left to comment on your text: 'So what?', meaning that the point of your discussion is lost on that reader.

If there is a need to digress from your main line of argument, signal this as a deliberate digression and give a reason for it, as illustrated:

Before continuing this examination of financial issues to do with setting up the test project, it is helpful to provide a brief overview of a series of political events that caused a departure from the original plan at this time.

Maintaining relevance

Relevance refers to the overall focus of your essay. Sometimes lecturers make comments in the margin of an essay such as 'I can't follow the point of all this', 'This seems to be a digression from the main thrust of the argument' or 'How does this relate to topic?' Comments of this type signal that the reader cannot work out the *relevance* of your ideas to the position supposedly being developed. In the process of ensuring your position is clearly focused on the set topic and deals fully with its central concerns, ensure that all ideas relate back to your position, as represented in Figure 5.1.

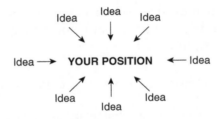

FIGURE 5.1   Ensuring relevance

Working up a conclusion

When pressured to submit an essay, it is easy to rush the ending so that there does not appear to be a proper conclusion. Do bring the essay to some resolution, perhaps referring the reader back to the topic for a sense of unity.

Remember, you are drawing together the findings of your essay, so you should not introduce new material that has not been previously discussed in the body of the essay. In summarizing overall findings, avoid merely repeating conclusions reached in various parts of the essay. The conclusion is another stage of thinking – a reflection on what has been uncovered during the course of your argument or, it might be said, what *you* have learnt from conducting the research. In effect, try to process your findings for the reader and put these findings into a new set of relationships.

Ask yourself questions of this type:

- What do I find most interesting, important or significant about my findings in terms of the topic and the position I have developed? And what seems to be of lesser interest or importance?
- Are there any interesting implications of my overall findings? (When answering this last question, you will probably be speculating, so use more tentative language such as: 'perhaps', 'it seems', 'it could be' and so forth, but do ensure your speculations are grounded in findings reached in the body of your essay.)

In these ways you let the reader know what you think about your findings, and perhaps leave her/him with something interesting to think about (see also → 'The thesis conclusion' in Chapter 10).

Cutting to meet word length

If the essay needs to be cut to meet word length stipulations, do not cut the very detail that strengthens the argument – look elsewhere, in places such as these (see → Figure 5.2):

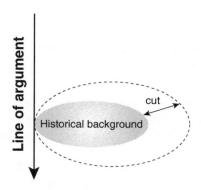

FIGURE 5.2   Cutting material to meet word length

- Introductions are often wordy, over-written and can stand considerable condensing.
- Lengthy arguments or discussions can fall victim to what is sometimes called 'the expository bulge', meaning that there is an unnecessary proliferation of explanatory information, with too much peripheral detail. Detail is important, but you need only as much detail as is necessary to secure your argument.
- It is often possible to cut material from the more descriptive or explanatory parts of an essay (for example, historical background), which need to be there but can be condensed.

Reviewing the essay presentation

The fourth and final criterion mentioned above is that your essay 'will be competently presented'. Consider these matters:

- Include a separate cover sheet (you may be given one by your lecturer) that includes information of this type: Name (yours); Topic (exact wording); Course details (for example, AL836); Lecturer (name); Length (as given); Due date of submission.
- Use double spacing or space and a half, and double this between paragraphs or indent them – much easier to read. Leave decent margins so that your lecturer can write comments.
- Do a word count to ensure your essay meets the designated length where this is stipulated, as there may be penalties (for example, marks deducted) for going over the limit.
- Carefully check the accuracy of direct quotations (these must be exactly as you find them in your source), and also all referencing details, as well as tables, figures, and so on. Ensure your writing practices are consistent. Carefully edit and proofread your essay.

All these matters are discussed in → 'Essentials of academic writing', Chapter 3.

further resources

Kane, T.S. (1988) *The New Oxford Guide to Writing*. Oxford: Oxford University Press. Essentially for afficionados of fine prose that takes you from blank page to the finished product via the various styles of great writers, and also provides an insightful chapter on essay writing.

'What is an academic essay?' Sussex Centre for Language Studies. A concise account of what an essay is all about, with some comparison to reports and embedded links to more detailed information, all of which could be useful for the first-time writer of essays because of discipline transfer.

Weston, A. (2009) *A Rulebook for Arguments*. 4th edn. Indianapoli, IA: Hackett. Based on a set of timeless rules, all clearly explained with illustrations, this is the best 'how to' reference on constructing strong, cogent arguments and evaluating those of others, but does not cover arguing from formal proofs.

6

Book or Article Reviews and Online Writing

developmental objectives

By applying the strategies, doing the exercises and following the procedural steps in this chapter, you should be able to:

- Gain insight into the nature of different types of book or article reviews, and develop capacity to focus and structure a review.
- Manage effectively writing for blogs and wikis.

This chapter continues with the focus on other common writing activities in graduate study: reviewing books and articles in different contexts and producing blogs and wikis.

Book or article reviews

While the focus here is on book reviewing, it should not be difficult for you to adapt suggestions to review of a journal article or some other type of writing.

The different types of reviews

Consider these different scenarios:

1. You have been invited to review a book relevant to your research field for a magazine or journal.
2. As a course requirement, you are expected to produce a book review that emulates professional practice, say, as if for publication in a newspaper, where focus and style of the review could be affected by how upmarket that newspaper is – you would need to check.
3. As part of course assessment, you have been asked to critically review some book or article.

In the case of **scenarios 1 and 2**, you will need to adopt a style of writing suited to the specific context and audience. You can teach yourself to do any type of writing if you have models to follow. Before drafting, study previously published reviews to orient yourself to the basics of structure, style and treatment of information expected of your review for that particular newspaper or journal – make use of the exercise under → 'Mastering disciplinary writing practices' in Chapter 2.

Scenario 3 is now addressed in more detail. In writing an academic review, it is almost certain that you will be expected to engage critically with the book or article (see → 'Treating information critically' in Chapter 2). Your review should not therefore be a summary of the content or argument of the book (unless your lecturer specifically requests this). Instead, it should state concisely what the book sets out to do and assess how well the author achieves that goal. Be prepared to give sound reasons for your point of view. These points are elaborated on next.

Conducting an academic review

Steps laid out in the following exercise should allow you to take a more strategic approach to the conduct of your review.

 exercise: steps in the review process

Step 1

Look at the title, the table of contents, and read the preface and introduction to gain understanding of the central focus and the coverage of the book.

Read closely the introduction and/or first chapter. This is to determine the author's purposes or objectives, to identify questions being engaged, hypotheses being examined or issues discussed, and also whether any limitations have been placed on the scope of the study. Even acknowledged limitations may give cause for critical comment, say, in terms of treatment of material (for example, the author has excluded information essential to a balanced treatment of the subject matter). At this point, identify whether there is any theoretical or methodological framework being used, or even important assumptions of this type, as these will affect the author's approach and interpretations.

Skim quickly through the whole book first, running your eye over chapter and subdivision headings, opening sentences of paragraphs, and glancing at any tables, or other illustrations, as well as indexes and bibliographies. Try to gain a general sense of the argument being developed, as well as the issues being engaged.

Read closely the final chapter, which should cover the author's conclusions and summarize the main reasons for them.

Step 2

Now decide on the aspects of the book you consider important to discuss. These aspects will probably cover the strengths and weaknesses of the book as you see them, in terms of the content and perhaps the style and presentation as well; after all, clarity and conciseness in writing can contribute to a more accessible argument or discussion.

Pinpoint the strengths as you see them. Weaknesses may centre on matters of this type: flaws in the general thrust of the argument – weak evidence or flawed reasoning; biases in the methodology, theory or modelling; the uneven treatment of important issues; the current relevance of the ideas put forward or even the whole thrust of the argument (for example, it may be somewhat dated); problems with underlying assumptions about the nature of things; discussions that are too broad or too narrow, and so on.

Step 3

The next step is to read more closely the sections of the book that are relevant to the strengths and weaknesses of the book as you see it. Note the main points you want to make, and identify key quotations or paraphrased material from the book that you can use to support your claims; even just page references will do.

If you are required to review this book in the context of other studies, then this is the time to read these, after you have a reasonably sound knowledge of the book you are reviewing, not before. To situate the review in the context of other studies, ask yourself questions of this type:

- How does the study fit into the broader literature?
- How does the author's position compare with those of other studies I have read?

(Continued)

- In what ways is the argument similar or different?
- What might be the reasons for these differences and similarities?
- What contribution does the book make to scholarship in the research field?
- How useful or not is it? In what precise ways is it useful or not and why?

Structuring a review

It is up to you how you structure your review, but you could follow this step-by-step approach if you wish:

1. Begin with an initial identification of the book (author, title, date of publication and other details that seem important). Indicate the major aspects of the book you will be discussing in your review – **your focus** in terms of its strengths and weaknesses.
2. This could be followed by a brief summary of the range, contents and argument(s) of the book, perhaps just two or three paragraphs in a shorter review of, say, 1,500–2,000 words.
3. The **core of your review**, the body of the discussion, will be a critical analysis of the aspects you have selected to focus on. Make sure you substantiate what you say by drawing on the book itself as evidence and other scholarly sources if this is appropriate.
4. In the conclusion, provide a summary evaluation of the overall contribution made by the book to the subject area, to your understanding of the topic and to scholarship.

Online writing

Lecturers are more frequently setting online writing assignments, and, in particular, assignments that involve contributing to blogs and wikis. Although these formats may be unfamiliar to you in the scholarly context, they nevertheless represent legitimate forms of academic writing that you should master when necessary. For many students, judging the correct style and tone for such online writing can be difficult; it can be easy to fall into the trap of believing that writing online is either a case of 'anything goes' or that you can simply replicate what you have successfully done in your research essays and that it will be acceptable. In fact, neither is the case.

As with other forms of academic writing, writing for wikis and blogs is a specialized skill that comes with its own conventions – and it needs to be practised. Although we present some general advice below, you should ask your lecturers to describe exactly what they are looking for and expecting of you *before* you start writing for these types of online assignment.

Blogs

In writing for blogs, you may be asked to write either **blog posts** or blog comments – or, indeed, both. If you are writing a blog post, then you will be responsible for generating a (usually) short piece of writing that may include commentary, critique or reflection on key course topics, or that provides links to other materials. Your post should have a catchy title that interests the casual 'web surfer' enough to read on, yet clearly describes the subject of the post. It is also generally acknowledged that in a blog post you will write shorter paragraphs and that bullet points will help both to break up your text and to get your point across. If your lecturer has set a blogging assignment then they are probably expecting you to inject a bit of life into your writing, so be sure to put some of yourself into it and to express your (reasoned-out) opinion. Including hyperlinks, tags, images and other rich media are also ways of demonstrating engagement with the topic under discussion.

In general, the language should be clear and simple, and not as formal as that used for a research essay. Having said this, however, some lecturers may be expecting you to write a mini-essay for a blog post and they are simply using a blog platform to access or share your work; either way, you should clarify expectations around language with your lecturer before you begin. The other problem that can occur is to use language that is *too* informal. Incorrect grammar, spelling and punctuation may be tolerated on a Facebook wall comment or in a text message, but is certainly not acceptable in blog posts.

Blog comments should be approached a little differently. In writing a comment on a post, you will not be prompting a conversation but rather responding to or taking part in one already started by someone else. Your comments should be short, focused, insightful and strictly limited to the issues at hand. People will not appreciate your comment if it is too long, off-topic, or ridiculous. Your comment should be friendly, civil and encouraging: the blog owner (who may very well be your lecturer) has every right to remove comments that are rude, offensive or insulting.

Wikis

Contributing to a wiki is an altogether different proposition from writing for a blog. Whereas a blog is all about the author and individual responses to thoughts and opinions, wikis are about groups of people collaborating to create an online resource for others to access. Lecturers will tend to set wiki assignments when they want you to produce group work online. For some students this can be challenging enough, without adding an unfamiliar online technology into the mix. However, wikis are simple to edit and, after some practice, you should have no trouble in making basic changes to a wiki.

In contributing to a wiki, it is important to remember that wikis are about collaboration and that you *will* be expected to edit others' work. Your lecturer is looking for (and can track) your individual contributions to the cooperative exercise. To this end, it is important that you add meaningful content to the wiki and that you do not simply attend to others' poor punctuation. Your group's wiki should be clearly structured and written; it may be worth getting your group together before you start your wiki to discuss the most logical layout of the content.

As regards language, wikis are predominantly written in standard English, although the tone is not as formal as that for research essays. It is important that you avoid jargon and that explanations are presented plainly and with relevant supporting media such as images, videos, audios or links. When you make a change to a page, the wiki system may ask you to give a reason for your edit. If you have only amended a punctuation mark, then you can ignore this step. If, however, you have made substantial changes to others' work, it is courteous to let them know why you have altered the material. It can be particularly difficult for some students to accept that it is allowable to modify the work of others, but if you have established a good group dynamic to begin with then group members will understand that it is the project that comes first, not the individual.

7

Coursework Exams

developmental objectives

By applying the strategies, doing the exercises and following the procedural steps in this chapter, you should be able to:

- Understand implications of different approaches to exams.
- Identify strategies for effective revision and the writing of different types of coursework exams.

There are different approaches to exams. Most common are **closed-book exams** into which, as implied, you are not able to take any reference materials at all. This approach contrasts with **open-book exams**, which do allow you to take in certain materials. Your lecturers will tell you which materials are allowed – perhaps notes, books or journal articles for reference. These materials, however, will only prove useful to you if they are well organized, practised with and thoroughly understood before you go in. Preparation is needed. In the exam there is no time to read these materials, only to find relevant information you know is there because you are already familiar with the content.

With **take-home exams** you will be given an exam paper to complete in a specified time (perhaps a weekend or a week). Take-home exams usually consist of essay questions. As you will have full access to sources (books, articles, and so on) in answering these questions, the opportunity to rework your answers and less restriction on the time you take to write them, lecturers will expect a higher standard than for a regular exam.

Pre-seen exams are different. Here you will have the opportunity to preview your exam paper beforehand and prepare your answers in the revision period. You might be told that you will have to write on all the questions on the paper; or maybe only some of them will be selected for the examination, though you will not be told which ones. In this case, you will complete your paper under the usual, formal examination conditions. Again, because you have been advantaged in previewing the paper, a higher standard will be expected.

Apart from there being different approaches to examination, exam papers can take different forms, three prominent types being:

1. **Essay exams**, which usually allow a choice of topics to write on.
2. **Short answer exams**, involving answers of a paragraph or half a page, and sometimes allowing choice.
3. **Multiple-choice exams** in which you normally have to answer (tick, circle or nominate an answer for) all questions.

Discussions to follow take account of the different communicative needs of these different types of exam. To communicate effectively in exam papers, you will need to prepare the ground – to revise effectively.

Setting up a revision plan

The following discussion walks you through three stages of the revision process.

Stage 1: focusing your plan

Grounding revision in course objectives

Exams test your knowledge of a particular course within your degree programme, and your ability to apply this knowledge under exam conditions. But it is easy to forget, when caught up in details throughout a semester or whole year course, why the course was offered and what lecturers envisioned you might gain from taking it – information that will surely be important in the design of the exam paper. So you first need to identify sources to clarify your understanding of the rationale underlying the course – its scope, aims and

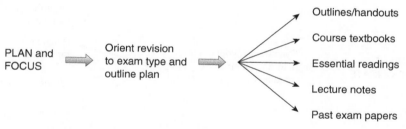

FIGURE 7.1   Orienting and outlining a revision plan

objectives, and the probable scope of your exam. So this is where revision should begin.

This information can be gathered from the sources indicated in Figure 7.1, and any other similar sources appropriate in your case.

From outlines or handouts that detail what will be covered and when, you should be able to see *why* the course was offered – its aims and objectives, and so what your lecturers hope you will learn from it, which will be tested in the examination. Look at the beginning of your 'Course Guide' if you were given one.

By scanning relevant textbooks, essential readings from seminars or reading 'brick' materials, as well as lecture notes that cover the whole sweep of your course, you should be able to clarify your understanding of basic content: the main topics covered, how those topics are broken down for discussion (for example, in lectures), key aspects of topic focus, issues of importance and so forth. Doing this should provide a clear overview of the *scope* of knowledge being covered in the course.

Reviewing past exam papers

Review past exam papers if these are available (also relevant for take-home exams). But before you do this, make sure that your exam paper will be of the same type as the paper of previous years. You want to avoid putting effort into past papers only to find the lecturer has changed the exam paper from the previous essay format to a short-answer paper.

In reviewing past exam papers, you are orienting yourself to what might be expected of you, with questions of this type being helpful to engage:

- What do the exam paper instructions say?
- Are you expected to answer all questions or to select from a range of questions? Are all questions compulsory in one section but subject to choice in others? Are some questions given different percentage weightings, which is not unusual in short answer papers? If yes, when writing the paper you should give less time to those questions worth less.

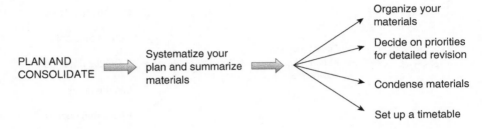

FIGURE 7.2   Systematizing a revision plan

- What sort of time schedule would you need to work out if you were to manage your time efficiently in the exam?
- Do you get a sense of the scope of knowledge being tested?
- What types of questions are being set and what sort of knowledge do the examiners seem to be testing? Go back to the aims and objectives of your course as a point of comparison.

You should be able to outline your revision plan from notes that you have taken during this first stage.

Stage 2: systematizing your plan

With the plan outline from Stage 1, you are now in a position to systematize your plan for intensive revision by using strategies noted in Figure 7.2.

The details of your revision plan will need to be adapted to the specific types of exams you will be taking.

Essay-type exams

Usually in this type of exam it is possible to specialize in revision, focusing on, say, nine or ten (but not three or four!) out of the 13 or so related topics covered throughout a semester. You will know you can do this if, in your review of past exam papers, you notice that the expectation is for you to select, say, three essay questions from a list of 12.

key points

The essay-type exam will not only test your knowledge of the course generally but also your capacity to reason about a topic in the process of producing an argument.

Having identified the set of topics you wish to revise, set priorities, allowing more time for topics you find most difficult, and establish a timetable so that you can monitor your progress in revision.

When condensing materials do not summarize in detail each journal article, essential reading, textbook, or any other source material. Rather, hold your sources in relation for the purposes of comparison and contrast. For example, with a theory topic, the revision process might involve taking notes towards understanding the principles of the theory, developments that have taken place in the theory over time, key figures who featured in these developments, criticisms brought against the theory and why, how advocates of the theory have answered these criticisms and supported their views, the theory's explanatory and/or predictive value, its limitations and strengths and why.

 **key points**

Use flow charts, diagrams and other visual aids to condense and plot comparative findings from sources.

Use your sources to extract the type of essential information that will serve you well regardless of the specific orientation of any particular exam topic or question that is set.

It is also important to understand the relevant issues or sets of issues, if you are to produce an argument, by tackling these questions:

- What are the points on which scholars agree or disagree?
- Are you clear about the reasons for their agreement or disagreement?

Be fully analytical in your approach to revision. Decide in the revision process what you think about a subject or topic and why, and what evidence you can use to support your views. There is no time to sort out your position in the exam room – whether you agree or disagree with other scholars' arguments.

With the above approach you should be able to achieve a balance between the depth and breadth of your topic coverage, which is necessary in all exam situations. You want to take to your exam a thoroughly critical, but *broad* understanding of the course subject matter.

Short answer exams

Some of the above advice also applies for short answer papers, though you may not be given a choice of topics to answer or be expected to produce a sustained argument. Still, you will need to establish priorities, set up a timetable for revision monitoring and develop a critical understanding of your material. You would have determined the nature of the questions from your review of past exam papers in Stage 1, the types of knowledge being tested, or the sorts of information needed to be able to answer the questions well.

key points

Papers of the short answer type often focus on problem-solving, concept or issue definition, modelling, design principles, knowledge application, and so on.

With problem-solving questions, for example, you will need to practise solving problems in the revision process; it is not enough to know your material thoroughly. First, identify a range of key problems in the revision material on which you need to focus. Then ask yourself as you revise:

- Why is this a problem? (Ensures understanding of the distinctive nature of each problem.)
- Which strategies (for example, formulae or techniques) would enable the best resolutions?
- Is there more than one viable strategy or approach?
- Why do you prefer these strategies/approaches and not others? Be prepared to justify your choices – give reasons for them.

Condense material along the appropriate lines (for example, as sets of problems) in flow charts, graphs, tables or diagrams – whatever appeals.

Multiple-choice exams

Multiple-choice exam papers are often designed to test how well you are building up basic knowledge of a disciplinary area. It is probably in the area of *fine* distinctions that the revision will prove most taxing. In the exam, a correct answer may depend on understanding subtle distinctions in the language, so if English is not your first language you will need to practise as much as possible, and perhaps check your answers with a native-speaking friend from your course.

key points

Multiple-choice questions test detailed knowledge and understanding, with questions that require recognition of fine distinctions in terms of definitions, understanding of basic concepts, models, stages or the sequence of stages in processes, cause and effect relations, comparisons and contrasts, explanations, and so on.

When revising, actively look for slight differences, for fine shades of meaning, for paradoxes and uncertainties. As with all exams, however, you are being tested on your general knowledge, so avoid sacrificing breadth of understanding to a detailed but narrow understanding of just a few topics. Prioritize revision tasks along a well-thought-out revision timetable.

The end of Stage 2 should leave you with a condensed set of notes that may include visual materials such as maps or outlines that chart important sets of relations or developments.

Stage 3: testing the efficacy of your plan

It is now time to test the efficacy of your revision plan by way of the strategies suggested in Figure 7.3.

Particularly important in the context of the above set of strategies is the notion of attempting a practice run with an old exam paper if this is possible. At this stage, much of your revision should be complete, so it is then useful to put this knowledge to the test. This is certain to highlight any strengths or weaknesses in your preparedness for the exam. Do you know enough to be

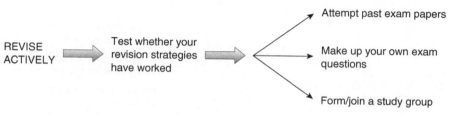

FIGURE 7.3   Testing the efficacy of a revision plan

able to answer the types of questions set? And do you think you could complete the paper in the given time?

Your lecturers may be prepared to look over a practice paper to give you feedback on how you are progressing, but if yours is a multiple-choice exam paper that is being recycled from year to year so that you have no access to past papers, then you may have to rely heavily on the **strategy of self-questioning**. Joining with a few friends in a study group can be useful to question each other, though this might be difficult if you have various other commitments in terms of family and employment, or you are studying off campus.

Exam room strategies

In most exams there is a 'permitted study period', where you will be allowed approximately 10 to 15 minutes or so to review the paper before the official start of the exam. This is where the next set of strategies, given in Figure 7.4, needs to be activated.

Interpreting exam paper instructions

Read the exam paper instructions carefully, and follow them rigidly. If you are to select questions, again read carefully the instructions for selection – you do not want to misinterpret these instructions. Work out what each question is testing by highlighting **key words** (take a highlighter pen with you to the exam) – read all questions very carefully. Now make your selection; do not delay with this.

Determining the order of your answers

Decide on the order in which you will answer questions. It may be best simply to begin at the beginning when you have to answer all questions on the paper. But

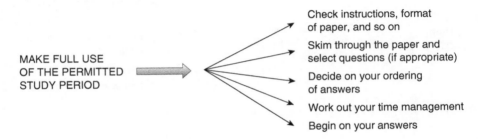

FIGURE 7.4   Making use of the permitted study period

120

when there is choice, you may feel more confident about some questions than others, and so choose to answer those you know best to see if you can get ahead of time, allowing extra for those questions about which you are less confident.

Indicate on your paper which question you are answering by noting this above your answer (for example, Question 2 or Topic B3 – use the exact wording from the paper). Doing this is most important if you change the given order when writing your paper. Protect yourself against reader confusion.

Working out a time schedule

Time needs to be rigorously monitored in the examination room, so wear a watch. Work out your time schedule during this preparatory period: calculate how much time you will give to each question on the basis of how many questions you need to answer and perhaps, too, their percentage weighting. For example: 20 short answer questions in a 3-hour paper where each question carries the same weighting means giving about 9 minutes to each question, but where there is a percentage weighting you might decide to give, say, 12 minutes to some questions and only 2 or 3 minutes to others. Or, if you have to write 4 essays over 3 hours, then you would have about 50 minutes for each essay. If your entire paper were multiple-choice with, say, 120 questions over 2 hours then you would have about a minute for each question.

Consider these strategies:

- Exclude 10 minutes of the allotted exam time in planning your time schedule. This gives you a little spare time at the end of the paper to at least jot down in note form any ideas for answers left incomplete on the way through the paper.
- In answering multiple-choice questions, mark on your exam question paper the halfway mark, preferably with a bright slash so it stands out. This will alert you to how your time is going.

Starting on answers in the 'permitted study period'

If you have any time left, you can begin working on your answers. You could jot down some notes, or, in the case of essay-type questions, perhaps begin to outline your first answer in the margins of the question paper (not the booklet for writing your answers).

Writing the exam paper

Regardless of your type of exam, make sure you attempt all questions you are required to answer. Also, monitor time regularly throughout the examination – stay with the time schedule set up in the 'permitted study period'. If you are starting to get behind, then move on quickly and see if you can make up time elsewhere in the paper. If you finish early, then read over your answers for a final edit.

In your answers, use actual words/phrases from the topics. Doing this will keep you attuned to topic requirements.

Essay papers

With essay-type questions, it is best to do some planning before writing. Repetition, labouring of points, narrow coverage of topic in too much detail (just a few points being discussed in great detail while other important points are ignored) are all tendencies aggravated by a lack of planning.

key points

What matters is the *quality* of your argument, not quantity – how much you write.

If, for example, you had to write three essays in a 3-hour exam, you would have 1 hour for each. Take 10 minutes of the hour for each question to produce a rough essay outline of the type shown in Box 7.1.

box 7.1 Outlining an exam essay can help you to stay on track with your argument

Introduction: two or three sentences indicating what your argument will be about (your position on the set question), and how you will order your discussion 'First I discuss … I then … Finally, I …'. Perhaps also, provide any necessary definitions of words, terms, etc. The introduction should be concise and to the point – it is your argument that matters.

Body of the essay: jot down main ideas or points around which to build your paragraphs – think about the order in which you want to present them: main idea 1 … main idea 2 … main idea 3 … and so on. Some of these ideas might take several paragraphs to develop. Think about what evidence you will use to backup the ideas you want to develop.

Conclusion: summarize the main points made in the course of your argument in three or four sentences – perhaps going back to your set topic or question in the process to round off the discussion – bring in actual words/phrases from the topic.

Remember, you do not need to be writing for every second of the exam. You will not be graded on the number of pages you produce but on the quality of your answers.

Short answer papers

With a short answer paper, also allow some time for thinking through your answers before writing – again, you do not need to be writing every second. With short answers there is considerable pressure to be concise; usually you will only have about a paragraph to perhaps half a page or so to write your answer (or maybe you will be asked to draw a model). Distinguish your points clearly (for example, first, second, third), and build paragraphs around main ideas you want to develop (see → 'Effective paragraph development' in Chapter 4).

Multiple-choice papers

If yours is a multiple-choice exam, read each question and all the suggested answers carefully. Note whether or not you are likely to be penalized for a *wrong* answer – as mentioned in the exam paper instructions. Avoid the temptation to pick the first answer that looks correct without reading the others. Some questions may have several correct answers (that is, 'all of the above'), no correct answer (that is, 'none of the above'), or a partly correct answer, one of which is more complete or more precise than the others.

Look for **key words** that might affect the meaning of questions – highlight words like conditionals ('if', 'when'), or modals ('might', 'could'), or qualifiers ('never', always', 'sometimes'). If you cannot answer a question, then move on to the next – at the end of the paper you can go back over the questions that remain unanswered, knowing how much time you still have left. As you move through the exam paper, mark clearly (for example, with a brightly coloured dot) those left unanswered so as not to waste time searching for them in the end-stage.

8

The Literature Review

To reduce the challenges typically associated with literature review production, the writing needs to gestate in the search, reading, critical appraisal and information-processing stages. As with all academic writing, however, you first need to be clear about the purpose and functions of this type of writing.

Purpose and functions of a literature review

Dena Taylor's description captures well the essential purpose of the literature review:

A literature review is an account of what has been published on a topic by accredited scholars and researchers. ... In writing the literature review, your purpose is to convey to your reader what knowledge and ideas have been established on a topic, and what their strengths and weaknesses are. As a piece of writing, the literature review must be defined by a guiding concept (e.g., your research objective, the problem or issue you are discussing, or your argumentative thesis). It is not just a descriptive list of the material available, or a set of summaries. (undated)

In short, an 'effective review creates a firm foundation for advancing knowledge' (Webster and Watson, 2002: xiii).

key points

The literature review provides a rationale for your research in terms of what has gone before, a justification of its value and significance.

Writing tasks engaged

In order to fulfil the purposes of a literature review, you will engage writing tasks of the following types (depending on the nature of your research):

- Demonstrating through engagement with the literature that you have a thorough critical understanding of the literature. That is, you will be critically appraising strengths and weaknesses of the literature relevant to your own research.
- Pointing out gaps in the literature, identifying problems remaining to be solved or issues needing to be addressed and so forth.
- Drawing together the main themes and arguments of a particular body or bodies of literature.
- Developing arguments in the process of reviewing the literature.
- Showing how your research fits in with what has already been done so as to justify its value and communicate the nature of your contribution (sometimes occurs in a separate section).

Review mode and orientation

With a formal literature review, review mode means moving from review of the literature to points being made in building your arguments, like so:

(**From:** review of literature) → (**To:** points abstracted from the review to develop your discussion)

In short, keep your eye firmly on the literature when writing your review.

All literature reviews have a strong research orientation in that they engage the relevant research and show how the individual student's research fits in. Your review could have a dual orientation, however: research and practical or professional. While developing arguments is standard practice in the process of reviewing the literature, producing a sustained argument throughout is more common in those reviews with a strong professional orientation. Definition and determination of interventions with the 'most beneficial impact' would obviously require sustained argument, as was indeed the case for this student:

> *This paper reviews some of the epidemiological literature on the high prevalence of non-insulin dependent diabetes mellitus (NIDDM) among Aboriginal and Torres Strait Islander People, and on the aetiology of diabetes in these communities. After examining the differing accounts of aetiology these are related to the interventions they suggest. The aim of the paper is **to define the kinds of intervention that will have the most beneficial impact**. Answers to these questions are sought in accounts of both cause and of action* (our emphasis).

Model yourself on this writer, who managed to avoid the trap of developing a thesis (as in argument) supported *from* the literature (more like a formal argument as discussed under → 'Research essays', Chapter 5), unless your lecturer requests this. Rather, let your point of view emerge from review of the literature itself – keep the literature in the foreground.

With an appreciation of what a formal literature review is, a next step might be to locate appropriate material.

Exploiting library and Internet resources

There are two main sources for academic literature: your institution's library and the Internet. You may tend to rely on the Internet as your primary source for scholarly materials because you are uncertain about how to use library databases. The problem with this strategy is that you can easily spend more time evaluating items for scholarly validity than you did in finding them. Even using Google Scholar cannot guarantee that the sources you track down are suitably academic in nature. Your institution's library, on the other hand, holds material that is almost certain to be scholarly and/or peer reviewed.

Your institution's library

Today's libraries hold more than just paper monographs and journals. Increasingly, digital assets are becoming a core component of any library's collection and many of the latest journals and even some reports are *only* published electronically. Because of the wide variety of formats that academic material is published in, it is essential that you know your way around your institution's library collection, catalogue, and, in particular, the specialist databases that help you search for materials.

Most libraries offer tours of their collection that can be finished in an hour or so, and it is in your best interests to sign up for, or attach yourself to, just such a tour. Alternatively, there may be a virtual tour offered that you can take in your own time. At the beginning of your degree or course, it would also be wise to attend any library workshops on how to make the most of the catalogue or on how to find research materials in your discipline or subject area. Subject and/or graduate specialists usually facilitate these workshops, and there is nothing better than having access to an expert.

key points

Gaining a solid understanding of your library catalogue early on can save you hours of frustration when it comes to locating the relevant literature.

Many students do not use the library to its full potential. Some focus solely on the physical assets they can pull off the shelves when, to reiterate, many scholarly materials these days are *only* published in electronic format: not to explore them could mean that you are missing out on the latest developments and ideas in your area. Other students do not visit the physical collection at all, preferring instead only to search for digital holdings that they can read or print out via their own computer. Although you might find the latest materials on your topic, this approach could impact on your ability to track the provenance of an idea, which, in turn, prevents you from demonstrating full engagement with the literature.

You should aim to be a fully rounded researcher when it comes to using your institution's library.

key points

Be aware that searching on the Internet is not the same as searching your library's electronic catalogue.

The Internet

Regardless of the limitations previously mentioned, the Internet can be a useful tool to help you locate thought-provoking articles or unusual perspectives or ideas that could help you expand your critique of the literature.

Google Scholar is, perhaps, the most obvious and frequently used source for searching for academic literature on the Internet. When you use Google Scholar, an underlying algorithm makes a 'best guess' as to whether or not a source is scholarly. It is then up to you to evaluate the source for academic authority. A Google Scholar search will, nevertheless, likely unearth a number of useful or interesting citations that you can follow up.

Do not limit yourself to Google Scholar, however. A large amount of scholarly material is now being published and aggregated in other digital formats, all of which are searchable via tags or search boxes. Many scholars, for example, keep **blogs** that can be searched for both links to useful material and for different angles on the literature (you can find blogs using Google's blog search). **Twitter** can also be a worthwhile source for current literature, not least because many Twitter users assiduously share links to reports and journal articles. Academics are also sharing their slideshows and PowerPoint presentations on services such as **Slideshare.net**, a quick search of which might provide a number of potentially useful citations. Searching people's **online bookmarks** can also be profitable: find a user on Delicious.com or Diigo.com who has similar interests to your own, and browse their bookmarks. The chances are that they have a number of 'favourite' sites that are also relevant to your own research.

Do remember though, that although these sources might provide stimulating or provocative material, none of them can be guaranteed to be peer-reviewed. You should not rely only on Internet searching for finding scholarly material, no matter how difficult using the university library might at first seem.

If you are enrolled in a lengthy research degree, you will need to do search 'updates' until submission of your thesis so as to ensure that you have not missed any relevant later publications.

Strategically managing the reading

The extent of coverage will of course depend on the level of your degree, and the nature of your research. For a **longer thesis**, you will need to provide a comprehensive review of all relevant literature, perhaps even an encyclopaedic one if that is required. For a **shorter thesis or report**, you will at least need to (1) focus on key writers in the field (you may not be able to survey all writers in the field, so limit your coverage to those authors who have contributed significantly to developing the research field); and (2) cover the most recent, relevant publications available. But do consult with your supervisor about expectations of coverage.

You may be working with a scant literature, the challenge being to critically evaluate that literature to show precisely what has been done, what has not been done, what gaps you will be filling and why it is useful or important to do so. Or, in having a clearly defined project in hand, you may be working with a localized, contained literature, where the challenge will be to situate that body of research in a broader knowledge base.

Or you may be in the situation where, having just started your research degree, you have not yet identified a research topic to work on. In this case, you will be reading for different purposes: (1) early stage skimming (see → 'Reading intensively and skimming' in Chapter 2 to discover what is going on in the literature or bodies of literature around your subject, and perhaps to identify a suitable topic for research (directions for future research in the conclusions of recently passed theses are also worth checking); (2) more focused reading to refine your project; and (3) intensive reading while appraising sources directly relevant to your project. Each of these reading modes, which you might find yourself circling more than once, is now discussed a little further.

Discovery mode

It is not a good idea to take detailed notes while in discovery mode, as you are just trying to gain a solid overview of what is going on in the literature to find out where you can slot in. So, most likely you are skimming across a great deal of material.

Still, in this stage you will be developing an appreciation of how the bodies of knowledge around your subject have evolved over time. So, begin generating useful categories. You can group studies around anything potentially relevant to your research: procedures, theories, models, methodologies, topics or themes of interest (perhaps in different settings), or whatever complements your (potential) research interests. Doing this will help you to partition information in a meaningful way and keep track of sources you may wish to return to later for closer scrutiny. You could try brainstorming or mind-mapping categories (see → 'Visual mapping of material' in Chapter 4) to break these down into further blocks of reading.

Refining mode

If you are in a research area where you are conducting on-going tests or experiments, perhaps over 1–2 years, so as to pin down your research, then the set of refining questions provided in Box 8.1, which can be used to progressively refine your topic or project when reading in terms of focus, purpose and method, may be less useful.

Otherwise, keep writing down your answers to these questions during reading. Your answers will surely change as you progress further in the literature, thus deepening and refining understanding of your subject.

---

box 8.1 Refining questions

Value and contribution: Why is it important to be undertaking this research at the level of your research degree? What is the nature of the contribution you expect to make to research/practice?

What? (Research focus): What precisely is your topic of investigation? Or what precisely is the focus of your research project? What exactly will you be doing? What work will you carry out?

Why? (Research purpose): Why are you covering this topic or doing this work? What is the big question driving your research enquiry? Or what precisely is your primary objective? If you have hypotheses, how do these relate to your primary research question or objective? What are the subsidiary questions or objectives underpinning your research? Jot these down too as they occur to you.

How? (Research approach): How are you going to conduct the research: Methodology? Modelling? Theoretical framework? Fieldwork? Data-collection instruments? Experimental or test procedures? Archival research? Other? What is the justification for taking that approach? How will this approach help you to achieve your research goals?

Appraisal mode

The more you refine your topic or project, the easier it is to identify material directly relevant to the subject under investigation. You will now be engaging with your material in a fully critical fashion (see → 'Critical appraisal of the literature' below).

Skimming does occur in the third stage, as it is not always easy to tell from an abstract or an introduction whether a source, or parts thereof, is relevant, or to what extent it is relevant. You do not want to waste time reading, for example, a 30-page article when only a few pages are directly relevant. Finding a good balance between skimming and reading intensively is aided by reading strategically.

Do think carefully about the *types* of information you want from more focused, intensive reading before setting out. You will not know the details of what will be found until you do the reading, but this should not curtail thinking through what you hope to gain from reading intensively any particular source.

Critical appraisal of the literature

Full critical engagement with the literature is a requisite of all literature reviews. Avoid either describing the literature when you write or becoming a detached observer, presenting a wonderfully complex vision of a world (the literature), which, exciting though it may be, floats free from your own research. If you are unpractised in critical appraisal, refer to the 'Critical appraisal checklist' in Box 8.2, which details practices that govern a critical approach to the literature when reading and taking notes (see also → 'Treating information critically' in Chapter 2).

box 8.2 Critical appraisal checklist

Develop an overview of the status of knowledge around your subject: What is known? What is not known? What do we think we know? What do we think we do not know? What seems to be contradictory, contested, problematic, uncertain or incomplete in the literature? Critical information of this type may need to be finely discriminated when writing your literature review.

Keep a balanced perspective: Identify what is useful in the studies under review: the strengths that you can build on, as well as any problems or gaps you encounter. Critical appraisal always involves due acknowledgement of other scholars' contributions, as well as criticisms of their work.

Remain open minded: Even when you think you know the answers, remain open to other possibilities as you explore the literature. Doing this will ensure that you do not miss important information that suggests you need to qualify, reshape or even abandon a position you hold. In short, it is not a good idea to approach the literature with the sole objective of finding information that will support a predetermined position or thesis, which unfortunately does happen.

Maintain a healthy scepticism: Probe for biases, problems, etc. How robust is the design of the research? Think carefully about theory, methodology, modelling, as all will influence authors' interpretations. Any problems with the approach: design principles, test or experimental procedures, data collection processes and instruments used, etc.? Examine terms and concepts; use specialist dictionaries/reference works if needs be. Definitional clarity is vitally important in all academic communication. Are there any problems in this regard?

Identify and evaluate key debates and issues: Raise questions as you read, lots of them: What do the important debates centre on? What are the key issues? Who are the key figures in the debates? To what extent do authors agree/disagree and why? How strong are their arguments? How good is their evidence? How sound are their interpretations of data presented? What do you think and why? Take notes on where you stand and why, any ideas you are developing and evidence to support them, which is so important when it comes to writing the review.

Map authors' viewpoints: Draw mind maps, graphs, whatever suits you to plot similarities and differences in authors' findings. It is not enough to show what these differences amount to in your literature review. You may need to explain what accounts for such differences, or provide possible reasons for these. One place to begin looking for explanatory reasons is in the design of the research. How robust is the design?

Position your research in relation to the literature: Are there problems inviting resolution? Issues that need revisiting? Changing circumstances that demand attention? New perspectives that could alter our understanding? Advances that need to be made? Research gaps that beg to be filled? Or what? How does your research fit in? Identify where you stand and why, and take notes to this effect.

Processing information to facilitate writing

It is a mistake not to give due consideration to whether or not the methods you use to process and store information will facilitate the writing of your literature review. You should not leave thinking about how you are going to develop and structure your review until you come to the writing. A number of suggestions for processing are now offered, but do discuss this matter with your supervisor, other academics, and students further progressed in their degrees, as they may offer more appealing suggestions.

Processing information

Useful as it is for identifying needed information, **key word searching** of imported databases is no more a processing strategy involving critical appraisal than is highlighting text when you read.

Annotating texts

Jotting down your ideas, thoughts, queries, uncertainties, etc., and perhaps summarising key points at the front of a paper you are reading is a sound processing strategy. Strategies of this type may suffice if the literature is contained, perhaps only 30 papers or so, but will need to be supplemented by more global strategies where the literature is extensive.

Category indexes

These allow you to group related sources while documenting summary critical responses to source material, and often appeal to students writing more unstructured theses in the arts and social sciences. Students have used electronic tools such as Evernote, Mendeley, Zotero, Word, Excel, and EndNote to build these, while others prefer boxes of index cards. You may want to build one or a number of indexes around key concerns of your research, as for example, themes, ideas, concepts, methods, etc. (see → the hypothetical illustration in Figure 8.1).

BIBLIOGRAPHICAL INDEX	THEME CARD INDEX: EUTHANASIA
Brown, P.Z. (2006) 'Living to die: debating moral right'. *Philosophy Today*, 12:4, pp. 234–65. Include your own evaluative comments (perhaps in relation to ideas of other authors), plus any direct quotations or paraphrases of interest. Also note whether or not you have photocopied the whole or parts of this article.	**Brown, P.Z.** – philosophical approach to the morality of Euth. practices – very good. Chin, K. – see bibl. for direct quotes (interesting case studies). Parker, T.Q. – dilemmas facing medical practitioners – 'medical' issues well covered. Paque, J. – unusual angle on supporters of Euth. – (yes – see paraphrase on bibl. reference). Smith, S.T. – weak challenge to Parker.

FIGURE 8.1   Indexing different types of information

Critical reading reports

These reports are like mini-literature reviews of only a few pages that are built around, say, four or five papers (often with competing views) on some specific aspect of your subject. These reports have distinct advantages: they help build confidence and reduce anxiety through practice; provide early feedback on where improvement might be needed; are an antidote to vagueness, as writing forces you to think through material; can contribute to agenda setting for meetings with supervisors about where your research is going, ideas and challenges; and, most importantly, will feed into the writing of your literature review.

Even though some reports may be abandoned as your research changes direction, the act of writing can speed up the project refinement process by filtering out what you do not want to get into while focusing your evolving interests.

The matrix method

This is a popular method in a number of research areas, particularly where evidence-based research is the norm. Useful as matrixes are, they sometimes read like an index or quantitative summary of papers in the literature with little or no actual processing unless this is deliberately built in, which is easy enough to do. Google 'the matrix method literature review' to find an example (see also → 'Further resources').

Software

If you are technologically inclined and enjoy using computer software, read the interesting article by Silvana di Gregorio (2000), which notes different software packages, and discusses the analytical advantages of using NVivo for the literature review. NVivo allows for deep-level analysis of qualitative data. If your work is more quantitative in nature, then there will likely be specific software designed with your disciplinary purposes in mind. Check with your lecturer, supervisor or lab colleagues to see which software is used in your department, which may help you analyse data for your literature review. Online software, such as Evernote, Zotero and Mendely can also be used for this purpose, but only if you use tags particularly well.

Processing and structure

During reading, processing and storing of information, bear in mind that the nature, design and objectives of your research will have a shaping influence on how you structure your review. The following discussion of different options illustrates the interconnection between students' approaches to structuring, their specific research interests and how they processed their information for easy retrieval.

The chronological approach

Reviewing the various studies, or groups of studies, in order of their appearance in time could be appropriate, say, for example, if it proved necessary for your research to chart, in some detail, technological or theoretical advances made over a period of time.

Key themes, concepts, issues or debates

It may be appropriate to organize your review around key themes, concepts, or indeed key issues or debates, as this student did:

> The purpose of this detailed review of the major debates surrounding market reform is to isolate a specific set of issues relating to policy development and implementation, the key focus of this dissertation.

Even then, your structure could be further influenced by the way in which the research field itself has developed, as signalled below by another student:

> *As these issues are discussed separately in the literature rather than being held in relation, I follow this practice in my Review.*

The methodological approach

Or it could be that methodology is the over-arching interest of your research, as was the case with the literature review chapter of a doctoral thesis that had only four main subdivisions. Each lead sentence of each subdivision clearly stated that a different aspect of methodology would be addressed, and why this was being done in the context of that student's research goals.

Shortcomings in reviews

Sometimes, even generally well-written reviews can display shortcomings of the following type in one or more areas.

Reader processing needs

As with all academic writing, you need to take care not to frustrate or alienate readers. Experts in the content they may be, but you still need to assist them to follow the aims and organization of your review by contextualizing your discussions where needed, and including adequate signposting. (See also → 'Attending to readers' needs' in Chapter 3.)

Contrary findings in the literature

When writing a review, it is insufficient to simply note differences in findings; you need to explain them. An explanation may not be self-evident, so probe deeper – start with design of the research. Below is an example of a student explaining contrary findings in her review:

> *These contradictory findings are indicative of differences in the assumed engine of growth. X and Y assume it to be capital per worker, whereas the empirical paper assumes it to be labour force participation: that is, the quality of workers and quantity of workers respectively.* (Economics)

The all-important: 'So what?'

As in all parts of the thesis, in the literature review you need to draw out the implications of your discussions, as this student does:

While these various arguments provide interesting insights into what caused the eruption of the conflict, none adequately engages the critical issue of the entrenched ethnic tensions in the region as a signature cause of the prolonged tensions. (Political history)

It is frustrating for readers to come across a fine piece of analysis of the literature only to be left wondering: 'But what is the point of all this'? 'Why am I being given this information'?

How your research fits in

Detaching your review of the literature from the research in hand can be problematic. It could be that you are expected to reserve detailed discussion of your own research for a separate section following your literature review. More likely, though, you will be expected to hold your research in relation to the literature during the review process at key junctures of your critical appraisal. This is a powerful strategy for drawing out key issues or questions you are addressing, while communicating the value of your research and your expected contribution, which is necessary with a PhD or Professional Doctorate.

Indicate at appropriate points how your research ties in with previous research, as these students from representative disciplines have done:

Sociology:

Insufficient attention is paid to the mobilisation and organisation of contenders. As the above critique suggests, this thesis will attempt to correct this deficiency through greater sensitivity to the politics of mass mobilisation and the struggle between the polity and contenders.

Computer Science:

It is not clear how much weight to give to the results. Further, most studies published so far have assumed search server cooperation, possibly including the running of homogeneous retrieval systems. By contrast X (ref.) and Chapter 5 compare vG1OSS, CVV and a modification of CORI. The experiment models an environment where servers do not cooperate and have heterogeneous retrieval systems.

Psychology:

The advantage of X's work is that these observations are lodged within a perspective built up in the course of a survey of processes that shaped the categorization of old age in a single culture, over a long period of time. ... X's work is important for the purposes of this thesis, not only because of. ... More importantly, the broad sweep of her study highlights the systemic changes that underpin shifts in the experience of old age and public understanding of it.

Linguistics:

The division by X and Y into numerous subcategories is inadequate to the overall function of modality. Such a division would in turn produce more subcategories such as anger, hesitation, sorrow, and so on. Hence, the classification of modality must be established by the characteristics of the function of modality related to the proposition in the sentence. The classification of modality is one of the subjects of this study.

Botany and zoology:

This thesis reports experiments aimed at extending this observation to crop and pasture species (see section 1.5).

 **further resources**

Fink, A. (2009) *Conducting Research Literature Reviews: From the Internet to Paper.* 3rd edn. London: Sage Publications. A great, practical resource that takes you through searching online databases, evaluation systems and techniques to assess research design validity, doing the write up and much more.

Garrard, J. (2007) *Health Sciences Literature Made Easy: The Matrix Method.* 2nd edn. Boston, MA: Jones & Bartlett. An excellent resource for those grappling with control of a fairly extensive literature in evidence-based research in the sciences.

9

Reports and Research Proposals

developmental objectives

By applying the strategies, doing the exercises and following the procedural steps in this chapter, you should be able to:

- Understand the complexities of report writing and appreciate the demands of the audience in some report writing.
- Identify strategies suited to focusing and developing the different types of reports discussed in this chapter.
- Appreciate the different purposes of proposals, and identify strategies for focusing and developing a proposal.

Students in taught courses are often expected to produce reports for assessment, and like those in research degrees may also have to produce a research proposal if proceeding to a thesis. These two types of writing are the focus of this chapter.

Reports

Reports are remarkably varied. The style, structure and treatment of information in a report can be strongly influenced by disciplinary practices, and by context and audience (particularly in the case of reports emulating workplace practice), all of which you will need to take into account when writing. There are the more traditional reports, such as field, experimental or laboratory reports; academic progress reports; the more consultative type, such as option viability reports or cost-effectiveness reports; and other reports that emulate workplace practice as, for example, in business, the professions or industry (for example, project management reports).

If you are required to write a report, take care to read any written instructions carefully, if you are given them; or ask your lecturer/supervisor if it is possible to review a model of what is expected, or to clarify what is generally expected in terms of the appropriate style and structure, and the expected length.

Possible audience considerations

As the nature of the audience can influence the style of a report, questions of this type often need to be addressed at the outset of writing:

box 9.1 Brainstorming audience considerations

- Who is my audience? Lecturers/supervisors? A single organization or industry body? A particular group – for example, farmers or environmentalists? A dual external/academic audience – for example, government ministers and academics? Or members of, say, two different professions – for example, doctors and engineers, or lawyers and business representatives?
- Who is meant to read the report? One person? Different people at different levels of an organization? Varied people from different organizations? Others?
- If the report is to be written as for oral presentation, who is my intended audience? (See → 'Planning for Success' in Chapter 11.)

Given your answers to the above, what factors do you need to take into account when writing? Think along these lines:

Organizational and other limitations for implementation? Countering anticipated opposition? The assurance of cost-effectiveness? Time or timing considerations? Policy alignment – for example, that the policy proposals are viable in terms of the current government's stated aims? Constraints to action by the intended audience? That the report will address the varied interests of readers from different levels of an organization, or readers from different professional backgrounds? That the report embodies awareness of cross-cultural communication issues? How logically persuasive will I need to be to convince my audience and what evidence can I use to aid persuasion? Anything else?

Features of prominent types of reports in different contexts are now discussed. These contexts illustrate a range of possible features that may appear in different combinations in a written report. An experimental or technical report, for example, may embody features of a formal report. You will need to adapt the advice here to the specific needs of your project.

Business reports

Your business report will likely involve analysis of a situation – historical, current or projected – so as to engage problem solving. As such, it will have a strong practical or workplace orientation.

Focusing a business report

In orienting business graduates to what was expected in their reports, a lecturer advised them to avoid 'academic argument' (that is, argument of the type discussed under → 'Research essays', Chapter 5) in favour of 'short, crisp reports', which focused the analysis of a 'situation' in sequential terms (see → Figure 9.1). Such advice invokes a medical discourse model in view of its obvious relation to the process of diagnosis, prognosis and cure. Superficially, the model looks simple, amounting to not much more than a summary introduction and a dot-point approach to detailing the information covered. But it is far more challenging on a deeper level of analysis as now discussed.

Diagnosis

Identifying what the problems actually are may be a moot point debated in the literature, a debate in which you would need to critically engage. Also, the symptomatic effects may be contested in the literature, or they may not be fixed but variable over time or context, and so again be difficult to pin down. As for causes, these may require analysis on both surface and deep levels. For example, on the surface the problem may appear to be due to incompetent management, but in probing deeper you find the real cause is the flawed structural organization of a company, which, in turn, demands you grapple with difficult organizational issues, perhaps of a theoretical nature.

Prognosis

After identifying the problems, you would then need to assess the probability of these being overcome – this is the prognosis part. This could involve in-depth

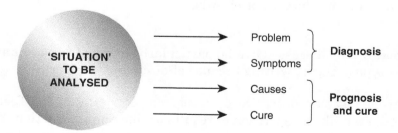

FIGURE 9.1   A model of a business report

analysis of a range of alternatives, including close examination of the positives and negatives of each and evidential support for conclusions reached.

Cure

Cure implies the need for recommendations to overcome the problems, perhaps in the form of an executive summary (see → 'Formal reports' later on in this chapter), or as a set of proposals. Again you could find that there are various choices needing analysis, perhaps in terms of short- and long-term benefits with further discussion of any projected disadvantages. This could also involve you in analysis of different theoretical perspectives, and perhaps prediction of a speculative nature. It would then be necessary to ensure your speculations arose out of your earlier discussions if they were to have any basis in fact. Throughout this process, you may need to include evaluation of the likelihood of specific proposals having the desired effect – this will be further prognosis.

Experimental or technical reports

Even if you are practised in writing experimental or technical reports, the following discussion could prove a useful refresher, if you are returning to study/research after an absence. This type of report conforms to the structural model, or some variation of it (and there are many): Introduction; Materials and Methods; Results; Discussion. Under disciplinary influences, results and discussion are sometimes combined in one section; sometimes there is a separate conclusion, or the discussion section acts as the conclusion – confirm what applies in your case.

The interlocking relationship of the structural divisions

The model in Figure 9.2 illustrates the tight, interlocking relationship of the structural divisions or parts of this type of report. All parts need to be held in relation at all times, and when writing the results and discussion sections you need to ensure that these line up with your stated research goals/questions, as laid out in your introduction, or elsewhere.

Issues

Issues now briefly discussed can be particularly vexing if you are unfamiliar with this type of report writing because of discipline transfer.

Coverage and treatment of information in different parts of the report   Discussions sometimes read like a repetition of results or like an introduction. Whereas the literature is foregrounded in the introduction as a means of providing

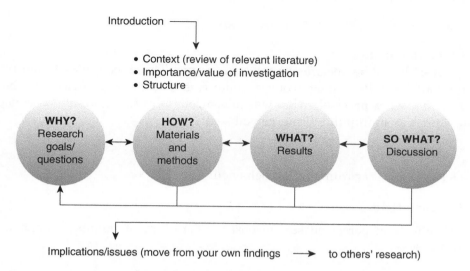

FIGURE 9.2   Typical parts of an experimental or technical report

'context' or background to the investigation, in the discussion it is the significance/implications of *your* results/findings that are focused on, with subsequent references to the literature to show agreement/disagreement with others' findings and reasons for these.

Alignment of stated research aims and presentation and discussion of results
Sometimes the results presented do not fully align with the stated research objectives or aims. There is a disjunction between reasons given for undertaking the research and the report of what was found. Every part of the report must relate back to the objectives or aims as set out in the introduction, or perhaps in a separate section.

Organizational flow of information throughout the report   Sometimes the ordering of discussions in different parts of a report is such that it is difficult to detect a coherent line of discussion (see → 'Developing texts' in Chapter 4).

Level of detail suited to different parts of the report   Sometimes there is insufficient detail to follow what exactly transpired in the conduct of an investigation, with even key details missing. While disciplinary/course practices can influence the level of detail to be included in different parts of a report, there can be unfamiliarity with fairly standard expectations in this regard. Discuss this with your lecturer/supervisor if needs be.

Each of the divisions or parts of this type of report is now discussed in more detail, with particular regard to focus.

Focusing the different parts of the report

Title (separate page)

Your title should be specific rather than vague. These examples taken from a handout for a Psychology course make this point: a vague title has been reworded to show precisely what was measured (infants' emotional responses) and what was manipulated (perceived sex):

> **Vague title:**
>
> Observer bias regarding infant behaviour

> **Focused title:**
>
> The effects of perceived sex on observers' ratings of infants' emotional responses

Abstract or summary (separate page and usually just a few paragraphs – provides an inclusive summary)

An abstract or summary may or may not be necessary. If it is, make sure it is self-contained and that it does at least the following:

- indicates clearly specific objectives, the hypothesis(es) being tested or problems investigated and why – the value of the investigation;
- provides brief information on how the experiments or tests (or anything else) were done;
- discusses more fully key findings and their implications in terms of the objectives or hypothesis(es) tested, perhaps in terms of future research and/or theoretical considerations.

Introduction (orients the reader to the aims/objectives and value of your investigation)

As the structure of the introduction can vary across disciplines, do clarify expectations. Usually the introduction includes information of this type:

- An initial statement of the topic of investigation and experimental objectives or test purposes, indicating why the investigation was undertaken, and why it was important. Sometimes there is also a scope statement, detailing limitations of the experiment/project.
- Definition of any complex terms or concepts used in the report.
- A succinct review of previous research findings (reference these) for the purpose of detailing what has been done and identifying any gaps, weaknesses or areas of extension leading to the formulation of research questions or objectives. Focus only on information specific to development of your questions; do not be tempted towards broad general discussion.
- A clear statement of the hypothesis(es) in the final paragraph.

From the writing of your introduction, it should be clear what previous research has been done, how your investigation arises out of this research (certifying its value) and what precisely you are investigating or testing, and why.

Separate theory section?

Sometimes in more technical reports (for example, in Engineering) a separate theory section follows the introduction. This section usually draws out theoretical issues relevant to the research presented in the report or outlines the theoretical model/s or framework/s being applied in your test/experimental analyses.

Materials and methods (explains how you conducted your investigation or tests)

This section is likely to include information of this type:

- Descriptive details of, for example, subjects tested, including the total number, pre-test or selection criteria applied, placement or assignment of subjects, and so on; or of the physical environment used, or of the materials, apparatuses, equipment and stimuli used in experiments.
- Explanation of the functional relationship between various devices or instruments used. Focus on only those details relating to your research objectives or the hypothesis(es) you have set out to test.
- A sequential description of the procedure. Consider a chronological, step-by-step description of what you actually did when running the experiment or conducting the test; organize your description around sub-headings if appropriate. It could also be necessary to include some explanatory information on why you made the choices you did, as this student did: *'In order to assess the amount of paint applied to the wood surfaces all specimens were weighed prior to paint application'.*

How much detail you include in this section will depend on whether it is expected that your experiment or test could be replicated from your description. Ask your lecturer whether this applies if you are unsure.

Results (tells what your findings were)

First consider the best way to group your results for discussion. Create appropriate sub-headings (see → 'Using sub-headings effectively' in Chapter 4). Review whether the results you present do tie-in with the hypotheses, objectives or research questions laid out in your introduction.

Next, think through how to order your results for discussion. One way is to direct attention to what is more or less significant about the results in terms of your objectives and/or hypothesis(es) as laid out in the introduction. Or organize discussion of your results around a set of illustrations (bar charts, tables, figures, diagrams, graphs, and so on). If you do use figurative illustrations, provide adequate explanatory description of them in this section, and draw out what is significant about these in your discussion section (unless you are combining results and discussion). **Appendices** can be included if your results are extensive, so that readers can refer to these for more detailed information as they wish.

Discussion (draws out the significance and implications of your findings)

This section represents a further stage in the thinking, in which you process your results to determine what they really mean. Begin by reviewing yet again your stated aims/objectives/questions/hypotheses as laid out in the introduction. Some compositional moves you could make in this section are as follows:

- Explain what you found in terms of expected or unexpected outcomes, or perhaps conflicting results.
- Determine the importance/significance of your results by situating these in the context of other scholars' findings. In the discussion section always work from your findings to others' findings.
- Deduce the degree of generality of particular results, whether or not these might apply beyond the particular experiments or tests carried out by you.
- Discuss biases (for example, in the methodology) that may have skewed your results. Determine the status of the hypothesis(es) in light of the results obtained compared to those of other studies.
- Formulate new or modified hypotheses from claims regarding the general applicability of particular results or because results show a need for these.
- Relate your findings to the theory from which your predictions were derived.
- Make recommendations for future research, perhaps by identifying gaps, difficulties and ways of clarifying or extending the present research.

In the process of discussing your findings you can draw attention to your final conclusions, although you may wish to present these in a separate concluding section.

Formal reports

A formal research report is often long and comprehensive. As the structure can be influenced by disciplinary preferences, be advised by your lecturer/supervisor as to specific requirements.

Two prominent structures

If you are a science student, your formal report could embody the structural divisions detailed under 'Experimental or technical reports' above. The formal report can also be similar to a mini-thesis in its general structure, in that it often conforms to the structural division of parts shown in Figure 9.3.

Distinctive features of the formal report

As most of these features are covered in various other sections of the book (see → in particular 'Principles of sound structure', Chapter 4 and 'Dividing up the text' in Chapter 10); only those features marked with an asterisk in Figure 9.3 are discussed further.

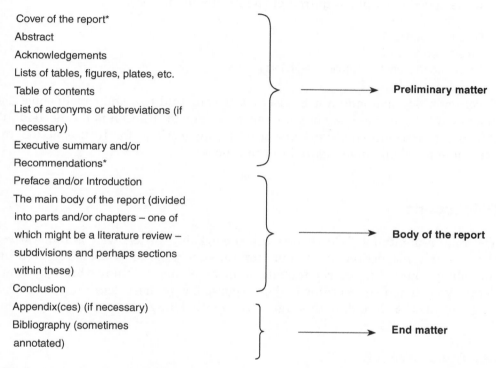

Cover of the report*

Abstract

Acknowledgements

Lists of tables, figures, plates, etc.

Table of contents

List of acronyms or abbreviations (if necessary)

Executive summary and/or Recommendations*

Preliminary matter

Preface and/or Introduction

The main body of the report (divided into parts and/or chapters – one of which might be a literature review – subdivisions and perhaps sections within these)

Conclusion

Body of the report

Appendix(ces) (if necessary)

Bibliography (sometimes annotated)

End matter

FIGURE 9.3   Structural outline of a formal report

Cover of the report (separate page)

If your report is meant to replicate a commission from an outside organization, then the cover page is likely to include this type of sequential information:

- The title.
- For whom the report was prepared.
- The department in which it was prepared.
- The date it was produced.

Otherwise, you may simply have a title page.

Executive summary and/or Recommendations

While positioning of the 'Executive summary' or 'Recommendations' in the report can vary, these sections usually appear just prior to the main body of the report.

An 'Executive summary' typically contains discussion of the major findings, the conclusions and (possibly) recommendations. This summary is often no more than one to three pages, although it can be longer. Or you may be required to include only 'Recommendations', which are then succinctly stated in a few lines, often with sequential numbering as follows (a single recommendation may also be divided into sub-recommendations using (a), (b), etc. to focus specific actions required of the recommendation):

Recommendation 1 ...
Recommendation 2 ...
Recommendation 3 ... (continue with this format)

Recommendations made must arise out of your findings and conclusions, as discussed fully in the body of your report; so substantiation is not needed at this point. Recommendations are usually suggestions for future action to overcome problems investigated in the report.

Field reports

The requirements for field reports are remarkably varied so it is imperative that you get instructions from your lecturer/supervisor on what is required in compiling yours. In general though, it is necessary to think through what details you should be recording and ask yourself: why these details and not others? (See also → 'Avoiding the urge to rush into data-gathering' in Chapter 2.)

Keeping precise records

In collecting samples, it might be necessary to keep records of dates, times of day, season, weather, locations and relevant physical characteristics, selection processes, sample dimensions and other characteristics, techniques of sampling and storage, and so forth. Or, in conducting interviews, there might be a need to record the time of the interview, the characteristics of those interviewed (for example, gender, status, etc.), the communicative content of non-verbal gestures, details of the interview setting, or perhaps indicators of relations among respondents where group interviews are taking place.

Carefully record your observations on what occurred, difficulties encountered, unusual occurrences, insights gleaned, emerging themes, hunches and possibilities, etc. Such records will be invaluable when you come to write the report.

key points

Be meticulous in your record keeping.

Progress reports

The purpose of this type of report, as its name suggests, is to report on how your research is progressing. Sometimes a (work in) progress report is rather like an updated research proposal, as discussed in the next section, which could be useful for you to review as well.

The purpose of a progress report

A progress report provides the opportunity to engage fully with the research you have already undertaken in order to demonstrate what changes your thinking has undergone and why; explain more fully your choices and the direction your research is taking; and obtain the type of feedback that will allow you to continue to progress.

Your report may include a full literature review (see → discussion above) with the length being governed by the level and stage of your degree, and perhaps disciplinary requirements. You may also need to include a timetable for completion.

In preparing to write, ask yourself:

- What have I done in my research so far?
- What difficulties have I encountered along the way?
- What solutions did I employ?
- How has my research changed in terms of my original research proposal as regards changes of focus, objectives or questions being asked, methodology, issues I want to look at, theoretical questions, experimental or test design and procedures, and so forth?
- Why have these changes occurred and what have been the consequences for my research?
- Do I see any continuing difficulties on which I need feedback? (You could, for example, be trying to make a decision between choices, each of which seems equally viable to you.)

The objective in writing the progress report then is to present an up-to-date account of the status of your research, to detail plans for the completion of the research and to get feedback on all this.

Research proposals

You could be writing research proposals at various points: prior to enrolment (perhaps as part of an application for a scholarship and/or as an application for entry to study at a particular institution); not long after enrolment in a research degree; at various stages in the first year or so of a research degree; or prior to beginning the research component of a degree that includes both coursework and research.

There are also various synonyms for a 'research proposal' produced during the course of a degree: for example, 'position statement' or 'statement of intent'.

The different purposes of proposals

The timing of production as well as the level of degree in which you are enrolled will affect the purpose, and therefore both the kind, and the extent, of coverage in your proposal. Proposals produced prior to enrolment or in the early stage of your degree may be quite limited and general, perhaps two or three pages. Those produced a year or more after commencement of, say, a PhD will be more comprehensive.

If you are producing a proposal to proceed to research after completing the coursework component of your higher degree, your proposal will vary in terms of length and complexity, so be advised by your supervisor as to requirements, and range beyond discussions here if needs be, perhaps even in → 'Thesis writing', Chapter 10. In certain areas of US study, for example, the research proposal produced on completing coursework constitutes up to the first three chapters of a PhD (introduction, literature review and methodology chapters), as discussed in some detail by Watts (2003).

One way to see the proposal is as a marketing exercise, its main function being to sell your research. In this perspective, the purposes are to allow your reader/s to assess the value and viability of your proposed research and to provide useful feedback on this. Your objective is to convince your reader(s) that the following apply:

- The scope and quality of your research is suited to the level of the degree. Clearly, the breadth and depth of research expected will be different for shorter and longer theses.
- The research as outlined is appropriate for the length. Again there is a vast difference between the extent of research required for a shorter thesis of, say, 15,000 words and that appropriate for, say, an 80,000 word PhD.
- The methods you propose to complete the research are appropriate, that is, it will be possible to access the resources needed to complete the research, to conduct the

interviews proposed, to carry out field research, to access suitable equipment, or to obtain necessary materials, etc.

- Your proposed research is viable in terms of time available to complete the degree.

With a research proposal, then, you will need to address a range of issues to do with the validity, viability and value of the research being proposed for your level of degree.

Focusing and developing a proposal

This section poses questions to think about when focusing and developing your proposal. Again, though, which questions are relevant and the amount of detail included in answering them will depend on the degree in which you are enrolled, the nature of your research, the stage you are at in your degree and any disciplinary requirements.

What is your field of research or topic of investigation?

This question addresses what you are setting out to investigate, what it is you want to look at or focus on. This could take the form of identifying the field of research in which you are interested, the general topic area, or a specific topic. These distinctions are chartered in Figure 9.4 by way of an example from Linguistics, which you can easily adapt to your situation.

A proposal is just that: what is proposed is not fixed for all time. Do not be overly concerned when proposing a topic that you will have to stay with it, particularly not prior to beginning, or early in your degree. Topics are sometimes changed or the focus shifts, along with other aspects of the study, as occurs during fieldwork on occasion. Do take care, though, as a radical change of topic might mean that an appropriate supervisor cannot be found, or that your designated supervisor no longer feels able to supervise your project.

Field of research:

Second language acquisition

General topic area:

Forms of address in different cultures

Scale of refinement

Specific topic:

Intercultural problems in teaching forms of address to Thai learners of English as a second language

FIGURE 9.4   Progressive refinement of a topic

What is the context of your study?

It is usual to provide relevant background information so as to contextualize your proposed research, to describe the broad context of your study – the big picture – and then say which aspects of the research field you want to consider. This can be done by way of a mini-literature review, perhaps even a full literature review if you are further on in your degree, which also allows justification of the foci and interests of your research, the issues you will be addressing and so forth.

It may be that you have only a limited, general knowledge of what research has been done, but that would be sufficient for a proposal accompanying an application, where you could provide background information by way of topic generalizations. Ask yourself: (1) what background information on my topic am I able to provide? And (2) how does what I want to do fit in with my general understanding of what research has already been done in the field?

What is the primary research objective or central research question?

This question addresses why you are undertaking your proposed research. There are different ways to encapsulate the why of your research, and perhaps you will use a combination of these: stating aims and/or objectives; proposing questions that you want to answer; setting up hypotheses that you wish to test, a hypothesis being 'a proposition put forward merely as a basis for reasoning or argument, without any assumption of its truth' (*New Shorter Oxford English Dictionary*); or 'laying out a problem' in some detail.

What is the value of your research project?

This question needs addressing if you are enrolled in a doctorate, but not necessarily otherwise. A PhD requires an original contribution to the research field. Answering this question allows you to convey the nature of the contribution you expect to make and say why you think it is important to conduct the research. The significance of your research project can be conveyed through discussion of the existing literature – its strengths and weaknesses and how your research fits in. Apart from providing information on the contribution you expect to make to research, it may also be important for you to mention practical or professional value attaching to your proposed research, as might be the case with industry applications, commercial uses, reform recommendations, and so on.

Will you be using theory, modelling and/or methodology?

If theory, modelling and/or methodology are likely to be a special consideration in your research, provide information to this effect, if you are able. If you are further along in your degree, you may be able to discuss fully and justify your theoretical framework or your choice of model.

Do take care with this term, 'methodology', which should not be confused with procedure (the next point discussed). As has been suggested, a methodology is:

> A rationale for the methods used to gather and process data, in what sequence and on what samples, taken together, constitutes a research methodology. This is not a grand term for 'list of methods', but an informed argument for designing research in a particular way. A research methodology needs to be appropriate for the research problem, and the justification that this is so should form part of a thesis. (Cryer, 1996: 45)

It is not just a matter of preferring some methods to others, but of choosing a combination of methods most appropriate to the research you wish to carry out, and being able to argue convincingly that this is indeed the case.

How do you intend to proceed with your research?

If yours is an early proposal, say something about procedure. This reveals how you intend to go about your research, what activities you will need to carry out and in what order. It might be appropriate, for example, to provide information about general plans for fieldwork if this applies (for example, locations, or populations targeted), to discuss experimental or test plans, or to identify primary sources to be accessed (such as archival materials). Of course, in a more comprehensive proposal, all these matters might be covered in a methodology chapter, justifying and validating your approach.

The idea is to provide an overview of what you think needs to be done to complete your research. Include as much information as you can so that a reader can determine any likely problems, unforeseen by you, in carrying out the research (for example, difficulty accessing and using materials or equipment, locating suitable source materials, undertaking fieldwork or anything else). Mention any potential problems you anticipate so as to get feedback.

Do you need to discuss relevant work experience?

Where appropriate, give a brief account of any work you have done and are presently doing, putting special emphasis on anything, including courses you might be teaching, relevant to the research you are proposing. Work experience may feature prominently, particularly if this is a key reason for receiving strong support in the proposed research from academic referees, and/or this experience is highly relevant to your type of degree (for example, a professional doctorate).

Should you include a timetable for completion of your research?

The answer to this question is probably yes, if you are at the end of or beyond the first year of research, but no if it is a proposal accompanying an application for entry.

Do you need ethics clearance for your research?

Ethics clearance is needed for various types of research using animals and humans, including, at times, conducting interviews and doing surveys on human populations. This will not concern you at the point of applying for candidature, but discuss the matter with your supervisor before writing a proposal during candidature.

Are you likely to need special training to undertake your research?

It is usual in a research degree to undergo training of various types. But if you are likely to need special training that could impact on time to completion (for example, learning a new language), then mention this, as you need to know that such training will be supported.

You should think about other questions you might need to ask (and answer) given your specific research interests, so as to ensure that supervisors, or potential supervisors, are fully conversant with your research interests and needs.

 **further resources**

Watts, M. (2003) *The Holy Grail: In Pursuit of the Dissertation Proposal.* Institute of International Studies, UC Berkeley. An insightful essay – available in pdf – based on a training workshop entitled: 'Dissertation proposal workshop: process and parameters'.

10

Thesis Writing

developmental objectives

By applying the strategies, doing the exercises and following the procedural steps in this chapter, you should be able to:

- Manage your project more effectively by orienting yourself to thesis writing in your discipline, taking advantage of online research management tools, and engaging anticipatory thesis management strategies.
- Avoid unnecessary work by settling typography and formatting decisions early.
- Think through the implications of writing for examiners.
- Understand a broad range of standard academic expectations of thesis writing – both shorter and longer theses – so as to develop more rigour in your writing.
- Identify strategies for dividing up the text and incorporating a thesis statement, structuring chapters in different ways, gaining overall thesis control, and developing the thesis abstract, introduction and conclusion.
- Organize a thesis writing group as a mutual support and learning forum.

The hallmark of thesis writing is rigour: rigour in foregrounding and developing a thesis, in treating the literature critically, in referencing all source material, in using theory and justifying methodology, in presenting test or experimental data, in mounting analyses, arguments and discussions, in attending to readers' needs, and in the overall style and presentation. This chapter considers some generic strategies to assist with effective communication of your research, whether in a shorter or a longer thesis.

A shorter thesis is seen here as roughly between 10,000 and 25,000 words, and a longer thesis as roughly between 60,000 and 100,000 words. As this division is somewhat arbitrary, scan the chapter to see what might be relevant for you. Where there is no distinction made between shorter and longer theses, advice applies generally.

Managing the project

Communicating original research can prove more demanding and time-consuming than anticipated. So, you need to put in place sound management practices early in your degree (see also → 'Managing your writing environment', Chapter 1).

Orientation to thesis writing

Orient yourself early on to the thesis as 'product' by browsing in one or two recently passed theses in the degree for which you are now studying. Students in your discipline may be producing different types of theses, such as case studies or topic-based research, so select those that approximate your type of research. Even then you could find that the same types of theses have different structures because of the specifics of the research. If you are uncertain, ask your supervisor to advise you on how to obtain appropriate theses for review, or, as a last resort, key in 'digital theses' or 'digital dissertations' to access online libraries.

If your thesis is to be a set of published articles, review the whole of Chapter 12 while browsing in this chapter and elsewhere in the book for useful material given your research interests.

 exercise: reviewing passed theses

As you review passed theses, you will need to avoid getting caught up in the interesting content, which is so easy to do. Keep focused on how writers go about the writing – the composition processes (see → the exercise under 'Mastering disciplinary writing practices' in Chapter 2 for suggestions about this type of focus). The idea is to get a feel for what constitutes a thesis at your level of study in your discipline. Do not be intimidated by what you find, as you are just starting out, and finished products never reflect the messy reality of research.

Having oriented yourself to what a thesis *is*, now activate strategies to ease the path towards producing your thesis.

Using online tools to manage the research project

While your supervisor will guide your research, developing online strategies for managing a larger research project can be effective in helping you to find, keep track of and analyse materials that are in digital formats. Many tools are available to assist you in this task, and there may in fact be tools developed specifically for your discipline or even for your department or school. Some of the most generic are now discussed.

RSS

Generally agreed to stand for either 'Really Simple Syndication' or 'Rich Site Summary', this is the key to directly accessing the most up-to-date information that is published on the web, and is a very powerful way of aggregating research content. Most websites these days come with an 'RSS feed' that allows you to subscribe to the latest content that is published on the site and then have it delivered to your 'feed reader' or 'aggregator'. This means that you do not need to keep checking websites for updates: instead, the updates come directly to you. By subscribing to feeds, you can view the latest research reports, blog posts, data streams, publications, notifications, photographs, bookmarks, tags, Tweets, weather forecasts, news items, and so on, all in the one place.

There are three main steps you need to go through in order to have such content delivered to you. There are other ways of subscribing to content, but this is how it works at its most basic:

- **Set up a feed reader through a feed reading service:** There are numerous feed readers freely available on the web. If you have a Google account, then you already have access to Google Reader. Netvibes.com and Pageflakes.com are also popular feed readers and allow you to customize your feeds into a kind of 'personal homepage'.
- **Find feeds that you want to subscribe to:** To find out whether or not a site has a feed, look for a small square and orange 'RSS' icon or some text that says 'RSS' or 'Subscribe' or similar. Click on the icon or text and you will be taken to a page that often looks very plain or that is seemingly full of code. Copy the URL or web address of this page. This is the RSS feed address.
- **Paste the RSS feed address into your feed reader:** Go back to your feed reading service and paste the RSS feed address into the 'add subscription' or 'add content' area. You will now receive directly to your feed reader any updates that are made to the site you have subscribed to – there is no need to visit the original site again.

Online note-taking and document management tools

These have largely been covered already in Chapter 1 (see → 'Electronic tools for increasing productivity') and in Chapter 2 (see → 'Strategies for information storage'), but it bears reinforcing that such tools should be part of your research management strategy to facilitate writing. Using a service such as Evernote.com, Mendeley.com, or Zotero.org will allow you to file, annotate, retrieve, and share the resources you both collect and produce throughout the course of your research project.

Online bookmarking tools

Being able to keep track of useful websites is a core skill for the modern researcher. Many students keep their bookmarked websites in a 'favourites' or bookmarks folder that sits on their local hard drive. This system is fine if you are working only from the one computer, but we are increasingly required to work across devices and on various machines; this means that if you have bookmarked or 'favourited' a site on one machine's hard drive, then you cannot access that bookmark or favourite on another machine. Keeping your bookmarks online can solve this problem.

Services such as Connotea.org, Delicious.com and Diigo.com allow you to save, tag, search and share your bookmarks on the web so that you can access them from any device that is Internet connected. By default, bookmarks that are saved to such services are usually publicly viewable, although you may set them to private if you wish. Searching or subscribing to (via RSS) other people's bookmarks can also be an excellent way of finding new or interesting research materials: if you find a user who is sharing similar content to your own, you can browse their collection for further resources.

Once your research management strategies are taken care of, you should concentrate on putting in place early in your degree, practices that will aid communication of your research in a thesis.

Anticipatory thesis management strategies

Keeping a research journal

During years of research, it is easy to forget important details of what transpired in the course of the research. So, just as experimental scientists keep detailed notes in a laboratory book, it is advisable to keep a research journal from the outset of research, regardless of your discipline.

The research journal can be a valuable aid to writing, as long as it is focused towards that end. Keep detailed notes on *precisely* what you did and why during the research phase, how you went about conducting the research (the details), and your findings. Note reasons for all decision-making, so that you will be able to justify what you did when you write your thesis, particularly as this influences the conduct of your research. Take notes on anything else that you think might possibly feed into the writing of your thesis.

Upgrading thesis production skills

Many libraries now have on-site and/or online training in getting the most from your computer during the thesis production process (for example, working effectively with long documents, using style templates, or formatting a print-based thesis). Take up such training if you do not already have the know-how, as it will certainly reduce frustration with the mechanics of thesis production.

Managing the project through regular writing

It is not enough to document details of your research, and take notes, important as these activities are. Writing skills atrophy if unused, which is a definite hazard when writing longer theses, so try to ensure that, from as early as possible in your degree, your research efforts issue in written outcomes that are sustained pieces of writing – properly developed academic texts.

 **key points**

Write early and write often.

In the first phase, you could write up methods/procedure sections or early test, experimental or field results, short comparative analyses of related sources on some aspect of your subject, thematic analyses of literary or art texts, analyses of archival materials or pieces of legislation – anything appropriate. You may then move on to an expanded research proposal (including an early literature review), progress reports, seminar and conference papers, or journal articles, all of which are discussed elsewhere in this book. Not only will such writing clarify your thinking and keep you practised, some of it will eventually feed into your thesis.

Setting up a thesis writing schedule

When you begin to write a first *full* draft of your thesis, set up a detailed writing schedule that includes time available for reworking chapters in the process of, or subsequent to, producing the first draft.

exercise: setting up a writing schedule

Step 1

Set up a time line that demarcates months to submission and includes an actual submission date, as below (based on eight months to submission):

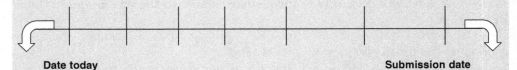

Date today   **Submission date**

Step 2

Now work backwards from the submission date allotting time segments to the different writing tasks (for example, chapter drafts) and activities, as specified here for the last month:

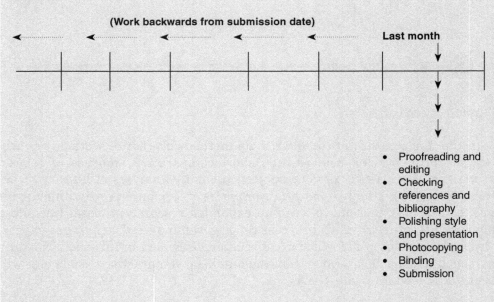

(Work backwards from submission date)

Last month

- Proofreading and editing
- Checking references and bibliography
- Polishing style and presentation
- Photocopying
- Binding
- Submission

Step 3

Set up a schedule that details dates for submission and return of drafts, revision of the whole thesis, and so on – everything you have to do to complete the thesis. Discuss the viability of your schedule with your supervisor to negotiate any changes needed to accommodate the supervisor's commitments.

Settling on typography and formatting

At the point of beginning your first *full* draft, if you have not already done so, clarify with your supervisor any institutional and/or departmental guidelines or policy papers relating to the writing of your level thesis. Such documents might be guidelines of a type that address general issues of style, formatting and standard expectations, and perhaps also more substantive issues in terms of focusing and structuring your thesis.

The few strategies now suggested complement the discussion on → 'The mechanics of academic writing' in Chapter 3.

Put in place all appropriate formatting, such as margins and spacing, *before* writing a first full draft. Changing aspects of formatting in later drafts can throw out figurative illustrations that are tedious and time-consuming to fix. It is best to set up a style template on your computer before drafting, and to stay with this.

You might also want to keep a record of practices settled on in a first chapter (for example, use of hyphenation, capitalization, or bold, italics, underline in the text if relevant) so that you can refer to this record for later chapters, as it is easy to forget when working across chapters, and time consuming to standardize practices in the editing phase (spell-checking helps little with 'consistency' matters).

Expectations of theses

While your supervisor will advise you on disciplinary-specific expectations, there are standard expectations that apply generally at any level of thesis writing.

Standard expectations

Your final draft will need to evidence at least the following features:

- Coherent development of the entire thesis (see → 'Principles of sound structure', Chapter 4).
- Adequate signalling of intentions and embodiment of audience needs (see → 'Bringing examiners into view' next).
- Evidence that the relevant literature has been thoroughly worked and understood. You may need to write a literature review (see → Chapter 8) and/or integrate the material you have read into your own discussions throughout the thesis.
- Logical rigour, sound reasoning and solid evidence in terms of analyses, discussions or arguments (see → relevant parts of 'The research essay as formal argument' in Chapter 5).
- (Perhaps) demonstrated knowledge and full critical appreciation of experimental or test procedures, relevant theories, models or methodologies (see → 'Treating information critically' in Chapter 2).

- Competent presentation of material. Do make sure the thesis is a scholarly presentation. Use appropriate citation and bibliographic formats as discussed under → 'Referencing and plagiarism' in Chapter 3. Proofread very carefully, and ensure that references are correct in the text and the bibliography – cross-check these. Check the consistency of legends for tables, figures, graphs, and so on, and that these are correct. Check that there is a table of contents page, an abstract and whatever else is required at the beginning, perhaps a list of abbreviations or acronyms if there are a large number in your thesis.

Bringing examiners into view

key points

It is useful to write your thesis with examiners in mind whether supervisors, internal or external examiners, or by way of a viva.

Taking care of examiners' needs is a further standard expectation, and one that can prove something of a challenge for thesis writers. Difficult as it can be to think beyond the sometimes obsessive intellectual processing that is thesis writing, bear in mind that your thesis is primarily a communication with the scholars who will assess it.

To recap in brief on 'Attending to readers' needs' in Chapter 3, always respect readers' processing needs by signalling your intentions at appropriate points throughout your thesis, as they know nothing about *your* decision-making. It is also often necessary to contextualize your discussions as you lead into subdivisions to ensure that your examiners are put in the picture as to the what, why, and how of the discussion to follow.

Writing with confidence and authority

Think positively about examiners – they are not out to get you. They will, however, be close critical readers concerned to maintain high standards in the research field. Regardless of their subject expertise, it is important to demonstrate that *you* have complete control and critical understanding of any subject matter under discussion in your thesis.

By the time you approach writing of later drafts you have certainly earned the right to a display of confidence and, as Ken Hyland argues, 'writers gain credibility by projecting an identity invested with individual authority, displaying confidence in their evaluations and commitment to their ideas' (2002a: 1091).

Authority resides in rigorous conduct of your research under the guidance of a supervisor, and in equally rigorous writing practices: fine-tuning arguments and discussions by providing solid evidence and exploiting logical connectors of the type given in the Appendix; using precise and incisive language (see → 'Clarity: the first rule of style' in Chapter 3); careful referencing of all source material (see → 'Referencing and plagiarism' in Chapter 3); clear structure at all levels of the thesis (see → 'Principles of sound structure', Chapter 4), and much more.

Taking control

During different stages of your research you may have found yourself in awe of your supervisor and other scholars with whom you have worked. It is now time to let that awe settle into collegial respect. As you write, respect your knowledge and trust your own judgement: it is up to you to anchor your preferred meanings when you write. You are in control of the writing, and in being so you have the power to guide your examiners towards the understandings you wish them to take up, to offset criticisms and get examiners on side (see → 'Engaging the reader' in Chapter 12). After all, at this stage you have become something of an expert, perhaps even the expert, on your topic.

Longer theses

This section discusses some distinctive features of communicating original research of the type presented in a longer thesis, in particular a doctorate.

The PhD needs to be seen realistically, particularly if you are researching in a climate that allows only three-year scholarships, if, indeed, you have scholarship funding at all. So do not make the mistake of pondering too much over the great work you feel you have to produce or the revolutionary contribution you need to make – you are not chasing a Nobel Prize. If the requirement is for an *original* contribution, you will need to uncover new knowledge so as to advance knowledge and (perhaps) practice in your field of research. In this case, your supervisor will guide you as to the suitability of a topic or project.

Quality indicators in examiners' reports

The information in this section is taken from examiners' reports, to which one of the authors of this book had access, and which were used in an in-depth pilot study done by Brigid Ballard (1995). The study analysed examiners' reports for 62 PhD theses. Each thesis had three external examiners, who were both national and international. The study covered reports from six disciplines – English and History in the humanities; Anthropology and Political Science in the social sciences; and Botany and Zoology in the life sciences.

This was a small, localized study (see also, the expanded study by Holbrook et al., 2004). It nevertheless has broader value in terms of *generic* quality indicators, to be augmented by disciplinary indicators, as advised by your supervisor; and some value too for theses other than PhDs. Examiners' commentary may also prove insightful if your thesis is to be examined by way of a viva or oral, a subject explored fully by Murray (2003). Engaging generic practices noted and valued by examiners will surely aid you in communication of your research.

Overall quality and contribution to scholarship

Among thesis qualities most commonly valued was the capacity to **contribute innovatively**. In the life sciences this was often communicated along the lines of an incremental advance on a commonly recognized problem, with summary comments like the following:

> 'Pioneering work' – 'stimulating' – 'breaks new ground' – 'important and valuable contribution to knowledge' – 'major piece of original research' – 'offers significant and useful insights' – 'advances scientific knowledge' – 'tackled problems difficult though intriguing to scientists'

Similar comments appear for theses in the humanities and social sciences:

> '… develops diverse and original methods which should exert an influence on other scholarship in the field.' 'This is a major piece of original research.'

> '… a major contribution both to ethnography and to social theory.'

> 'This thesis is an important contribution to the history of the domestic economy in X [country named], to women's history and to the agricultural history of X.'

> 'This thesis breaks new ground that will, I think, prove to be significant to the scholarship in the area.'

> 'As an original contribution to knowledge … this thesis qualifies twice over.'

In assessing the nature of the contribution, examiners also considered 'justification' for the research undertaken, the importance of the 'questions' being addressed and 'issues' canvassed; the capacity to relate research concerns to those of the broader discipline; and the grounding of the research in the relevant scholarship.

Whether there was a formal, separate review of the literature or not, thorough knowledge and **critical understanding of the relevant literature** was extremely important to examiners, engendering such comments as:

'Takes account of all relevant literature' – 'close critical review of others' investigations' – 'relates findings fully and forcefully to extant literature' – 'judicious use of a wide range of sources'.

But, more critically:

'failure to review and take up relevant literature across disciplines' – 'appears not to be fully conversant with the literature'

Evidence of publication in quality journals was highly regarded by examiners in the life sciences in assessing the overall quality of a thesis. Examiners in the humanities and social sciences also considered, and provided advice on, publication, either as journal articles or as monographs, but did not attribute the same importance to there being existing publications from the thesis in assessing overall quality, though this may have changed in subsequent years.

Scope, viability of topic, breadth and depth of study

Examiners were also concerned about the **appropriateness of the chosen topic** for the level of a PhD and the time frame:

'To tackle such a topic is clearly to undertake a task "involving a comprehensive study of a scope and size that could normally be expected to be completed in the equivalent of 3 years' full-time study".' [This latter quote is taken directly from the university instructions sent to examiners.]

'The candidate has identified a viable topic, researched it with appropriate techniques and methodology, and reached results with care and clarity rarely accomplished by a doctoral candidate.'

'... although "viable", the topic is also extremely difficult to address.'

Some topics were clearly thought beyond the scope of a PhD, and others not viable:

'Neither the supervisor nor the student seem to recognize that they were tackling a major problem that was probably too difficult.'

'This is a monumental thesis involving, in my view, too much effort for the degree of Doctor of Philosophy.'

'Undoubtedly, the thesis adds an appreciable amount of detail to what is already known ... Yet it is doubtful whether the material is significant enough to warrant a reference to the thesis in any future publication … It may be that this is not the candidate's fault. Assiduous though the research has been, it is possible that material of the desired significance is simply not there to be found.'

Examiners further took account of the breadth and depth appropriate for a PhD, sometimes commenting on the scope and quality of the **bibliography** or **list of references** in the process of determination.

Research techniques and methodologies, results, discussions, analyses and arguments

The importance attributed by examiners in the life sciences to **competence in research techniques** and procedures is evident in the following summary remarks:

'Has mastered a diversity of procedures' – 'high technical expertise' – 'displays competence in the variety of techniques' – 'demonstrates acquisition of the art and techniques of research science' – 'maturity of scientific approach' – 'employed intelligently a wide range of current techniques' – 'used a range of experimental techniques with great effectiveness' – 'data analysed by appropriate statistical methods' – 'well designed piece of research'.

But also this:

'Each of the other topics investigated in the thesis are at a low level of technical expertise and not carried through to conclusions.'

Many examiners from the life sciences complimented students on the quality of their data and the **logical rigour** of their discussions. For example:

'Good solid empirical data' – 'data suggests careful observation' – 'careful selection of data for presentation' – 'the logical rigour of the discussions is extremely impressive' – 'logical and systematic throughout'.

The more negative comments tended to be of this type:

'… too often prepared to reach firm conclusions in the light of insufficient data.' '… there are observations in the Discussion that were not mentioned in the Results.'

'… gets caught up in the minutiae of the results and has failed to highlight the significance of many of his findings.'

These reports suggest you need to be realistic about the importance of your results – grand speculations are not appreciated. You will also need to draw out the *significance* of the results in the discussion section, and their *implications*, as doing this was thought essential by examiners.

Examiners of theses in the humanities and social sciences were no less careful in their scrutiny of analyses and arguments, with many praising and detailing evidence of **'critical thought'** (or remarking on the lack thereof). One noted 'the subtlety and brilliance of analysis' in a thesis; others commented as follows:

'The whole thesis is vigorously argued. It is one of the strengths of this work that it repeatedly provokes argument and, indeed, invites debate throughout the text.'

'The structuring of the argument is, indeed, one of the most reassuring and impressive aspects of the thesis.'

'The quality of the analysis is excellent throughout – the present work represents a well researched, well argued study.'

'The author almost always appears aware of alternative explanations and [the] reasoning is frequently ingenious.'

But also:

'The first two models are in danger of functioning as straw men in the argument ...'

There was also this type of comment, which highlights the value examiners attributed to **overall coherence**:

'The connecting discussion throughout the thesis is almost always clear and intelligent.'

'The weakness of the thesis lies in its inability to maintain a common thread of argument throughout what is a very long and detailed piece of work.'

Where **theory** was an important consideration, this too was carefully assessed. One examiner praised the candidate's awareness of 'alternative theories and explanations'; another, the 'theoretical sophistication' of the study; and yet another, the 'creative' and 'rigorous' use of theory in the thesis under examination.

The importance of 'sound' **methodology** and its careful application in context was another vital consideration for many theses, as was 'clear definition of concepts' – one examiner displaying considerable annoyance because of a student's failure to define seminal concepts.

Academic style and presentation

Details of style and presentation were consistently referred to in the commentary, with examiners in the life sciences being particularly meticulous about these aspects. Examiners were enthusiastic about 'clarity and simplicity', 'conciseness', a 'succinct' thesis, 'consistency of style', impressive 'flow and cohesion' of discussions, with further comments like this:

> 'The physical presentation of the material, the quality of the line drawings, charts, and illustrations are of outstanding quality.'

> 'Let me observe in conclusion that this thesis is not only full of original insights and judicious syntheses but also impeccably written and presented as a material object, which makes the task of reading much more pleasurable.'

There was strong disapproval of 'discursive and unfocused' writing, a 'journalistic style', 'long-windedness', 'frequent repetition' (on several occasions), and labouring the point:

> 'There is a tendency to "overkill". When the candidate proves a point [the candidate] continues to prove it again and again.'

Some examiners were clearly irritated by excessive numbers of typographic errors and spelling mistakes, many of them meticulously listing these for future correction. Careful proofreading is indeed important.

Summary implications of the reports

All examiners took careful account of the instructions for examination sent to them in making their judgements, often framing comments regarding assessment in terms of the phraseology of that university's instructions. So, if your thesis is to be examined externally, try to obtain a copy of these instructions to which your supervisor could have access.

Examiners were keen to pass students, and felt bad, displaying irritability, when struggling to find positive comments to make about a thesis. They did not expect perfection, and sometimes easily accommodated both high praise and strong criticism of aspects of a single thesis. On occasion, more serious criticisms were tempered by examiners' making allowances for probable causes of perceived weaknesses in a thesis. Generally, they seemed to see the candidate as an 'apprentice' at the beginning of a career in research, not at an end. (This is despite the fact that many of you will not continue with research careers.) Mostly, these reports show considerable encouragement and support for doctoral candidates.

Examiners perceived the role of the supervisor(s) as extremely important, congratulating both student and supervisor on an excellent thesis, and often including the supervisor in criticisms of a problematic thesis. Also, some examiners thought they were not the best person to examine, or had insufficient knowledge to do so, which highlights the importance of choosing external examiners carefully, where this applies.

Coverage of the thesis being examined was, in all instances, comprehensive. The 186-plus reports (there were extras because of resubmissions) show that all examiners were diligent and detailed in their assessment of the research and writing on both the levels of the overall thesis and individual chapters. It would seem, from these reports at least, that very little escapes their eye.

Shorter theses

Shorter theses can have distinctive topic orientations, which, in turn, will affect expectations of your thesis.

Different topic orientations

The issue-driven topic

One dominant orientation across many disciplines is the issue-driven topic. In this context, engaging key issues of interest to scholars in your discipline will be central to the development of the discussions/arguments presented in your thesis (see → 'The research essay as formal argument', in Chapter 5).

The data-driven topic

Perhaps yours is a data-driven topic, where the accumulation and presentation of new data (for example, through fieldwork, local surveys, interviews, the generation of statistics, participant or non-participant observation, conducting trials or tests) is paramount. (See → 'Avoiding the urge to rush into data-gathering' in Chapter 2.)

It could also be that your interest has led you to improve, even marginally, on an existing model or product by way of a series of practical tests. Data generated by way of these tests might then be used in your thesis to critique that model or product.

The literature review orientation

Orienting the topic to a review of the literature also seems to be an attractive option for many shorter projects. In Box 10.1, the student signals this orientation in the thesis introduction.

case study example

box 10.1: Signalling a literature review orientation

Thesis title

Community participation: A key element in mother and child primary health care activities

Extract from the introduction

This literature review aims to present, in the context of health care, a synthesis of the major themes and arguments relating to the concept of community participation and PHC [Primary Health Care] and MCH [Maternal and Child Health Care]. It is acknowledged that there is a wealth of literature on the general concept of community participation; however, this review will be confined to community participation as it relates to MCH/PHC. First, literature on the different theories, practices and approaches to community participation will be reviewed in the PHC context, along with the debate on the vertical/horizontal approaches to PHC. Second, current issues relating to MCH and its correlation with women's participation and health will be reviewed. Third, a framework for further research will be formulated. This will be followed by a summary of the major themes and future directions for research.

There may be other possibilities available to you. Or it may be that your orientation is decided for you by way of disciplinary expectations.

Constraining factors

Regardless of orientation, a shorter thesis should also be a critical (see →
'Treating information critically' in Chapter 2), but not necessarily an exhaustive investigation of a topic. The scope of the study is likely to be limited along the following lines:

- The review of literature will be selective, perhaps confined to essential readings and recent research only that allows you to position your study in the research context.
- Data-gathering is likely to be small-scale and localized. You will probably be working with easily accessible subjects, conducting interviews or tests, doing short surveys, or carrying out manageable experiments.

- Arguments and discussions will necessarily be limited, though logically sound, so that generalizing from findings to other contexts is not likely to be an aim, though speculating about these findings might be warranted (see → 'The thesis conclusion' below).

Structuring a thesis

Structuring a thesis is an emergent, growing, developmental process of drafting and re-drafting: it is the bringing to full maturity of your ideas, the details of which are progressively refined during writing.

Strategies presented in the remainder of this chapter are designed to help you with macro-structuring – dividing up the text, overall structuring, structuring thesis chapters, gaining control of the thesis as a whole – and structuring individual parts of the thesis – the abstract, the thesis introduction and the thesis conclusion. Do review → 'Principles of sound structure', Chapter 4, which covers brainstorming and mind-mapping techniques, sequential outlining and using sub-headings effectively, controlling paragraph development to capture the main ideas that push along your thesis or overall point of view, and manipulating sentence structure to focus important points so that readers do not miss them.

Dividing up the text

The thesis text is usually divided along the lines of Figure 10.1, although variations do occur and shorter theses are unlikely to require a statement of originality.

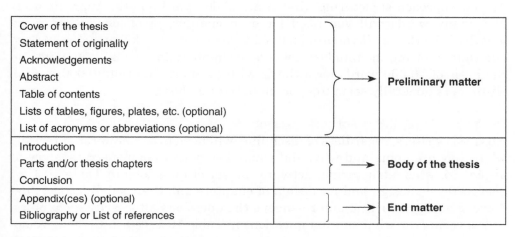

Cover of the thesis Statement of originality Acknowledgements Abstract Table of contents Lists of tables, figures, plates, etc. (optional) List of acronyms or abbreviations (optional)	→	**Preliminary matter**
Introduction Parts and/or thesis chapters Conclusion	→	**Body of the thesis**
Appendix(ces) (optional) Bibliography or List of references	→	**End matter**

FIGURE 10.1   Basic divisions of a thesis

key points

Check whether the ordering of preliminary matter and wording is standardized in your institution by way of policy or guidelines.

These are a few points to keep in mind:

- On the table of contents pages indicate the page number of the start of each chapter, and perhaps those of subdivisions or sections within these – practice varies. Include also page numbers of appendices and bibliography or references list.
- Pages of the preliminary matter are usually numbered with Roman numerals (i, ii, iii, iv, v, vi, vii, and so on). On rare occasions though, pages in the preliminary matter appear unnumbered, so review theses in your discipline.
- Consecutive page numbering in Arabic numerals (1, 2, 3, 4, 5, 6, 7, and so on) is used for the body of the thesis, from the first page of the introduction to the last page of the thesis.

Key structuring strategies

Structuring and developing writing on the scale of a thesis can be intellectually hard work. These two strategies will complement the many suggested in → 'Principles of sound structure', Chapter 4.

Strategy 1: Capitalize on word length
As you approach structuring, first think about word length. Approximately how many words will you need for each chapter, given designated word length of the thesis? If you are inclined to overwrite, work from a lower word length in allotting the number of words to chapters (for example, estimate on the basis of 70,000 words for a thesis with an upper limit of 80,000 words). Examiners generally seem to appreciate tighter theses.

Strategy 2: Apply this set of core questions
All thesis writers, regardless of discipline, will need to communicate precisely what they are doing and why, and what they wish to demonstrate, show or argue. So, when structuring, activate the set of questions in Table 10.1 for overall thesis design and for design of chapters and their subdivisions. Just do your best pre-writing and re-engage the questions after writing chapters.

Answering the what/so what questions in Table 10.1 feeds into the development of a thesis statement, as elaborated on next.

TABLE 10.1   Core questions for structuring at any level of the text

WHAT? (Research focus)	WHY? (Research purpose)	HOW? (Research method or procedure)	WHAT/SO WHAT? (Implications of your research)
How do chapter titles line up in terms of the overall research focus laid out in your thesis introduction? Does each chapter title actually capture essential coverage in that chapter (may need adjustment after the chapter is written)? Can you provide a succinct précis of *precisely* what you will be covering/ doing in the introduction of each chapter? Do your subdivision headings seem to capture the essential coverage of each chapter (list subdivision headings and do a print out)?	Why are you covering this subject matter in each chapter? What precisely are your research objectives, the hypotheses you are testing, or the questions you wish to answer in each chapter? How do chapter objectives fit in with your overall aims and objectives, as laid out in your thesis introduction? Have you identified clearly your objectives in dealing with specific topics in the different subdivisions? (Check printout and review → 'Using sub-headings effectively' in Chapter 4 to ensure that headings do capture the *true focus* of each subdivision – adjust if necessary).	How are you going to order your discussion in the subdivisions of each chapter? What precisely are you going to do and in what order are you going to do these things? Why? This will involve considering chapter titles and the *logic* of their ordering within the thesis, as well as subdivision headings and the *logic* of their ordering within each chapter. The best arrangement is one that ensures a coherent line of discussion throughout each chapter and across the thesis.	What are the main ideas/ points you want to make in developing your discussions or arguments in each chapter – review 'Developing texts' in → Chapter 4? You may be uncertain about these ideas/points until you write a first draft. But, if you are clear about some, jot them down now when structuring. Answering the 'So what?' is vitally important when writing. You need to draw out the implications of your discussions so that your reader is not left thinking: 'Well I take your point, and this is all very interesting (e.g. a great piece of analysis with good critical insights) but, so what? Why are you telling me all this – what is the point of it?'

 key points

Pause frequently when writing to consider that critical question: 'So what?' Keep asking yourself as you write: what are the implications of my arguments/discussions?

The thesis statement

The notion of a 'thesis' as in 'argument' does not resonate with all researchers. Still, if your thesis is required to be a connected piece of writing, then it is useful to think in terms of 'argument', as this notion embeds the idea of substantiating all knowledge claims made in your thesis, while ensuring a coherent line of development throughout the thesis.

key points

Put a 'working thesis' into a header so that it turns up at the top of each page of your draft. This is a useful way to refine it as you write and remind yourself that each chapter should somehow be contributing to thesis development where this is required.

For some students, pinning down a thesis can be like trying to hit a moving target – difficult. Perhaps it will help to think about it in different ways:

- What do I think my overall argument actually is?
- What is the big message I want to communicate to readers?
- What is the overall point I am trying to make that underpins what I say throughout my thesis?
- Why should somebody want to read my thesis? What is new/different/important about it?

Your thesis is your answer to that BIG question driving your research (for example, a why is it so question, or what caused it, or how can it be done or improved). Even a rough, working thesis can help guide your early structuring efforts. Confine your thesis statement to a single short sentence, no more than two or three lines:

MY THESIS IS THAT ....
(This always takes the form of a big general assertion – a statement.)

The example below constitutes a thesis statement, as laid out in the introduction:

I will argue that X's [country named] poor record of environmental law enforcement and compliance by industries cannot be explained solely by reference to specific aspects of environmental law, but rather, is a result of the very nature of X's social, political and legal system.

174

Everything done in this shorter thesis (the product) was meant to advance the above thesis (the argument).

Chapter structuring options

Often PhDs have as many as eight or nine chapters; a shorter thesis might have about four. Word length will affect the number of your chapters and/or parts, but so too can the principle of structuring used, the type of research and so forth. It could be that there is a preferred basic structure in your discipline, which should take precedence over suggestions to follow. Or perhaps your supervisor will refer you to one of the useful resources that target structuring and writing theses in cognate disciplines, such as that by Perry (1998) on marketing and related fields.

A science model

If you are researching in the experimental sciences, you will likely use some variation of this model in structuring core chapters: introduction, materials and methods, results, discussion, a model that is discussed in detail under → 'Experimental or technical reports' in Chapter 9. This might be called a science model of structuring, though certainly not all science theses evidence this modelling, and disciplines other than those in science use the structure.

A social science model

This model, which is not confined to researchers in the social sciences, has a pre-given partial structure for the first three or four chapters: introduction, literature review, methodology, and perhaps theory. Subsequent chapters will be organized around themes or sets of issues identified in reading the literature and/or from collation and analysis of data – organization of these chapters will depend on the orientation of your research (start experimenting with how to structure later chapters as soon as possible).

An illustrations-based model

Some students (and supervisors) have reported the value of taking this particular approach to structuring. First they process their data, producing different sets of illustrations (for example, tables, graphs, plots, figures, bar or pie charts) for each chapter. They then consider the order in which they want to present the illustrations in a chapter, and structure accordingly.

This is a model in which a considerable intellectual effort is expended before the writing of each chapter begins. Research in which a mass of data is processed as illustrations will certainly lend itself to this type of structuring.

A sequential model

Your research might be of the type that easily lends itself to the sequential model of structuring chapters, where there is an inbuilt logic to the sequencing of chapters, as was the case with the historical chronology underpinning the nature of one student's research. Moving successively from landmark changes pre-contact through landmark changes occasioned by European contact to ongoing changes in the present – was the underlying principle of a structure of his thesis that had both parts and chapters.

An open-ended model

There is no pre-given structure behind this model, which can indeed be notoriously challenging because of the inherent formlessness of the nature of the research (usually reading based).

 case study example

box 10.2 Early structural experimentation is vitally important with this model

One student's solution to this challenge, arrived at towards the end of the first year through structural experimentation, was a photographic model of structure: Chapter 1 provided a broad overview (*wide-angled shot*) of the two distinct traditions of Western supernaturalism to which the two poets under examination inclined, and the conceptual implications of their different preferences. There was then a move in Chapter 2 to a *middle distance shot* of the conceptual tie-in of these two traditions with other areas of the Western metaphysical tradition, which in turn were linked to the literary movements attracting the two poets as well as the types of literary criticism they espoused. Chapters 3 and 4 then zoomed in for *close-up shots*, detailed analyses of the early poetry to show how each poet's conceptual framing of reality was influenced by the different traditions of Western supernaturalism to which they held. The Conclusion then built on these four chapters to show how conceptual changes in the poetic output of each poet mirrored progressively changing attitudes to their preferred forms of Western supernaturalism.

If there are no disciplinary requirements for thesis structuring, be creative and experiment during the research phase, perhaps coming up with more than one likely structure to discuss with your supervisor. Let your research objectives determine the best structure for your thesis. It could be that your chapter structure will evolve from central themes covered in your research, or the seminal issues you wish to engage, as happened in the example discussed in the next section under → 'Visually mapping core chapters', which was a case-study type thesis.

Gaining overall thesis control

Different strategies are now suggested for gaining control of the overall structure and development of the thesis.

Visually mapping core chapters

Visually mapping core chapters on paper, or with a computer, appeals to some students. Take time to study Figure 10.2, which is an example of a student's

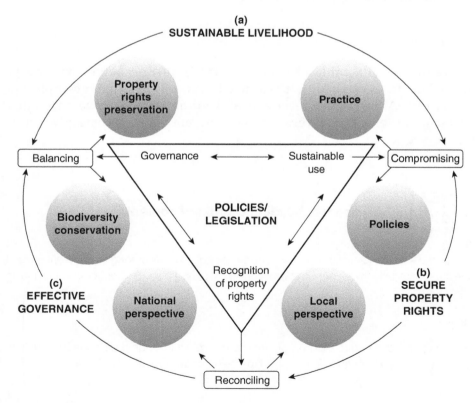

FIGURE 10.2   Computer modelling of thesis chapters

successful attempt at doing this, as he set out to determine the logical relationships among his thesis chapters. His topic was *The legal/policy framework for integrating indigenous peoples in protected area management in X [country named]*.

Each fundamental issue in the central triangle – governance, sustainable use and recognition of property rights – was covered independently in successive chapters (chapters 4, 5 and 6). These were the chapters analysing data from the case studies. In each case, there was analysis of the dichotomies pictured in the relevant circles: the balancing of property rights preservation and biodiversity conservation in terms of 'Governance'; the compromise of practices and policies in terms of 'Sustainable use'; and the reconciliation of national and local perspectives in terms of the 'Recognition of property rights'.

Chapter 7 then provided a comparative analysis of the implications of these three issues and chapter 8 expanded the discussion to determine an appropriate policy framework that would allow for (a) Sustainable livelihood, (b) Secure property rights and (c) Effective governance. (The first three chapters of the thesis, not included in the above model, covered the introduction, theory and methodology, respectively.)

The table of contents

Do attempt a solid table of contents (TOC) outline before writing your first *full* draft, even though it will need some reworking on completion of the writing. A TOC outline is a useful guide as you move through the writing of different chapters, which you may not necessarily want to write in sequence.

 exercise: building a table of contents

The purpose of this exercise is to determine the logical relations among the different parts of the thesis, not just to work out what you want to cover (see also → 'Sequential outlining' in Chapter 4).

Step 1

Some supervisors require that their students produce a full, rough draft of the introduction; others are happy with questions of this type being answered in dot point form:

What is your topic of investigation? What problem are you tackling, what are your research objectives or questions? Why is it an important topic of investigation? What contribution do you expect to make to the field of research (if relevant)? What subdivisions do you need in your introduction?

Try to answer these questions as clearly as you can, and then mock up chapter outlines.

Step 2

Now apply the set of core questions – What? Why? How? What/So what? – annotated in Table 10.1 to determine the logic of relations among the parts. Doing this will allow you to assess the following:

- How the foci and objectives of the different chapters fit in with your overall research focus and objectives as laid out in your thesis introduction.
- Whether the order in which you have placed your chapters, subdivisions and further sections within these, is best after all – whether they evidence a *logical* flow.
- Whether that main ideas (if you know them) that you wish to bring forward in the different chapters are likely to contribute to the coherent development of a thesis or unifying point of view.

Discuss your outline with your supervisor. Make any suggested adjustments, and then move on quickly to the writing itself. Spend no more than two or three weeks on this task.

The detailed thesis outline

With a detailed thesis outline (DTO), the table of contents is expanded in two ways:

1. A two or three page thesis introduction is attached, which develops more fully what is to be covered (for example, different foci, research aims/objectives/questions, hypotheses tested, discussion of the problem at the heart of the research, issues addressed, methodology or theory, outline of the thesis structure, a statement of the thesis (as in argument).
2. A paragraph or two precedes each chapter of the table of contents in order to provide detail on what you will be doing, why you are doing it, how you will go about this, and what you want to show or demonstrate – overall arguments within individual chapters.

When producing chapter introductions, students make multiple use of such words and phrases as: *introduces, outlines, examines, presents, analyses, provides an overview, discusses, concludes, purposes, objectives, summarizes, reviews, illustrate, this shows, it is shown, in order to demonstrate, I argue.* We see this happening in this example:

> **Chapter 3 explores** *the historical context of forestry development in X from industrial forestry to social forestry, to community forestry in the context of the ideals of sustainable forest management.* **Specifically, this chapter analyses** *forest-based development in X within five major periods in order to understand various reasons for forest degradation as experienced in the country.* **This chapter shows** *how forestry development in X is administered in a technocratic fashion that has failed to take into account the social dimensions of forest management.* **Finally, this chapter introduces** *the development of the SEP for Y as a new forest management approach for sustainable forestry.* (Our emphasis)

How far you will get with a DTO depends on the stage at which you write it: before producing a first full draft; to gain more control of the writing after you have produced a first full draft; or when you have come unstuck during chapter drafting. Just do your best.

Students do find producing a DTO demanding (a lot of hard thinking is involved). Still, the effort is considered worthwhile in the end.

 case study example

box 10.3 Students report many benefits from producing a detailed thesis outline

One group of research students approaching the thesis write up were encouraged to produce a detailed thesis outline. Doing this, they said, had 'reduced anxiety' and 'increased confidence':

- This was because they now had a stronger sense of 'how the whole thing hung together', to quote one.
- Or as another student commented: 'The best thing about the detailed thesis outline exercise for me was that I was able to concentrate totally on the bits [of the thesis] I was writing because I sort of knew how everything fitted in.'
- And another had this to say: 'My table of contents was pretty good but I still didn't know where I was really going with the argument until I did the detailed thesis outline. It helped me sort out my argument – what I really wanted to do with my chapters. It was great.'

The writing of a DTO is formulaic. You can shape introductions more creatively when you come to write them, while still communicating clearly foci, objectives and procedure, parts of your argument, and whatever else is needed.

The thesis abstract

Abstracts are differently focused and vary in length from about one third of a page to three pages. Shorter abstracts tend to focus only on findings, while longer ones usually evidence broader coverage of the type in Figure 10.3.

The abstract, often dashed off at the last minute, is important in that it could be the first imprint of your research on examiners. It could also be used by other researchers to decide whether or not to take the trouble to view your thesis in full, which might be the only avenue for accessing your research if you do not publish. Avoid a poorly constructed PhD abstract, which is also there for everyone to see in such international directories as *Dissertation Abstracts*. Consider the set of core questions offered in Figure 10.3 and take up what is appropriate for your research and discipline.

Often about one-half to two-thirds of the abstract is reserved for discussion of findings/conclusions and their implications for past and future research, though, again, you may wish to devote more space to different aspects of your research that you consider vitally important.

About ⅓ of space	{	Why was it important to undertake the study? (And for PhDs: what does it contribute to scholarship in your field?)
		What is the scope of your enquiry? Were any delimitations placed on the study? (While you will undoubtedly point this out in your introduction, it is also helpful to restate this concisely in the abstract.)
		What did you actually do?
		What were your research objectives/questions/hypotheses?
		What approach did you take? (If you need to, discuss your methodology, how you went about fulfilling your objectives, what models, or theories, etc. you used.)
About ⅔ of space	{	What were your findings? Set out clearly the main conclusions reached and provide some discussion of how you arrived at these.
		Also draw out their implications. Mention too any inconclusive findings, giving reasons for them.

FIGURE 10.3   Core questions for structuring an abstract

The thesis introduction

The purpose of your introduction is to introduce readers to the research presented in the body of your thesis: to the foci and parameters of your research, justifications for choices made, thesis procedure and so forth. While considering the following issues, bear in mind that the introduction is functionally significant in shaping reader expectations of what to expect on reading your thesis. Do consult with your supervisor on length, focus and development of the introduction *before* writing to gauge if any preferences prevail.

 **key points**

Align what you say you will do in the introduction with what you actually do in the body of your thesis.

Timing the writing of an introduction

If you have produced a well thought through table of contents or detailed thesis outline, it should not matter when you write your introduction. Still, supervisors frequently recommend that students write an introduction prior to producing a first full draft, although this will eventually need to be rewritten, or tidied up, in order to accommodate changes made during the writing process.

Focusing an introduction

Deciding what information to include in the thesis introduction and what to include in the introductory sections of individual chapters can prove challenging. This is primarily a matter of scale, as shown in Table 10.2.

The set of questions now presented is designed to help you focus and develop your introduction, perhaps using sub-headings in the process – engage those relevant for your type and length of thesis, and include additional questions if needs be:

- What is your topic of investigation, your research focus? It is helpful to state this up front in a paragraph or two leading into the introduction, so that readers can easily contextualize discussions to follow.
- What are the aims/objectives and/or hypotheses informing the research? Do you need to provide a problem statement as well?

TABLE 10.2   Information scale for the general and chapter introductions

Thesis introduction	Chapter introductions
The purpose of the thesis introduction is to orient the reader to the research presented in the body of your thesis.	Chapter introductions perform a similar orientation function in that they introduce the reader to the foci, aims, procedure and argument of each specific chapter, and provide any other necessary reader information for that chapter.
The introduction should include all information necessary to prepare the reader, to put the reader in the picture as regards the specifics of your research project: what the thesis focuses on, the context of the study, the research questions or objectives driving the investigation (should be broad enough to encompass those in specific chapters), the methodology applied, the argument you intend to present, etc.	
It may be necessary at times to reserve more detailed discussion of issues etc. for specific chapters and signal where these will be discussed in greater depth.	

- Do you need to justify the scope of your study (delimitations)? You may need to tell your reader precisely what you are covering and what you are not covering and why, perhaps to offset potential criticism for not having done something you never intended to do.
- Why is the research you have undertaken important? Can you demonstrate its centrality? Or how is your study different from others done in the research field? What contribution will your research make to knowledge? What is your thesis, as in argument? (All of this may be conveyed through context, the next point.)
- How much context, background information, do you need to set the scene, provide the 'big picture'? (This can be extensive in some theses, even up to 20 or more pages.) Consider the relevance of what to cover in terms of reader needs: what and how much background is needed to ensure your examiners will be well positioned to enter the body of your thesis.
- Should there be a formal literature review in the introduction (sometimes used to provide context) in which you draw out the issues you will be addressing, or elsewhere, or not at all?
- Do you need to explain your methodology, field or experimental procedure, or provide a discussion of the theoretical framework of your thesis here in summary form, in separate chapters, or not at all?
- Should you include a chapter-by-chapter outline of your thesis? If not, how might you otherwise convey the overall structure of your thesis? How will you indicate what you are going to do, in what order you will do these things and what you want to show or demonstrate in various chapters?
- Are there any other questions relevant to your research or disciplinary needs that you want to add?

The thesis conclusion

The thesis conclusion is your opportunity to step back and reflect globally on your completed research project with a view to communicating what you see as important and meaningful about it. A basic function of the conclusion is 'to summarize the progress which has been made in achieving the aims of the research' (Oliver, 2004: 151). Higher-level research conclusions extend to showing how you have advanced knowledge in the subject area, perhaps demonstrating the value of your research in terms of practical implications/application, and considering the possibilities for future research.

Thesis conclusions vary greatly in terms of titles, length and complexity, depending on disciplinary/research requirements, as pointed out by Bunton (2005), who provides an insightful discussion of thesis-oriented PhD conclusions in science and technology, and in the humanities and social sciences. Your conclusion may be fairly short and straightforward; or it may be long and complicated, and very demanding to write in drawing out and discussing fully findings and conclusions of individual chapters. In more complex conclusions, students often return to the aims/objectives/questions/hypotheses that informed the research as an aid to structuring when processing groups of findings and drawing out their implications.

Processing the thesis findings

Merely listing or repeating your findings from various chapters – chapter 1 shows, chapter 2 shows, etc. – gives no insight into the meanings you attach to these findings. Not only do you need to draw chapter findings into a coherent whole, you need to think about the weight and significance you attach to these.

Conveying significance

Not all findings will be equally important, so think about them in terms of a scale of significance by considering questions of this type:

- What do I consider most important about my findings in general and why?
- Which findings seem to be of greater or lesser significance and why?
- Are there any specific findings to which I want to draw particular attention and why (perhaps because they are unusual, striking or unexpected)?
- Has my methodology or anything else affected the validity or reliability of my findings and is this something that needs to be discussed (for example, biases inbuilt into the research design)? (Do not overlook discussion of limitations if applicable, even if these were outside your control, as examiners will not.)

By processing thesis findings in this way, you are bringing them into a new set of relations, providing a global synthesis of what your research means in the final analysis.

Drawing out implications

Processing involves carefully drawing out the implications of your findings. Your findings may have significant implications in terms of **research** (for example, theoretical, methodological or modelling implications), or **practice** (for example, application to industry, policy or legislation).

It is usual to situate findings in the contexts of past and future research: the extent to which your findings align with, question or challenge other scholars' work and why (in the conclusion, work from your findings to the literature – the reverse mode of a literature review); and the implications for future research – perhaps your research raises further questions or issues that need to be addressed, exposes previously unrecognized problems or the need to reconceptualize these, or calls for revised hypotheses, and so on.

As a writer of a shorter thesis you may not be in a position to suggest future research, but this does not mean you should avoid thoughtful discussion of implications.

case study example

box 10.4 Drawing out the implications of your findings can add zest to a conclusion

A shorter thesis examined the fall of a democratically elected government to determine whether the key actors participating in the downfall had acted within the framework of that country's Constitution. The student concluded that they had done so. But in her view, a major implication of her findings was that there was perhaps a need for review of the Constitution itself in the context of twenty-first-century society. This she aired in the conclusion, giving thought-provoking reasons why she believed such a review might be warranted.

Grounding speculations

The implications of your research project may be complex and variable, leading you into the realm of speculation. Some findings, for example, might appear to have implications beyond the parameters of your research, and they may do. But you need to be judicious. Ensure that such speculations are contained within the boundaries of the arguments and discussions developed in the body of your thesis. Keep your speculations grounded; do not let them float free from these boundaries so that they appear wildly improbable or even questionable.

key points

Use the more tentative language (for example, it seems, perhaps, maybe or it could be, possibly/possible, or it is likely/unlikely) suited to speculative uncertainty.

Organizing a thesis-writing group

Your fellow graduates can be a great personal and academic resource when writing your thesis. A thesis-writing group is a fruitful learning forum providing opportunity for reflection on the complexities of structuring and developing a thesis, and the sharing of ideas and helpful feedback from peers on your drafts. It is also a motivational stimulus in providing regular opportunities to share your grievances, frustrations, challenges, and, of course, your triumphs with fellow research students. Furthermore, such a group can reduce the sense of isolation that you and fellow students may be experiencing, if you are doing solitary research.

If there is no existing group of this type in your research environment and you feel it would be useful to form one (either on campus or online), follow these steps.

exercise: organizing a thesis writing group

Step 1

First approach an appropriate authority (for example, a graduate coordinator) to gain an email distribution list for research students in your group. Then send out a friendly email to determine level of interest. To work well such groups do need commitment from those involved.

Step 2

Having determined a sufficient level of interest, then organize a first meeting to sort out conduct of the group. Consider matters of this type (adapt suggestions for online groups):

- Whether you want it to be a students only group in which you will read each other's outlines and drafts, meet regularly to provide feedback on these, and to discuss strategies to address writing challenges, and so forth.

- Whether you want to reserve the possibility of inviting writing experts or scholars to address your group on occasion.
- How often you want to hold meetings, venue for meetings, length of meetings, prior distribution of materials for meetings, whether refreshments will be provided or not, and so forth.
- What organizational protocols you will follow. Usually the organization of such groups is democratic, with members opting to take charge of their own sessions by distributing copies of their draft to fellow students, identifying what specifically they would like feedback on given the stage they have reached in the writing, and perhaps organizing the procedure for their session. People also like to chat and have a bit of fun. While you and other students may initially be tentative about critically evaluating each other's work, well-intentioned criticisms will always be welcome, as will more positive comments on a draft.

 further resources

Biggam, J. (2008) *Succeeding with your Master's Dissertation: A Step-by-step Handbook.* Maidenhead: Open University Press. An excellent reference for the first-time author of a shorter thesis, with detailed process information and discerning comments on the common mistakes made by students.

Bolker, J. (1998) *Writing Your Dissertation in Fifteen Minutes a Day: A Guide to Starting, Revising, and Finishing Your Doctoral Thesis.* New York: Henry Holt. Pre-Internet days, but is nevertheless encouraging, embedded in sound writing principles, and provides timeless 'how-to-do' tips on such matters as developing self-reflection and regularizing writing to promote productivity.

Dunleavy, P. (2003) *Authoring a PhD: How to Plan, Draft, Write and Finish a Doctoral Thesis or Dissertation.* Basingstoke: Palgrave Macmillan. Not one to dip into for targetted information, but an immensely readable journey through thesis production, which contains many insightful comments, stimulating ideas and practical suggestions.

11

Presentations

developmental objectives

By applying the strategies, doing the exercises and following the procedural steps in this chapter, you should be able to:

- Understand and distinguish key expectations of tutorial and seminar presentations.
- Focus and develop an abstract to increase your chances of getting a conference paper accepted.
- Identify key factors influencing poster design and develop capacity to design your own posters.
- Identify practices influential in successful planning.
- Understand how to make the best of formatting options available to you in different situations of presenting.
- Avoid some of the technical problems associated with slideshows.
- Identify strategies to effectively manage a listening audience, the presenting venue, dealing with the unexpected and nervousness.

This chapter covers common types of presentations: tutorial, seminar, conference and poster presentations. It is advised that you first read the section referring to your particular type of presentation in the first half of the chapter, and then the general advice contained in the second half. Throughout the chapter, a distinction is made between text (any written material) and graphics (for example, images, photographs, diagrams, figures, plots, tables, charts, maps, and photographs).

The nature of oral presentations

The oral presentation is an interactive mode of communication that has a variety of functions. Its basic elements are configured in Figure 11.1 so as to convey the set of relations common to situations in which you will be presenting.

A presentation is often accompanied by a paper to be submitted to lecturers/supervisors, or circulated at a conference you are attending and/or published in the conference proceedings. Nevertheless, what you present orally is likely to be different from what you write in an accompanying paper, which is why the two are kept separate in Figure 11.1.

Distinctive features of presenting

In presenting, you will need to:

- (Possibly) handle the demands of multi-media presentations.
- Design your talk to fit the time available to you.
- Tailor your language and organize your talk to suit a listening audience.
- Control the presentation of your work and interaction with an audience.
- Employ strategies to attract and hold audience interest.
- Develop the ability to 'think on your feet' when responding to questions or feedback from the audience.
- Manage nervousness, which often accompanies speaking to an audience.

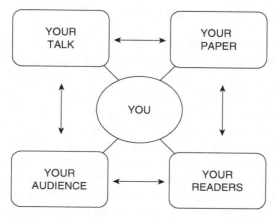

FIGURE 11.1   The basic elements of an oral presentation

Note the repeated mention of 'audience' in these points, a dimension given much emphasis in this chapter. Having a live audience both constrains and opens up your possibilities.

Tutorial and seminar presentations

Tutorials and seminars are two prominent types of presentation within graduate coursework and research.

Coursework and research students will not necessarily have the same objectives or interests in presenting their work. Nevertheless, there are some commonalities to consider whether, as a coursework student, you are giving a talk in a tutorial meeting to fellow students and your lecturer, or, as a research student, presenting a more formal seminar paper to departmental and/or other students and staff of your institution, and perhaps invited guests from the community.

Clarifying expectations

Prepare in advance of your tutorial or seminar by clarifying expectations.

Identifying formatting requirements
Clarify with your lecturer/supervisor whether there are special requirements for the format of your presentation. These may be set out in course guides, or they may be formalized in departmental/centre guidelines. In other situations your lecturers will simply tell you what is expected. Or you may be left to your own devices, in which case a useful starting point is to generate ideas/ strategies by reflecting on what impresses you about other speakers and their presentations (take some notes to this effect).

Determining assessment procedures
Clarify the criteria by which your presentation (and paper?) will be assessed. In **coursework** you may be asked to submit a paper, either before or after your talk, as part of the assessment and there may be different criteria for assessment of your presentation and your paper. Lecturers may also give different weight to various aspects of your presentation (for example, ability to initiate group discussion of important ideas; evidence of clear understanding of key issues, procedures or theories; clarity of structure and delivery of the talk) and of the accompanying paper (for example, breadth and depth of reading; the quality of the argument; and methodological soundness).

As a **research student** you are likely to be presenting as part of a progress review to showcase your work and gain useful feedback from peers and other colleagues.

Forestalling criticism in progress review seminars

Research students often report a fear of undue criticism in progress review seminars, and unfortunately such fear is occasionally borne out, which is why this subject is treated separately from strategies for managing nervousness at the end of this chapter.

key points

You cannot be expected to have all the answers with research that is still in progress.

If your research is still in progress, there will be uncertainties, perhaps incomplete developments or gaps in your research of which you are aware. Try these strategies to offset criticism:

- Remind your audience at the outset that it is work in progress in order to elicit their understanding and forestall criticism of the type that assumes you are already the expert.
- Assign the audience a useful role. Tell them on which aspects of your project you would particularly like feedback so that you can benefit fully from their expertise.

Assigning the audience a role can help forestall undue criticism and provide you with valuable feedback, just the feedback you want. Furthermore, if you have concerns that the nature of your coverage or the structure of your talk might invite criticism, again tell the audience why you are covering that material, or why you have structured the presentation in the way you have. Others will not necessarily see the sense of what you have done.

Conference presentations

As material in the second half of the chapter is relevant to producing a conference paper, this section focuses only on getting a paper accepted.

Getting a paper accepted

In some research areas, a fully written paper has to be submitted for a conference. More commonly, papers are accepted on the basis of abstracts, which are called for by conference convenors, usually by a set date. There may be standard expectations as to the formatting of your abstract, which you will know about (for example, using the introduction, materials and methods, results, discussion format). Or you may be given instructions as to the formatting of your abstract and designated word length, though often the only directive given concerns length.

As your abstract will compete with all others – perhaps with those of senior academics as well as, in some cases, senior people from many other areas of endeavour – you need to give thought to its composition.

Composing the abstract

Where there is a **conference theme** it is usually expected that an abstract address that theme. Demonstrate the link between your subject and the conference theme by building the theme wording into your abstract. But is this enough? One study suggests not. While the specifics of this study may not seem relevant, it does have interesting general implications for many research areas and disciplines.

Berkenkotter and Huckin (1995) report on 'gate keeping' at a particular academic convention, the large annual conference of the professional US organization called College Composition and Communication. In 1993 approximately 4,000 proposals (one-page abstracts) were submitted from which about 1,000 were accepted for presentation. Initially, a pilot study (of 96 abstracts) was conducted to isolate distinguishing features of successful abstracts as opposed to general features evidenced in most abstracts received. A later extended study issued these results (Berkenkotter and Huckin 1995: 102):

1. The high-rated abstracts all addressed topics of current interest to active, experienced members of the rhetoric and composition community; the low-rated abstracts often did not.
2. Almost all of the high-rated abstracts clearly defined a problem; the low-rated abstracts often did not.
3. The high-rated abstracts all discussed this problem in a way that would be seen by experienced insiders as novel and therefore interesting, whereas virtually none of the low-rated abstracts did.
4. The high-rated abstracts usually projected more of an insider ethos through the use of terminology, special topoi [traditional themes; rhetorical or literary formulas], and/or explicit or implicit references to the scholarly literature of the field than did the low-rated abstracts.

As detailed in Table 11.1, there are at least three important implications that can be drawn from the two studies that may have general application in many areas of research.

TABLE 11.1   Implications for focusing a conference abstract

Implication 1	Implication 2	Implication 3
• It will help to review abstracts from previous sessions of the conference at which you will present, if these have been published. • Try grouping their distinguishing features (see exercise below).	• You should be on top of what is going on in your research field: know the literature well, the shifts in research directions, the hot topics and issues. • Demonstrate your knowledge of all this in your use of the disciplinary language and by way of scholarly references.	• It is important to lay out a problem clearly and propose to treat it in a new or different way that is likely to prove exciting (or at least, attractive) to experienced researchers in the field, and be manageable within the time allowed for presentation.

exercise: workshopping the abstract

Before writing your abstract, examine abstracts from relevant, published conference proceedings and consider questions of this type:

- Why might these abstracts be of interest to the audience targeted?
- Does the writer make an effort to situate his/her audience by providing appropriate background information or context? (The extent of background information given will depend on the nature of the audience – the more general the audience, the more context needed.)
- Does the writer convey explicitly or implicitly the value/significance of the research being reported on in the paper?
- How are the abstracts organized? Review two or three and break them down into moves like so: first, s/he does this, second, s/he does this, third, s/he does this, and so on. Also, consider the level of detail provided with the different moves.
- Do you consider that these are confident writers on top of the research field? How is this confidence conveyed in the writing?
- Do all abstracts make a strong impact on you? Or do some impress more than others? How would you rate the abstracts you are reviewing, say, on a scale of 1 to 10?

Poster presentations

Poster presentations are popular at some conferences. You could consult professional graphic designers to advise you (some institutions have such people) or get help from those experienced in poster design in your department; or, like most students, you could design your own. Some students use computer software such as Photoshop, Adobe Illustrator or InDesign, and many simply use word processors or PowerPoint.

Find out if there is a graphics area or technology support centre on your campus that might give advice and allow you free or cheap access to such equipment as a colour printer and photocopier, lamination facilities, and so on. You can achieve a striking and attractive poster with some care and thought.

Factors that might influence design

As external factors might impinge on your design, do some prior research along these lines:

- Find out if there will be a large display of posters, where yours might be one of a hundred, or just a small display.
- Enquire whether the exhibition of posters will stand alone, or whether you will be expected to stand beside your poster to give additional information and talk with interested people.
- Find out what space will be available to hang your poster if you do not already know. You will need to know both approximate dimensions and the orientation (that is, vertical or horizontal).
- Find out what you will need to hang it with – Velcro fasteners or what. (You can be caught out by not taking your own.)
- Consider whether the poster you have in mind will be portable if you have to carry it long distances, say, for an international conference.

Design principles

Above all, a poster is a visual composition, or as some prefer including Woolsey (1989), a 'visual grammar', your key concern being how to utilize text and graphics to aid comprehension.

 **key points**

When it comes to poster design, bear in mind the *golden rule*: simplicity, clarity, brevity – less material rather than more is best.

exercise: designing posters

Step 1

Before you begin design, think back to posters you may have seen and found attractive. Can you pinpoint striking features that you could draw on?

Decide on what type of poster you want. Do you want a poster that is a large single entity (most popular) or one that consists of various bits (not that popular)? If a single entity, what size is the poster to be? What backing do you want to use? Your choice of material, its type and thickness, may be affected by whether or not you want lamination – matt is better than gloss. Now follow the dot points and suggestions in the next three steps.

Step 2

- Decide on the ratio of illustrations to written text that you need to fill, but not crowd, an A4 sheet of paper.
- Decide on what to include in the written text, perhaps a title, sub-headings, dot points and/or continuous text. Consider a short, pithy title. Strip all text ruthlessly so that only the most essential information is conveyed. The written text should complement the graphics.
- Reproduce the separate bits of text for your poster in appropriate type fonts, sizes and variations as discussed below under 'Pitfalls of using graphics'.
- Decide on what graphics you will use (for example, pictures, photographs, graphs, diagrams, tables, maps or figures).

At this point ask yourself: how readable will my text and graphics be from a distance of, say, 15 or 20 feet? Look at the difference between READABLE and **Readable.** Enlarged fonts vary in the space they take up and in their readability depending on the style chosen. BLOCK letters are not a good idea, as they do not allow for the definition afforded by a mix of upper and lower case letters, which is easier on the eye. Also, what size should your graphics be?

Step 3

Assemble the separate bits (the title, sub-headings, blocks of information, graphics, and so on) in an imaginative and creative way, experimenting with design proportions of space, graphics and text. Try not to get stuck in the groove of 'linear' arrangements. Another possibility is to carve up the poster using sweeping curved lines or circles of information, which can be most effective.

(Continued)

Now experiment with the positioning of texts, graphics and space to produce a scale model of the overall design on a piece of A4 paper. Although people's gaze tends to move from left to right, and often gravitates towards the centre of a design, some effective posters are not centred and can be read in more than one direction. At this point be prepared to go back to the drawing board to rewrite text, alter graphics, or find substitute ones if necessary. Leave a suitable amount of blank space or your poster will look too crowded; about a quarter of the total space available should be blank.

Consider what mix of colours you want: as background, to give emphasis to key points, or to ensure communicative consistency in the overall composition (for example, the same colour/tone being used to highlight all key points or for headings). Experiment with the colour spectrum on your computer; try strong contrasts (for example, bright yellow on blue or purple on green) or sharp tonal variations in a single colour. Consider two or three colours with tonal variations, as an overuse of colour can distract from rather than help communication. Colours can change from computer monitor to colour printer, so do a test print. Get a colour printout of your assembled A4 poster before you enlarge it.

Move back from your display to try to gauge the overall communicative effect – ask a colleague's opinion. Are there changes you could make to improve communication? Is it easy to read from a distance? Do the graphics increase or detract from the overall communicative effectiveness?

Leave it for a few days and return for another look.

Step 4

Scrutinize every detail of your poster. Edit ruthlessly and proofread very carefully, as you want to avoid errors appearing at the enlargement stage.

Now that you are sure all is in order, proceed with the enlargement. A4 to A2 is equal to double the enlargement in text height, and A4 to A0 is equal to four times the enlargement in text height.

This next part of the chapter contains generic advice intended for students making a presentation of any kind. As a general rule, invest 90 per cent of your energy in planning, preparation and rehearsal, and 10 per cent in delivery to improve the likelihood of a successful presentation – make it a triumphant occasion.

Planning for success

Design of a presentation should always begin with a thorough analysis of the audience, unless of course there is a highly specialist audience from your research area.

Audience analysis

If you are presenting in a course, you will know your audience – fellow students and your course lecturer. As a seminar presenter you could have a mixed audience: staff and students from your discipline and possibly from other disciplines, and perhaps invited public guests, such as practitioners in the field. Determining audience make-up could be challenging if you are presenting at a conference. You may be able to deduce this from the nature of the conference itself or from materials sent to you on registration, but if not, ask the conference convenors about the likely audience composition. You may also be taking courses that require you to develop skills for presentations in your future professional life. A psychology graduate, for example, had to design a presentation with an audience of young children in mind.

 exercise: audience profiling

The idea here is to generate as much knowledge about your audience as possible prior to preparing your presentation.

Step 1

Profile details of the audience for each of your presentations by considering these types of matters (where relevant):

- Audience size?
- Cultural background? (For example, English-/non-English-speaking background; other cross-cultural sensitivities to note.)
- Gender balance?
- Age make-up?
- Education level? (For example, tertiary, technical, school leaving certificate, mixed.)
- Make-up of the group? (For example, disciplinary or interdisciplinary academics/graduate students, disciplinary area specialists, university administrative staff, professionals, practitioners, business people, government representatives, mixed group.)

(Continued)

Step 2

With your profile before you, now consider the following questions, the purpose being to determine whether your particular audience will really want to *hear* what you wish to present, which has nothing to do with how controversial or not your paper might be:

- What three assumptions can you make about the likely interests of your audience in general? Jot these down.
- At what three points might your research interests and knowledge converge with those of your audience? Jot these down too. (Exercise your creativity with a mixed audience – you may be surprised at what you uncover.)

Language appropriateness

With an audience profile in hand, consider adjustments you may need to make to the language of your presentation in order to accommodate your audience.

All disciplines have specialist languages, specialist terminologies, special ways of speaking and communicating, which is fine for initiates but not for a mixed audience with varying levels of knowledge and expertise. If, for example, you are working in a highly theoretical or technical field, modify your use of terminology to accommodate all members of a mixed audience.

Listening effectively requires thorough understanding of the language of delivery. If your audience is likely to be from different language backgrounds, embody respect for this in your language choices, and in your delivery by enunciating clearly, slowing down and speaking up.

A lower level of formality is better suited to oral communication. Keep the language clear, simple and concise, less formal. First (I) and second (you) person usage is common in presentations. As you are interacting with an audience, remember to speak to that audience, certainly not as casually as you would with friends, but informally, which does not mean that you cannot also sound competent and professional.

Venue considerations

Also give brief consideration to venue in terms of what you may wish to do with your audience (we return to the subject of venue later).

Will the setting and room layout be suitable for your type of presentation? For example, you may want your audience seated at tables for workshop activities, or if you wish to have the audience engage in group discussions a formal theatre with fixed chairs would be unsuitable.

Building 'time' into a plan

A demanding feature of all oral presentations is staying within the allotted time. You need to take full account of the time you have to speak (be it 10 or 20 minutes, an hour or more) in developing your talk if you are to manage time effectively. In short, make special allowances for the fact that you are presenting to a listening audience; building in redundancy to help the audience follow; moving between media; or explaining graphics in slideshows.

key points

Do remember: it takes longer to speak from a paper than to read it through at your desk.

Be specific in drawing up a timeline: so many minutes for the introduction, outline, different parts of the talk, conclusion, and do a test run to ensure it will work for you on the day (see → 'The value of prior rehearsal' later on in this chapter).

Formatting options

Popular formats are slideshows, particularly PowerPoint, or multi-media presentations combining formatting options featured below, as well as other media not discussed here (for example, video or DVD). Still, where there is choice, canvass a range of formatting options before making a final decision on how to organize your presentation.

Using scripted notes

If your talk is to be fairly short, say 10–15 minutes, you may decide to speak from scripted notes. This situation is akin to having to write a 1,000-word essay; it might seem easy, but it is actually quite difficult.

key points

With a short talk, try to uncover what is *significant* about your topic for that audience rather than cover the topic.

Having a short time to speak exerts considerable pressure on *selection*, deciding what is most significant to include in your talk. Begin with these questions:

- What is significant/important about my subject?
- What is new about it and what might be especially interesting for my particular audience (return to your audience profile)?

All your effort will be directed to this matter of selection, after which you may decide on an outline of main ideas or key points around which to build your short talk. Or you may decide to develop the talk around a set of graphics (for example, tables, figures, or charts), or as a PowerPoint presentation (note comments below under → 'Slideshow technicalities').

Reading a paper as a presentation

If you are presenting a formal, longer paper and speaking for, say, 50 minutes, you may feel too insecure to work from scripted notes and prefer to read your paper. Or it may be that you are expected to read your paper, word for word.

Coursework students

In a course, you may be asked to read, in a 20–40 minute time slot, a written paper of, say 1,000–2,500 words, to be submitted at the end of the session for assessment, or reworked after feedback from the presentation. Usually, this type of presentation occurs in a tutorial where your audience is homogeneous – fellow students and the lecturer. There is then little to be said in terms of formatting, except to stress that you structure the paper in a way that it will not be too difficult for the audience to follow – you still need to take account of audience needs.

Also, review strategies discussed below under → 'Fine-tuning and rehearsal' (outlining papers, making objectives clear, building in repetition, summarizing key points for emphasis, pausing for effect, projecting voice and varying modulation, and so on).

Research students

You could be asked to produce a substantial written paper as part of a progress review and give a presentation. Some aspects that may concern you about this situation are:

- Trying to reduce a lengthy paper, sometimes 40–50 pages or more, to fit your presentation time.
- Addressing an audience of mixed disciplinary/academic interests, which may include other research students and departmental staff as well as staff and students from

outside your department and/or invited guests, or even audiences with a more complex make-up.

- Handling questions and criticisms from the audience.
- Managing nervousness.

All these challenges are discussed in the remainder of this chapter. Seek advice too from your supervisors and lecturers, other staff members and more advanced students. Many of them will be experienced speakers who have had to work through similar concerns.

Reworking a lengthy paper to present

Some graduates feel they have neither the time nor the inclination to rewrite a lengthy paper to accommodate reading for a specified time, and so decide to highlight certain parts of the paper to read and leave it at that. You may adopt this approach, or you may prefer to rework the paper. As it is impracticable here to include an example of a reworked paper, these few strategies for condensing are offered.

Condensing the material of your paper

Making your full paper available to the audience prior to a presentation will leave you in the enviable position of not having to provide detailed support for all that you say. So cut excessive detail, the very thing that can make the reading of a paper tedious, however imperative it is that such detail be included in the writing. While you can take liberties with evidence, referring the audience to your paper if more detail is requested, do be prepared to refer them to precisely where in your paper that detail can be found.

While you may wish to read some sections, you can break up the presentation by drawing on strategies of this type:

- **Condense** – for example, summarize a lengthy argument as key points on an overhead or slide, or isolate and list key issues to discuss.
- **Outline** – for example, model or picture the framework of your argument, theoretical discussion, experimental procedure, methodology.
- **Use graphical material** – for example, tables, graphs, figures, and drawings, to convey information succinctly.

Slideshow (PowerPoint) presentations

PowerPoint is the standard medium for slideshows, and may even be a mandatory requirement in your research area. Well done PowerPoint presentations are visually aesthetic and exude an aura of sophisticated professionalism.

Used by an audience-sensitive presenter, such presentations can be exciting and powerful. But not all is golden in this realm; presentations can also be boring for audiences, a complaint one hears too often.

Yale Professor Edward Tufte, who has published a monograph on the cognitive style of PowerPoint, notes (2003):

> At a minimum, a presentation format should do no harm. Yet the PowerPoint style routinely disrupts, dominates, and trivialises content. Thus PowerPoint presentations too often resemble a school play – very loud, very slow, and very simple ... PowerPoint is a competent slide manager and projector. But rather than supplementing a presentation, it has become a substitute for it. Such misuse ignores the most important rule of speaking: Respect your audience.

A curious effect of this audience/content neglect is a type of memory stasis – the audience fails to remember anything much about the presentation 10 minutes later, which defeats the point of giving the presentation in the first place. Full critical appreciation of audience interests/needs as discussed at different points in this chapter is as vital as it is with other presentation formats. Where choice does exist, considering possibilities inherent in other formats covered above, should help you to decide whether PowerPoint is the best option given the specifics of your presentation situation. Study the next section as it contains many considerations that are applicable to presenting using PowerPoint.

key points

Mastery of the slideshow medium does not equate with a successful presentation.

Online slideshow options

Popular as PowerPoint is, students are also choosing to use online slideshow services to host and/or create their slideshows. Slideshare.net and Slide.com provide popular online platforms for hosting and displaying slideshows in PowerPoint, Keynote, pdf and other major formats. Uploading your presentation to one of these services provides you both with an online 'backup' (see → 'Backing up your work' in Chapter 1) and with a public platform for sharing your work and raising your profile (do not forget to tag your presentations so that people can find them).

Other tools allow you to create slideshow presentations in a non-linear, more flexible fashion. With Prezi.com and Vue.tufts.edu you can create free-flowing slideshows that easily incorporate rich media. But again, be careful not to become besotted with the 'wow' factor of such tools: clarity of presentation must be your priority.

Pitfalls of using graphics

Watch that you do not fall into the trap of using graphics as a substitute for thoughtful content selection and structuring of your talk. This can lead to presenters failing to make critical connections, or including too much information for audience comfort, or zooming through graphics too fast, all of which can happen with PowerPoint presentations. It is frustrating for audiences to have a presenter show a complex table or figure that is information dense, only to have it whipped away before it can be read; or for the audience to realize that the print is too small to read; or for them to find that there is too much information to process and the speaker cannot manage this either; or to have a single table conveyed in eight slow-moving slides or bites of information so that the audience loses sight of the overall picture.

Slideshow technicalities

When designing and presenting a slideshow, consider the following points:

- Aim to **fill the frame** of each slide.
- In choosing **colours**, consider combining opposite colours on the colour spectrum for best effect. Do take care with reds and greens together as this combination might confound colour-blind people.
- Work towards **consistency** of design – for example, repeating colour and font sizes for different levels and types of information – in a set of slides. Your audience will soon tune in to the communicative meanings thus embodied.
- Experiment with *fonts*, as some are better than others. Courier New (as in the example below) gives good definition, as does Arial or Helvetica Neue. Avoid using all upper case letters, which are hard to read. It is important that people will be able to read your visuals:

    Headings (about 34–36 point)

    Sub-headings (about 28–32 point)

    ***Text Of Visual** (No Smaller Than 20 Point)*

- Consider no more than about **five points** for the text of a slide. Condense information in each point so that the point itself consists of no more than 10–12 words.
- Ensure **graphic materials** (for example, tables, figures, diagrams, and maps) contain only essential information. If these are necessarily complex, be prepared to draw out in a concise way what is significant about them.

- Use abbreviations where your audience will understand these – this saves space.
- Consider incorporating **other media** (for example, rather than waiting while the audience reads, say, a lengthy quotation, include an audio recording of the quote to switch them to the listening mode).

If you are doing a slideshow presentation, be sure you **have a reliable backup** just in case something goes wrong. It is prudent to have a copy of your presentation on a hard drive (for example, your laptop), on a thumb drive, and also on a networked drive (for example, on the Internet in a service such as Slideshare.net or Dropbox.com, or even emailed to yourself).

You should save your presentation in pdf format. Pdf will ensure consistency in formatting, regardless of the version or brand of software available at the presentation facilities.

Fine-tuning and rehearsal

A key factor in the success of any presentation, including poster presentations, is meeting audience expectations in terms of their interests and processing needs, so give this matter close attention in both the design and delivery stages.

Encoding audience management

Essential to a successful presentation is effective audience management. Strategies for addressing the key aspects noted in Figure 11.2 can be encoded in the planning of your presentation.

Attracting audience interest

In all situations of presenting, you will need to work at attracting audience interest.

Enthusiasm   Avoid seeming unenthusiastic about your topic (perhaps as an unfortunate effect of nervousness). Enthusiasm is indeed very catching, as

FIGURE 11.2   Key aspects of audience management

illustrated in this academic's opening comments to a broad general audience, who appeared riveted:

> Science is sometimes mysterious, sometimes impenetrable, sometimes frustrating, usually hard work, and often hard work for little result. But science is always exciting. Fascinating and exciting.

Humour   If it seems appropriate, and if you feel comfortable with it, build some humour into your talk. For example, an academic presenting to a broad academic audience began her talk by silently putting up an overhead of a humorous newspaper cartoon on a highly topical issue of the time regarding academic salaries (generating much laughter), and then said: 'I know you would all rather talk about this, but I'm going to talk about ...' She certainly caught the interest of her audience, and there was substance to follow.

Everyday analogies and metaphors   These are great devices because they are easy for the audience to relate to. Take the engineer who began his rather technical talk by humorously detailing the types of structural mismanagement that would ensure collapse of the family home, and captivating his audience in the process.

Linking your paper to prior papers   Another strategy is to link your conference paper to those presented prior to your own; even a few casual references in passing can be a useful way to engage, and re-engage throughout, the audience. This is particularly impressive where there is a conference theme, as it helps give a sense of continuity to ongoing presentations.

With **tutorial and seminar presentations**, remember not all people will be equally interested in your topic, so you may have to work a bit harder to generate audience interest. On a course, you will be guided in this by what you think will interest and stimulate students taking the same course as you. As a researcher, you could mention in your introduction how you think your paper might be relevant to the discipline as a whole, or how it complements work being done in other areas of the discipline. Ask yourself:

- Why might the advances I am making in my research interest members of the wider discipline? (You can assume that 'outsiders' have come precisely because they are interested in your topic.)

Orienting the audience to your talk
Start by thinking about these questions:

- What is my talk about?
- Why am I talking about this topic to this particular audience (return to your audience profile)?
- How will I approach the talk?

Build into your talk an overview of the paper you intend to present; keep it simple and clear. Remember that your audience is listening, not reading. Audience members are not able to backtrack, but instead rely on you to make the information easily accessible by adopting strategies of this type:

- Use an overhead/slide to outline or model the talk before you begin.
- Give the audience a written outline before you begin; keep this tight and compact.
- Circulate your paper the day before your presentation so that people have an opportunity to read it before your presentation. (Circulating a paper at the beginning of a presentation is not a good idea. People then tend to read the paper instead of listening to your talk, distracting both them and you. Sometimes, unfortunately, conference convenors request distribution of the paper at this point.)

Holding audience interest

Your audience is alert and listening – they know what your talk is about. Now, how will you hold their attention? In the main, try to remain sensitive to audience reactions, and consider the following strategies:

- **Let your eyes roam across the audience**. Make eye contact with many, not just one or two.
- **Modulate your voice**, change pace sometimes and pause for effect. Presenters often speak too fast. For a mixed audience of English and second-language speakers you should deliberately slow down, which is a good idea anyway. Speaking too fast can be a side effect of nervousness, which needs to be managed.
- **Speak up**. Make an effort to project your voice, particularly where there is no microphone. Audiences tend not to be forgiving of the softly spoken.
- **Alter the pitch of your voice** to avoid tonal monotony, which can be soporific or an incitement to daydream. Sometimes audiences do need a wake-up reminder and a change of pitch can achieve this.
- **Pause frequently**. Give the audience time to absorb your ideas, to have these implanted.
- **Summarize and recap** – look backwards and forwards – help the audience to remember and to follow. While redundancy or repetition is a negative in writing, it is a positive in presentations.
- **Try not to turn from the audience when speaking** to graphics (a big problem with slide-shows). A laser pointer might be available, but could be distracting if it is left to wander randomly as you glance up from your computer at the audience.
- If you notice someone snoozing in the audience, do not be thrown. Not all members will stay with you all of the time (particularly not those who have had a heavy night out!), but some may be completely engaged and listening intently.

Make reminder notes to yourself about all these matters on your paper or on prompt cards, particularly if you are prone to any of the above (for example, 'SPEAK UP').

The value of prior rehearsal

The value of a full rehearsal prior to presentation cannot be overemphasized. To manage time effectively, you will need to practise the delivery of your talk, preferably in front of an audience.

If you are located on campus, the best option is to get together with fellow students and borrow a room at your institution with the requisite equipment and other venue needs. Ask your lecturer/supervisor about this; it is usually possible for short periods. Fellow students can be very helpful in providing useful feedback before the official presentation takes place – remember to inform them about the nature of your audience, if needs be. A trial run can be relaxing and fun, alert you to the necessity for last-minute changes, help quell nervousness and increase confidence.

Family or friends might be willing audiences but, if you will be using equipment unavailable at home, you could be misled as to the effectiveness of your time management. Or, as a last resort, you could record yourself speaking your paper, and play it back so as to act as your own critic. But this is unlikely to give you a secure sense of how long it will take to deliver your paper, particularly if you will be moving between written text and visuals.

On the day: issues of delivery

By this stage you should be well prepared, rehearsed and brimming with confidence. But other issues may arise in relation to delivery.

The presenting venue

Whenever possible, visit in advance your venue for presentation. Look over the equipment and consider matters of this type:

- How big is the room? Will all audience members be able to hear if there is no microphone (do you need to get one?). Is the screen for visuals positioned so that those in the back row will be able to see it or does it need some adjustment?
- Will all your equipment needs be met and can you operate the equipment? Test equipment beforehand. It can throw your timing out if you have to fiddle with equipment to get it to work, and this can cause anxiety, though the audience is bound to be sympathetic. All equipment in the room may be operated from a complex panel, and there are differences in such panels. It will be disconcerting if the panel is one with which you are unfamiliar.

Dealing with the unexpected

Anything can go wrong with a presentation, and it often does: the equipment breaks down; or the room you are scheduled to speak in is changed at the last minute and you find it has no computer outlet for your PowerPoint presentation; or you realize you are running out of time and you have far from finished your talk; or a speaker on your panel has run way over time so your talk needs to be cut short on the spot; or the format of your panel session has been changed and you suddenly find you have less time to speak (it never seems to be more!).

As regards this last point, two useful strategies are:

1. Always think through beforehand how you might cut your paper short if you were to discover your speaking time had unexpectedly shrunk – actually mark out what you could cut without disturbing the overall coherence of your talk.
2. Learn your opening remarks by heart – not merely the polite or funny bits, but the intellectual lead-in. Do the same with your concluding remarks. A rambling conclusion or no conclusion because you are out of time can increase anxiety. Be able to cut straight to the conclusion if you run out of time.

You may have to make quick adjustments to cope with a new situation, but most presenters have had to confront the unexpected at some time, and are likely to feel sympathetic if this should happen. Draw your audience into your dilemma; make the best of the situation, and do not let it throw you off balance.

Canvassing audience questions

Question time often makes students nervous. It is easy to feel such relief at having finished your presentation that it is hard then to concentrate on questions. But do try to listen carefully because question time can be complex, as indicated by the situations mentioned below.

The belligerent or antagonistic question

Often the reasons behind aggressive questioning go beyond the scope of a paper, perhaps to a preferred ideology, theory or methodology, and there is little you can do except to respond if you can and move on quickly. Avoid engaging in argument in question time. Or, if your interest is aroused, offer to continue the conversation in a coffee or lunch break.

Uncertainty about what is being asked

Sometimes questioners are themselves uncertain about what it is they are really asking and so tend to be circuitous in putting questions. If you think there *are* questions being asked but you remain confused, ask politely for a rewording of the question(s), or for just one question at a time.

When you do not know the answer

You may be presenting work in progress that is incomplete, so you may not have all the answers. That aside, no one is infallible and it is easy to be caught out on occasion. You should admit you had not thought of that point and thank the questioner for drawing your attention to it. But be sure that the question is not simply irrelevant.

The irrelevant question

Some questions might be outside the scope of your paper, in which case just say so in your response. Or the question might imply the need for further research, beyond your scope, and you could say that. Or, if the question is more in the nature of a comment or observation of little relevance, then say so, or perhaps smile, nod and move on.

When there is not actually a 'question'

There can be a tendency for audience members to want to share their views and ideas rather than ask specific questions; others want to have their say. That is fine and can be interesting. But overlong, rambling speeches from audience members can be a problem too, unless there is a good Chair. When this happens, it might help to glance at a Chair who is not intervening, or you might have to politely intervene yourself to end the one-way 'conversation'.

Managing nervousness

Many presenters (students and academics alike) experience nervousness. Some nervousness is good – it keeps you alert and focused. But excessive nervousness can be terrible; all your careful preparation can collapse under a feeling of enormous strain.

key points

Take charge of your audience – lead them towards appreciation of your paper.

Be realistic

Try not to place impossible expectations on yourself. It really does not matter if your presentation is not perfect, if all does not go quite according to plan. Presentations rarely do, as seasoned presenters know well.

Think positively

Avoid engaging in self-sabotaging 'inner talk' of the type that predicts difficulties and failure – for example, 'I've never been any good at presentations', or 'They're going to hate my paper'. Instead, visualize your past successes and triumphs, your many past achievements – focus on a specific academic achievement that made you feel great.

Value your work

Remember that the conference convenors found your paper interesting enough to include. You do know a lot about your particular subject, and the audience can be persuaded that they want to hear what you want to tell them.

Keep your presentation in perspective

It is not the whole of your life, just a part of your overall academic endeavours at this time.

Nervousness usually decreases with further experience, but if you think the problem serious enough to warrant help, take steps to control it by contacting your counselling centre for professional advice. In the main, do not place impossible demands of perfection on yourself. Prepare well, do a practice run of your talk with fellow students if possible (help each other out), think positively, try to enjoy the opportunity to present, and do not be too concerned if everything does not go perfectly on the day – it rarely does.

 further resources

Alley, M. (2003) *The Craft of Scientific Presentations: Critical Steps to Succeed and Critical Errors to Avoid.* New York: Springer-Verlag. An engaging, rich resource with great illustrations that is relevant for anyone who wants to master the slideshow medium and technical presentations.

Shephard, K. (2005) *Presenting at Conferences, Seminars and Meetings.* London: Sage Publications. A highly practical guide to presenting across disciplines that complements and expands on material covered in this chapter, and contains a chapter dedicated to a subject not discussed here: the advantages and disadvantages of videoconferencing.

Sprague, J. and Stuart, D. (2008) *The Speaker's Compact Handbook.* 2nd edn. Belmont, CA: Wadsworth. More of an introduction to effective public speaking that provides essential information, great tips, checklists, learning tools (including speechbuilder express and infotrac), and discrete chapter access to specific topics of interest.

12

Publishing and Raising Your Profile

developmental objectives

By applying the strategies, doing the exercises and following the procedural steps in this chapter, you should be able to:

- Appreciate the advantages of self-publishing some of your work online.
- Understand how to raise your profile by building an eportfolio.
- Take a constructive approach to the sensitive issue of co-authorship with supervisors.
- Identify strategies for targeting an appropriate journal and shaping a paper for publication.
- Understand the peer review process and possible outcomes, and identify strategies for dealing with calls for substantial revision, or rejection of your manuscript.
- Identify strategies for contacting book publishers and focusing a book proposal.
- Form a publication syndicate with fellow students in your research group as a mutual support and learning forum.

As a graduate, publishing may be a new endeavour for you. This chapter initially considers online publishing and setting up an eportforlio to raise your profile before turning to two major avenues for disseminating your research: journal article and book publication.

Pre-publishing or self-publishing online

Many students are choosing to 'pre-publish' or 'self-publish' their work on the web in various formats, including in blogs, wikis, podcasts, slideshows, videos and even on Twitter. All of this counts as self-publishing online.

Advantages of distributing work online

The advantages of distributing your work online are many (see also →
'Raising your profile: setting up an eportfolio' in the next section for more information on the types of tools and services that you might use for self-publishing).

 **key points**

Self-publishing online can be a valuable way of disseminating, and getting feedback on your work, before sending it out for formal consideration.

Testing ideas and staking a claim to them

In formal publishing, the processes of peer review, editing and revision mean that there is normally a significant lag time between the time you submit work for consideration and the time it actually appears 'in print'. If you publish your work online, however, you can disseminate your material immediately and attract comments and criticism from the online community, including from your peers and colleagues. This can be especially valuable if you want to test a controversial thesis or idea for coherence and relevance before sending a paper off to a journal for formal consideration.

Because of the time it can take to have your work published via formal channels, you may want – or need – to assert your rights to your intellectual property sooner rather than later. This is especially the case in fast-moving areas, such as Computer Science or Engineering, where methods, designs and technologies quickly become obsolete and where a year or two's delay in publishing your ideas could cost you the advantage. Publishing online can help you stake an early claim to your work.

Increasing your visibility

As with presenting at conferences, self-publishing online increases your visibility in the research community and can be an important part of your networking (see → 'Networking for support' in Chapter 1). The more material you disseminate online, the more 'searchable' you become.

There will always be times during thesis writing when your belief in your ability to produce good ideas and to write well will be tested. Self-publishing your work can lift your morale, especially when you receive positive feedback on the material you have posted.

Writing your way to clarity

Throughout this book you are advised to write early and write often. Of course, you can always generate material by putting written matter into a Word document and keeping it on your hard drive, but producing items for an online readership (or viewership or listenership) can be a strong incentive to the intellectual and creative processes.

Writing regular blog posts or making frequent additions to a wiki helps form the writing habit and can even help you overcome writer's block (see → 'Managing common writing concerns' in Chapter 2). Neither do you have to write enormously lengthy tracts when self-publishing in this manner – simply a few hundred words might be all you want to add at any given time. This can reduce some of the pressure you might feel when you tell yourself that you have to write extended arguments in order to be producing worthwhile material.

Expanding possibilities

Publishing in the digital age need not be limited to text-based or 'paper' formats. Online publishing provides multiple and more flexible formats for communicating your work. You will probably produce at least one or two slideshows throughout your research degree and these can easily be added to a slideshow hosting service (see → the next section), as a way of expanding your online, self-published profile. If you are more adventurous, you might want to publish videos or audios related to your research, or you might consider Tweeting your ideas.

Some points to watch

Be selective about what you put online. Although you can, in theory, self-publish anything you want, it is nevertheless good practice to think carefully about your purpose in publishing online, and to edit and proofread all materials before hitting 'publish', 'save' or 'upload'.

key points

It is not advisable to publish online anything and everything you write.

Before you self-publish any of your research or ideas online, you should also consider that self-publishing is not typically regarded as 'proper' publishing in the academic community. Although it is easy to publish your own work online, doing so lacks the prestige of having your work published in a peer-reviewed journal or by a well-regarded publishing house. You need to be strategic about which material is suitable to self-publish and which material would more usefully be sent away to a journal.

You may need to 'pitch' your work at a different level online. Work that you produce for a journal article or book is usually in-depth, highly developed and complex; online environments do not generally sustain this approach to communication. If you are self-publishing online to attract audiences that you expect to give feedback on your ideas, then make sure that you express yourself clearly and simply so people can grasp your main points quickly. If, on the other hand, you are self-publishing as a way of generating material for formal publication in the future, then you must adjust your style and tone to suit the requirements of conventional scholarly discussion when you later submit a paper for peer review.

You might get negative reactions to or comments on your work. In publishing anything for general consumption on the web, there is always the possibility that you may encounter more criticism than anticipated. If the criticism is fair and helpful, then graciously accept it and use it to improve your thinking (this should be one of the reasons why you choose to self-publish in the first place). If the criticism is rude, abusive or genuinely unmerited, then you are within your rights to ignore it and even remove it from your site or profile.

Raising your profile: setting up an eportfolio

As a research student, you should start to think now about raising your profile within your chosen field of study. A simple way to do this is to set up an online portfolio, an 'eportfolio', that brings together your various writings, presentations and other research-related materials. The idea of an eportfolio is to introduce yourself to the research community and to promote your work. Providing a web link to your online portfolio can also impress potential employers no end, and it may be what distinguishes you from the competition when it comes to applying for a job.

There are two main choices in constructing an eportfolio: (1) build a basic eportfolio using only the tools provided by the service you use for your eportfolio; or (2) create an expanded eportfolio by placing your eportfolio materials on a number of different specialist sites and then 'feeding' them into a central gateway to your online presence.

Basic eportfolio

A basic eportfolio will find you using a single service to host all your eportfolio materials. You might choose a blogging service such as WordPress.com or Blogger.com (blogs make for excellent eportfolios), or you might prefer for the task a dedicated eportfolio service such as Mahara.org. These services are very powerful and offer a large range of functions, but with a basic eportfolio you will only be exploiting their capacity to upload documents, files and images, and to create written blog posts. Choose this model if you want the simplest of online presences, or if you lack confidence in drawing together a variety of sites into the one location. Do note, however, that because of the limited use you are making of your eportfolio, valuable ways of promoting your work, as now discussed, are being overlooked.

Expanded eportfolio

The idea of developing an expanded eportfolio is that you distribute various bits of content across the web and then draw it all together in the one place. At first glance, it might not seem to be a good idea to have all your portfolio materials in disparate online locations. There are, however, distinct advantages in choosing this format over its alternative.

This approach allows you to choose the 'best tool for the job'. With a basic eportfolio, you are only using the functions provided and/or supported by the service that hosts your material. But if you expand your approach, and distribute your work amongst a number of specialist services (for example, you upload your slideshows to Slideshare.net and your Word documents to Scribd.com – these are all described below), then you are able to embed visual, 'scrollable' displays of that work into your central eportfolio. This makes for a richer, more accessible – and more impressive – experience for visitors to your site.

Having your work distributed across sites and services also makes you more 'searchable'. If you have a presence in Twitter.com and a résumé on LinkedIn.com, for example, you are increasing the chance of having your expertise recognised by potential employers at the same time as increasing your exposure to your audience.

You can, furthermore, include a much greater variety of content. For example, you could share interesting research articles or websites that you have found by adding a feed to your online bookmarks or you might want to embed a YouTube video that you find useful or instructive. This adds to the dynamic, 'rich media' nature of your eportfolio and will make visitors want to explore further.

Some tools and services you might consider when setting up your expanded eportfolio are now discussed.

Blog

Running your own research-related blog can be an excellent way to promote both yourself and your work. Writing short entries (between, say, 200 and 600 words) can become an important part of your eportfolio in that such writing can communicate to your visitors what you are 'about' as a thinker and researcher. And the more you blog, the more you increase your searchability on the web. Using a blog as your main eportfolio site is discussed below.

LinkedIn

LinkedIn.com is somewhat like Facebook for professionals and is a great way to control your professional identity online. If you want to keep your personal and professional lives separate, then you could use Facebook for friends and family and LinkedIn for colleagues. LinkedIn allows you to create a profile, add updates, connect with and search for others in your field, and generally expand your networks. As with all elements of an expanded eportfolio, though, you need to keep your profile up to date.

Facebook

Many students already have a Facebook.com account, so you may consider connecting your Facebook to your eportfolio. This would work if you feel confident that your Facebook already presents a fairly professional account of yourself to the world (as opposed to one that might be more personal or private in nature), or if you feel that you can handle Facebook's privacy settings well enough to manage your public image. Be careful, though: Facebook's privacy settings are complicated and change frequently, so there is no guarantee that you will always be able to control what others do and do not see. If in doubt, use a service such as LinkedIn for your professional life.

Twitter

As with all the social media described in this book, it is how – and how well – you use them that matters to your research and writing. Twitter.com may be a way of relaying to the world the most inane happenings in your everyday life, or it may be a way of conveying research-related discoveries, pointing to the latest report in your field or networking with like-minded scholars.

Slideshows

As a research student, you will likely give several oral presentations throughout your degree and those presentations will, in turn, likely be supplemented by a PowerPoint or slideshow presentation (see → 'Slideshow (PowerPoint) presentations' in Chapter 11). Do not allow this excellent material to be limited by the time and space of the actual presentation itself: increase your audience by uploading your presentations to a slideshow and document hosting service such as Slideshare.net. Slideshows and documents hosted on Slideshare can be embedded and displayed in your eportfolio. This allows visitors to view and click through your presentation there and then, without having to download, unless they wish to and you have provided the option for them to do so.

Documents

It might be adequate to upload a Word or pdf document to your eportfolio but in order for visitors to view your material they must first download and save it, which can be inconvenient at times. A more elegant solution is to host your documents on a document hosting service such as Scribd.com and then embed a viewable version in your eportfolio – just as you would do with slideshows, as described above. All of this adds to your online presence and increases your searchability.

Video and audio

If you are a more advanced web user, you might even consider producing some audios or videos to embed in your eportfolio. Depending on your field of studies, and depending on whether or not you have the skill, means and time, you might create videos of laboratory techniques you are developing, of field sites you have established, or even of interviews you have recorded with informants (with ethics approval and their permission, of course). Audio formats can also be effective in an eportfolio and are excellent vehicles for discussions of theory-related topics, or of interim research findings. Not only does adding video or audio to your eportfolio demonstrate your thinking around your discipline area, it also shows off your skills in producing these kinds of media.

Choosing a service to host your eportfolio

In choosing a service to host your eportfolio, you should select a robust, reliable platform that allows you to export or backup your content. Blogging services provide a near perfect means for creating an eportfolio, whether you are using a basic or expanded format. You do not have to turn into a full-blown blogger, though; you are simply using the platform to assemble your eportfolio. Nevertheless, it should be remembered that blogs are designed to display dynamic content in the form of blog entries or posts in reverse chronological order.

WordPress.com and Blogger.com (Blogger is owned by Google) are perhaps the two largest blogging services. They have each been around for several years, are dependable and reputable, and provide excellent functionality for free.

In terms of features, WordPress has almost everything you can think of, so if you are looking for the most powerful and flexible platform for your eportfolio, then you might choose WordPress. Blogger, on the other hand, does not have quite the same level of functionality, but it is a little simpler to use. Both services allow you to customize the appearance of your eportfolio, offering many different 'themes' to choose from.

What to include in your eportfolio

What goes into your eportfolio will be up to you, but you should have at least a curriculum vitae (CV), some examples of your work (whether they be papers or presentations or both), and your contact details. Anything less than this, and your site will hardly be worth visiting.

Your CV
Include your employment history (past 10 years is normally enough), your higher education history, a list of any publications or conference papers, professional memberships, awards or any other relevant information. Do not include the contact details of referees as you are publishing your CV on the web, and your referees may not want their details made known. It is best if you provide your CV in both html (web page) and pdf versions. Avoid uploading Word documents, as they do not always print well.

Contact details
Think about how you would want people to get in touch with you. If you prefer email, then use an email address that you check regularly. Keep your contact details up to date.

Presentations, keynotes, and conference papers
Add a section to your portfolio that provides copies of any presentations you have given in the past. A short abstract on each, as well as the venue and date for your presentations should also be provided. Any slideshows should also be saved in 'handout' format and in pdf. Visitors do not want to have to print out 60 pages at one slide per page.

Scholarly papers
Provide copies of, or links to, your published and unpublished papers. Remember, though, that if your work has been published in a journal, then the journal probably owns the copyright on your paper, which means you should only provide a link to the paper, not a copy of the whole paper itself.

Awards

Let visitors to your eportfolio know of any awards or nominations that you have received. Include PhD or research scholarships under this heading.

Blog

As stated earlier, it can be strategic to write the occasional blog post, even if you do not see yourself as a dedicated blogger. Blogging raises your profile at the same time as letting people know about the great ideas you are developing.

Of course, how much material you choose to include, and the variety of tools and services you draw into your central eportfolio, will be up to you, but you must keep your site up to date. Even if you have all the skill and wherewithal to create the most elaborate expanded eportfolio, visitors will not return to your site if there is only 'old stuff' on it.

Journal publication

Publishing papers in scholarly, peer-reviewed journals remains a major avenue for disseminating your research. You may be writing a paper from scratch, perhaps because you are doing a thesis by publication, or wishing to publish papers from completed thesis chapters. Where the research reported on in a chapter is focused on a single experiment or test, as in some sciences, there is high compatibility between chapter and manuscript design. In the arts and some areas of science and the social sciences, however, thesis chapters are more complex and are not easily converted to publishable papers, because as Sadler (2006: 8) points out:

> An article needs a **clear, unitary focus.** It is often difficult to lift an intact section [let alone a full chapter] from a thesis, extract the relevant entries from the references and publish it as an article. How an article can be developed from a thesis depends on the thesis topic and the structure of the dissertation itself. (Our emphasis)

In such cases, a chapter may contain two or more potential papers, and considerable rewriting to reshape material for publication. Strategies presented in subsequent sections should help you with this.

ejournals

There are many well-established, top-class ejournals. If, however, you are thinking to publish electronically, take a little care to establish the duration of the journal and its scholarly status – whether or not it is peer reviewed – as there is an element of instability in this avenue of publishing. One student reported that a new ejournal that looked promising in her social science discipline disappeared after publishing just two issues, consigning the papers published in it (including hers) to oblivion.

Open access journals

The advantage of these journals is that anyone can access their articles free, which could increase the breadth of your readership and, subsequently, your chances of being cited by other authors. Just confirm whether or not you will have to pay to publish in such a journal.

Including supervisors as co-authors

Including supervisors as co-authors can be an excellent learning experience, and bestow reflected prestige from publishing with well-known, respected scholars in your research area. Still, co-authorship is an issue for some students. While the following discussion draws on a student publication that issued from a survey of students and supervisors in one science discipline, the observations are more generally applicable.

The authors observe:

> ... students and supervisors [in the survey] agreed on the basis for co-authorship of publications. Most students and supervisors thought that co-authorship was appropriate only when the supervisors had contributed both intellectual input and had written sections of the manuscript. (Christian et al., 1997: 30)

key points

If the issue of co-authorship is worrying you and others in your research group, meet and decide on strategies to resolve the situation.

Christian et al. suggest discussing this issue with supervisors early in the research to avoid conflict. As a guide to determining a supervisor's contribution, they also advise using Galindo-Leal's table (cited in Christian et al., 1997: 30) to assess the percentage input of a supervisor in five categories: planning;

executing (for example, a test or experiment); interpreting; analysing; and writing, which you can try if you wish.

A further issue turns on whose name should go first on the publication – presumably yours if you have done most of the work, though practice can vary. While co-authored publications from thesis work are unlikely to negatively affect the requirement of originality, you could also discuss this with your supervisor.

Targeting an appropriate journal

Although rejections are part of the business of publishing, you can minimize the possibility of rejection by avoiding inappropriate journals. If your research is highly specialist, there may be only one or two journals in which to publish. Otherwise, before you act, consult with your supervisor about suitable journals for publication. A journal's impact factor may be a consideration, but there is some controversy around this (see, for example, Van Aalst's (2010) discussion of impact, especially as it relates to Google Scholar). Also, take note, during reading, of where significant scholars in your research field are publishing.

Profiling the targeted journal

To determine the fit between your paper and the targeted journal, construct a profile of that journal. Doing this will also aid the writing process if you are a sole or first author on a joint publication.

 exercise: building a journal profile

Consider carefully the following questions (add your own too) and take some notes on your findings:

- How often is the journal published? Might time delay in publishing, say yearly, affect the relevance of your paper (in fast-moving research areas material becomes dated quickly)?
- What are the scope and aims of the journal? This information is usually provided at the front end of journals (online and print); if it is not, quickly review abstracts and/or introductions to see what types of content are favoured. Does your content seem to fit the

(Continued)

journal's profile (for example, a theoretical versus a practical focus, a preference for more multidisciplinary-type articles, professional or academic)?

- What appears to be the reach of the journal's audience – broad general interest? Inter- or cross-disciplinary interest? Disciplinary interest or a specialist audience within your discipline? Would your paper have the right appeal?
- What quality indicators or scholarly attributes can you isolate to help determine the status of the journal – is it well known in your research area?

Shaping a paper for publication

Having identified an appropriate journal, obtain instructions to authors for publication. These are sometimes printed at the back of journals, or you may need to write for them or download them from the Internet if the journal is online. These editorial instructions are highly prescriptive and cannot be negotiated. Follow them meticulously, and make sure your paper conforms in all respects before forwarding it to the publishers. Instructions may consist of several pages covering many details of journal house style and formatting preferences, all of which will need to be incorporated in your paper.

Being professional

Do adopt a professional approach to preparation of your manuscript for, as suggested: 'Traits of successful research and practitioner authors include being systematic, persistent and amenable to editing and revising their manuscripts in order to make them publishable' (Chisholm, 2007: 139).

Focusing the abstract

Give the aspect of persuasion careful thought when writing the abstract (or the introduction if an abstract is not required).

 **key points**

Convey the value or significance of your research to journal readers.

Ask yourself:

- What potential body of readers of this journal might be interested in my article, or aspects of it, and why?
- How can I convey to those readers what is innovative, different, important or exciting about the research presented in my paper?

Do think carefully about these questions. The idea is to attract as many potential readers as possible. You could review and compare abstracts of published authors in your journal of interest by applying the → exercise on 'Mastering disciplinary writing practices' in Chapter 2, which is designed to direct your attention away from content to composition practices and processes – take up what seems appropriate.

Reviewing scholarly practices

The value of the exercise just mentioned is reinforced by a seminal linguistics study that is contextually relevant. In his substantial investigation of the introductions of published articles in mainly science disciplines (some social sciences), John Swales proposed the CARS (Creating a Research Space) model of journal article introductions (Figure 12.1). The arrows on the right indicate the declining persuasive effort required by a writer in moving from the point of convincing a reader of the significance, value or importance of the research, to explicit statements on the nature of the research presented in the paper.

Compare this CARS model with introductions of articles in the journal you have selected. Not all science articles evidence these types of successive moves, or even different ordering of the moves, in their introductions, but many do. Many of the moves indicated also appear in the introductions of articles in areas other than science, and in many theses too. The CARS model is at least a fine example of how to go about uncovering composition or organizational strategies being applied in the writing of journal articles (not just the introduction), or any other type of writing for that matter.

Engaging the reader

Over 15 years of linguistic research in academic writing has shown that academics work hard to engage readers and get them on side, and that academic writing is not as impersonal as might be thought:

> ... while impersonality may often be institutionally sanctified, it is constantly transgressed. This is generally because the choices which realise explicit writer presence ... are closely associated with authorial identity and authority. (Hyland 2001b: 209)

223

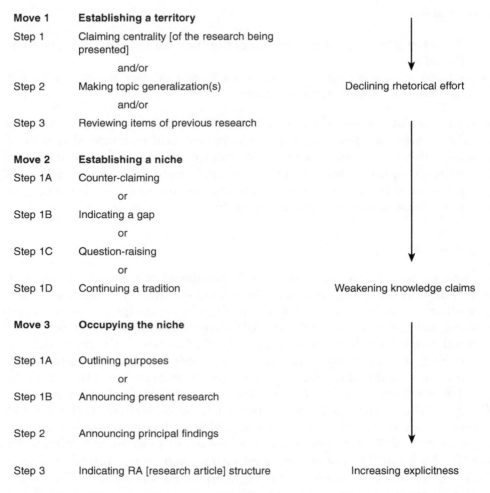

Move 1	**Establishing a territory**	
Step 1	Claiming centrality [of the research being presented]	
	and/or	
Step 2	Making topic generalization(s)	Declining rhetorical effort
	and/or	
Step 3	Reviewing items of previous research	
Move 2	**Establishing a niche**	
Step 1A	Counter-claiming	
	or	
Step 1B	Indicating a gap	
	or	
Step 1C	Question-raising	
	or	
Step 1D	Continuing a tradition	Weakening knowledge claims
Move 3	**Occupying the niche**	
Step 1A	Outlining purposes	
	or	
Step 1B	Announcing present research	
Step 2	Announcing principal findings	
Step 3	Indicating RA [research article] structure	Increasing explicitness

FIGURE 12.1   Creating a Research Space – the CARS model of journal introductions (Swales, 1990: 141)

Ken Hyland, a noted linguist and scholar, has studied different aspects of what might be called 'the insider ethos' of writing papers. Presently relevant is his study of reader engagement (2001a). Hyland points out: 'Writers construct an audience by drawing on their knowledge of earlier texts and relying on readers' abilities to recognize intertextuality between texts' (2001a: 551). (By intertextuality, he means the way in which the same practices recur in different disciplinary texts, and sometimes more generally in academic texts.)

Constructing an audience involves varied aims that can be summarized in paraphrase from Hyland (2001a) as follows:

Soliciting reader solidarity, trying to encourage particular reactions, securing reader agreement, inviting reader collusion, manoeuvring readers to see things in the same way as you do, positioning readers as fellow-travellers, appealing to collective understandings, predicting and responding to possible objections and alternative interpretations, and so forth.

Drawing on a corpus of 240 research articles and interviews with academics from the same disciplines, Hyland identified strategies for how academic writers engage their readers to achieve these aims. Table 12.1 is a tabulation of his characterization of these strategies, which contribute to a strong

TABLE 12.1   Strategies for engaging the reader

Strategy	Examples
Using inclusive first person, indefinite and second person pronouns	'**One might argue** that in order to understand the codes, the learner needs to become …' '**We know**, however, it is only in the last few years that …' '**We can readily see** that there are two kinds of …' 'If you concede that mental properties have causal powers … then you **must consider** the causal role of mental properties to be somehow dependent on the causal role of physical properties.'
Making references to shared knowledge – perhaps to concede a point only to turn the reader towards your own argument	(The adverbial phrase *of course* seems important here.) '**Of course**, we know that the indigenous communities of today have been reorganized by the Catholic church in colonial times and after.' 'The **obviously** correct relation between these two lengths is …' 'Chesterton **was of course wrong** to suppose that …'
Using directives	(Includes imperatives, and obligation modals referring to actions of the reader – for example, must, ought, should, have to, need to, etc.) '**A distinction must be made between …**' '**What we now need to examine is** whether there is more to constancy than this.' '**Hence it is necessary to understand the …**'
Using questions both real and rhetorical	('Real' questions are not all that common, but are sometimes set up to generate interest and provoke reader thought in concluding comments.) 'Do these findings mean that the current approach needs to be modified or that an entirely new approach needs to be developed?' (The 'rhetorical' question is more commonly found. It may be used in an introduction to 'establish a niche'.) 'How can these findings be reconciled? Our goal in this paper is to offer an explanation of these …' (Or as a transition device, say between paragraphs.) 'What is it then that the Zapatistas want?' (Note comments in 'Strategies for linking paragraphs' in Chapter 4 on using the rhetorical question as a transition device.)
Using asides addressed to the reader (sometimes marked off from the ongoing flow of the text)	'And – **as I believe many TESOL [Teaching English as a Second Language] professionals will readily acknowledge** – critical thinking has now begun to make its mark …' '**It is worth noting in passing**, that the conscience of those engaged in the moral condemnation that accompanied such reporting does not seem to have been greatly troubled by …'

Source: Collated from Hyland (2001a).

authoritative voice. (See → 'Bringing examiners into view' in Chapter 10.) There are also other strategies, such as 'boosters' (for example, indeed, it is clear that, undoubtedly, in fact), as discussed in Hyland and Tse's later reappraisal of such strategies (2004: 168). Hyland's body of work has much to offer the diligent, interested student (see, for example, Hyland (1996) on the significance of 'hedging' in scientific articles, or Hyland (2002b) on argument and engagement in academic writing).

It is the use of strategies of this type that demonstrates the extent to which all communication, including academic writing, is indeed a 'social process' (Bazerman, 1988: 251), or, better still, a social practice of the academy.

exercise: identify disciplinary practices for engaging the reader

Step 1

Select two or three journal articles in your discipline, articles you are reading for your research.

Step 2

Skim them with a view to identifying and highlighting any practices of the type in Table 12.1. Think about the impact such practices have on you as reader.

Approaching a book publisher

While finding an interested publisher is certainly not easy, the degree of difficulty could depend on the *marketability* of your proposed book. Occasionally, students have had publishers interested well before completing their theses because their research was topical and of high interest to a wider audience. But this is not usual. If you are writing a thesis with a view to turning it into a book, discuss early on with your supervisor and other colleagues ways in which you might reasonably modify the writing of your thesis to cut down on the amount of rewriting you will have to do for book publication.

Strategic considerations

If you are planning to approach a publishing house, there are a few matters to consider upfront.

Publishing houses have different requirements. They are not likely to welcome whole theses being forwarded, although some might accept electronically a full manuscript of a reworked thesis at the point of approach – you would need to check. Well-known publishers have websites, so do clarify the precise steps you need to take in approaching any particular publisher.

The proposal

You will need to produce a 'proposal'. Again proposal formats are different for different publishing houses; you should be able to download a set of guidelines from the relevant website. Be sure to write to specific requirements under the given sub-headings. You should also be able to identify on the site the appropriate editor to whom your proposal should be sent, and whether or not it is acceptable to do this by email. Proposals usually contain information of this type:

- A synopsis of your intention in producing the book – its justification, its importance or its topicality.
- A comparison of competitive publications in your area: how your manuscript differs, what it has to offer that others do not, its unique qualities.
- A table of contents outline; perhaps an introduction and/or a sample chapter.

 **key points**

Your proposal will be important in sparking initial interest, so do give it careful thought.

You will certainly need to address the issue of the **intended market** (publishing houses care about sales) – some questions you will need to grapple with being:

- Who do I see as my potential audience?
- How broad might the base of this audience be? Is interest likely to be generated beyond my subject speciality (a good idea in the current marketing climate)? If yes, among what types of readers and why?
- Why might people want to read my book instead of another on the same or a cognate subject?
- Why might they want to read my book alongside already published books on the subject? What am I adding in terms of value?
- Is my book likely to be included as a compulsory or recommended text for any course/s?

Talk over these questions with colleagues before writing your proposal. If your proposal is accepted (perhaps after being sent for peer review – see → the next section), you will then confront the challenge of turning your thesis into a book.

At this point, stop thinking in terms of your thesis, and start thinking in terms of a manuscript you want to publish. Talk to as many academic colleagues as you can (particularly those who have published books) for advice on what they think you will need to take into account during the rewrite for publication.

As you have an entirely new audience (no longer your thesis examiners), the introduction will need to be reshaped to address their interests. Also, a book typically has less detail and a less rigorously formal style than a thesis. The nature of your audience, however, will impact on the extent of rewriting required. A more specialist academic audience would involve less reworking than would be the case for a broader, more general readership.

The peer review process

It is highly likely your paper will be sent to referees (reviewers) if you are approaching a scholarly journal, and almost certain your book proposal will be sent for review.

Journal editors are concerned to select papers they consider most representative of the journal's interests (scope and aims), and the best available to maintain their reputation. Publishing houses too have reputations to maintain, and they are very interested in the market place, so your intended market *will* matter. The higher the status of the journal or the more prestigious the publishing house, the more advantage the editors have in selection, and the more care they are likely to exercise in ensuring they make the best possible choices. This is where referees come in.

Many quality journals are called refereed journals, meaning that articles published in them have been reviewed by outside referees or readers before acceptance for publication. Editors of these journals select papers from those they receive and send them on to reviewers who are scholarly experts in the field of research being addressed in your paper. Publishing houses have a similar procedure with book proposals.

Questions addressed by referees

Referees of your journal manuscript or book proposal will be asked to address questions of this type (articles and books have not been separated out here because for more academic publications similar types of questions will be asked, although questions specific to your particular book proposal or article will be included):

- Is there a relevant and informative title – 'eye-catching' may also be appropriate in some cases?
- Is there a clear and concise abstract? (An abstract is not always required, even for certain peer-reviewed journals, as some students in both the arts and sciences point out.)
- Is the article likely to have the right appeal for journal readers? Or is the book likely to appeal to the intended market as laid out in the proposal? Do you think people would actually buy it and why?
- Does the research reported on contribute new, innovative and/or significant insights? As suggested above, this needs to be foregrounded in your abstract and/or introduction.
- Does the introduction provide appropriate and sufficient context, in terms of breadth and depth, to put the audience in the picture?
- Are the foci, objectives and (perhaps) methodology or procedure all clearly laid out?
- How sound is the methodology or how well integrated is the theory (if relevant)?
- Does the paper/book evidence logical rigour? (For example, in terms of the validity of arguments, or interpretations of results or data, including speculations that arise from these.)
- Are the coverage and use of references in the paper/book adequate, and are the referencing details correct?
- Is the paper/book well-written? (For example, clearly focused, well organized and coherently developed, concisely written, and correct grammar/spelling.)
- Does the style of the book have the right appeal for the intended audience? (For example, use of sophisticated disciplinary terminology will not suit a broader, more general audience.)
- What do you see as the strengths/weaknesses of this paper/book?
- Are there any ways in which the paper/book can be improved?
- Should the paper/book be published? Revised? Not published? Why or why not?

Dealing with the outcome of peer review

Accept

Your paper has been accepted as it is, or with only minor revisions, after review by referees. Or you have been offered a contract on the basis of peer review of your book proposal. Congratulations.

Revise and resubmit

They are interested – great – but you are asked to make substantial revisions. As you read the reviewers' reports, you could experience a confusion of feelings (outrage, embarrassment, anger or disappointment), as does happen. Do not be surprised if the criticisms of both content and style are extensive; this is not unusual. Put the reviewers' reports aside for a few days until you have calmed down; until you have recovered from having your work picked over in such a humbling way; until you have regained your equilibrium and a bit more objectivity.

When you return to your manuscript, consider following these points:

- Attend to minor criticisms.
- Consider carefully all substantive criticisms. Then, implement worthwhile suggestions, noting precisely what you have done to address criticisms and where (give page numbers). Do be prepared to justify your position, probably to the editor, with respect to suggestions you do not wish to take up. Some criticisms might seem to you to miss the point, to be off the point, or to be unbalanced or biased.
- With a book, you may be asked to write a response to reviewers' reports detailing how you will address criticisms and suggestions for improvement. It could be that not until you have done this will your proposal be taken to a 'Proposal meeting' where it will be decided whether or not to offer you a contract.
- Be prepared for the possibility of having your manuscript go back and forth between yourself and editors more than once as you try to meet suggested improvements and negotiate with them.

Peer review can sometimes be harrowing. But it can also be a great learning process if you approach it that way. Of course, if your thesis is to be a set of published articles, peer review prior to publication is bound to secure positive examination.

Reject

Your paper/book proposal has been reviewed and rejected, and you are discouraged. This is understandable. But do not let the rejection bruise your confidence too badly; even experienced authors have confronted rejection at times. This need not be the end of the story for you, and will not be if you think of the process of getting published as a tough training course, with you just starting out.

With the feedback you receive from editors and/or reviewers, you can now consider reworking your manuscript to send elsewhere, or the editors might already have suggested more appropriate journals or publishers to contact, which we strongly advise you to do. You now have the advantage of scholarly input in your second attempt at publication. Keep trying. Do not give up too easily.

Forming a publication syndicate

A variation on organizing a thesis-writing group, as discussed in Chapter 10, is to form a 'publication syndicate', as laid out by Sadler (1999). Doing this would be particularly useful if you and other students in your research group are producing a set of published articles as a thesis.

The general idea is to discuss members' draft manuscripts in structured meetings organized by the convenor of the group. As Sadler (1999: 144) points out:

The syndicate itself simply consists of a group of like-minded [students/academics] who agree to act cooperatively to further their mutual scholarship and publication. The members should be committed to the task of accelerating the production of either manuscripts for publication in academic journals, or chapters for publication in edited books.

In such a group, it would be possible to take up many of the issues discussed in this chapter at relevant points in the publication process, to give each other feedback on drafts, to encourage each other, and to share difficulties and triumphs along the way.

 **further resources**

Belcher, W.L. (2009) *Writing your Journal Article in Twelve Weeks: A Guide to Academic Publishing*. Thousand Oaks, CA: Sage Publications. An excellent resource for those of you starting out or struggling to get your work published that takes you inside journal publishing processes and enables you to embed daily writing around all else that you may have to do.

Caro, S. (2009) *How to Publish your PhD*. London: Sage Publications. Provides valuable insights from an insider perspective into the fluid world of academic publishing and practical guidance on the processes involved – a must if you want to maximize your chances for book publication.

Cohn, E.R. (2004) 'Beyond the electronic portfolio: a lifetime personal web space', *Educause Quarterly*, 27(4): 7–10. A short article that may be a little old, but it nevertheless points to some of the basic principles of developing an ongoing web presence.

Appendix: Words and Phrases for Developing Discussions

To list, or show 'time' relationships

First/second/third, etc.
After that
When
Before

At the same time
Initially
Thereafter
Proceeding from

Previously
Last/Finally
Next/My next point
Earlier

Simultaneously
Already
Subsequently

Now
Afterwards
Meanwhile
Presently or
currently
Concurrently
Later
Following

To add information

Furthermore/Further
Moreover
In addition/Additionally
Likewise

Also
As well
Similarly
Supplementary to this

Besides
Another reason
The factor/point is

To endorse others' work (or to use theirs to endorse yours)*

Affirms
Concurs
Validates
Approves

Verifies
Ratifies

Agrees
Confirms
Supports
Conforms

Validates
Vindicates

Endorses
Makes clear
Corroborates
X is of the same
opinion
Repeats

To question or problematize others' work*

Accedes	Assumes	Claims
Concedes	Confirms	Makes clear
Conjectures	Contends	Contrasts
Dismisses	Generalizes	Presumes
Speculates	X goes so far as to suggest	Denies
Contradicts	Surmises	Professes
Declares		

To present a neutral stance on others' work*

According to X ...	Analyses	Cites
Comments	Compares	Considers
Defines	Demonstrates	Believes
Details	Elaborates	Explains
Indicates	In the view of X ...	Justifies
X makes the point that ...	Notes	Observes
Points out	Posits	Postulates
Predicts	Proposes	Puts forward
Reports	States	Theorizes
X's approach indicates that ...		

To show a causal (cause and effect) relationship

So	Since this is so	Therefore
Consequently	Hence	Due to
Thus	Because of this	It follows
For	As a result ...	The 'if/then' construction
Accordingly	Correspondingly	That being so

To draw a 'conclusion'

This implies/suggests/indicates/shows/establishes/demonstrates/confirms, and so on.

It can be inferred that	To sum up	In summary
In conclusion	It can be concluded that	To summarize
Finally	In closing	Lastly
In ending		

To clarify a previously stated idea

In other words
To put this another way

Put succinctly
That is

In effect
By this I mean

(Or simply restate the idea in a different way)

To introduce a 'contrasting' or 'qualifying' idea

In contrast
However
Even so
Unlike

Conversely
Nevertheless
On the other hand
Yet

But
Although
Alternatively
Whereas
(then bring in
contrast)

Nonetheless
Regardless

In spite of this
Despite

Notwithstanding

To provide an 'example'

For example
..., including ...

For instance
..., such as ...

To illustrate
..., as is illustrated
by ...

* Based on Coffin, C., et al., (2003) *Teaching Academic Writing. A Toolkit for Higher Education.* London: Routledge.

References

Alley, M. (2000) *The Craft of Editing: A Guide for Managers, Scientists, and Engineers*. New York: Springer.

Alley, M. (2003) *The Craft of Scientific Presentations: Critical Steps to Succeed and Critical Errors to Avoid*. New York: Springer-Verlag.

Bakhtin, M. (1986) *Speech Genres and Other Late Essays*. Eds C. Emerson and M. Holquist. Trans. V.W. McGee. Austin, TX: University of Texas Press.

Ballard, B.A. (1995) 'The quality of the ANU PhD thesis: an analysis of a sample of examiners' reports', occasional paper, The Graduate School, The Australian National University.

Bazerman, C. (1988) *Shaping Written Knowledge: The Genre and Activity of the Experimental Article in Science*. London: University of Wisconsin Press.

Belcher, W.L. (2009) *Writing your Journal Article in Twelve Weeks: A Guide to Academic Publishing*. Thousand Oaks, CA: Sage Publications.

Berkenkotter, C. and Huckin, T. (1995) *Genre Knowledge in Disciplinary Communication: Cognition/Culture/Power*. Hillsdale, NJ: Lawrence Erlbaum.

Biggam, J. (2008) *Succeeding with your Master's Dissertation: A Step-by-step Handbook*. Maidenhead: Open University Press.

Bolker, J. (1998) *Writing Your Dissertation in Fifteen Minutes a Day: A Guide to Starting, Revising, and Finishing Your Doctoral Thesis*. New York: Henry Holt.

boyd, d. (2011) 'Social network sites as networked publics: affordances, dynamics, and implications', in Z. Papacharissi (ed.), *Networked Self: Identity, Community, and Culture on Social Network Sites*. New York: Routledge. pp. 39–58.

Bunton, D. (2005) 'The structure of PhD conclusion chapters', *Journal of English for Academic Purposes*, 4(3): 207–24.

Burton, R., Barlow, N. and Barker, C. (2010) 'Using visual tools for analysis and learning', University of Huddersfield. http://eprints.hud.ac.uk/7843/ (accessed 20 October 2010).

Caro, S. (2009) *How to Publish your PhD*. London: Sage Publications.

Cham, J. 'Piled higher and deeper: a graduate student comic strip collection'. http://www.phdcomics.com/ (accessed 20 December 2010).

Chisholm, K. (2007) 'Strategies for publishing in scholarly HRD journals', *Human Resource Development Quarterly*, 18(1): 139–47.

Christian, R., Davies, K., de Chazal, J., Krebs, E. and Melbourne, B. (1997) *PhD Supervision: A Guide for Students and Supervisors*. Canberra: The Australian National University.

Clanchy, J. and Ballard, B. (1997) *Essay Writing for Students: A Practical Guide*. 3rd edn. Melbourne: Longman.

Coffin, C., Curry, M.J., Goodman, S., Hewings, A., Lillis, T.M. and Swann, J. (2003) *Teaching Academic Writing. A Toolkit for Higher Education*. London: Routledge.

Cohn, E.R. (2004) 'Beyond the electronic portfolio: a lifetime personal web space', *Educause Quarterly*, 27(4): 7–10 .

Covey, S. (2004) *The 7 Habits of Highly Effective People: Powerful Lessons in Personal Change*. New York: Free Press.

Cryer, P. (1996) *The Research Student's Guide to Success*. Buckingham: Open University Press.

Davis, L. and McKay, S. (1996) *Structures and Strategies: An Introduction to Academic Writing*. Melbourne: Macmillan Education Australia.

Denscombe, M. (1998) *The Good Research Guide: For Small-scale Social Research Projects*. Buckingham: Open University Press.

Di Gregorio, S. (2000) 'Using NVIVO for your literature review', paper presented at 'Strategies in qualitative research: issues and results from analysis using QSR NVIVO and NUD*IST' conference, Institute of Education, London, 29–30 September. http://www.sdgassociates.com/downloads/literature_review.pdf (accessed 25 October 2010).

Downes, S. (1995–2000) 'Stephen Downes guide to the logical fallacies'. http://web.uvic.ca/psyc/skelton/Teaching/General%20Readings/Logical%20Falllacies.htm (accessed 25 November 2010).

Dunleavy, P. (2003) *Authoring a PhD: How to Plan, Draft, Write and Finish a Doctoral Thesis or Dissertation*. Basingstate: Palgrave Macmillan.

Fairclough, N. (1992) 'The appropriacy of "appropriateness"', in N. Fairclough (ed.), *Critical Language Awareness*. London: Longman.

Fink, A. (2009) *Conducting Research Literature Reviews: From the Internet to Paper*. 3rd edn. London: Sage Publications.

Fowler, H.R. and Aaron, J.E. (2001) *The Little, Brown Handbook*. 9th edn. New York: Longman.

Garrard, J. (2007) *Health Sciences Literature Made Easy: The Matrix Method*. 2nd edn. Boston: Jones and Bartlett.

Gillett, A. (2011) 'Using English for academic purposes: a guide for students in higher education. http://www.uefap.com/ (accessed 8 November 2010).

Gilmore, J., Strickland, D., Timmerman, B., Maher, M. and Feldon, D. (2010) 'Weeds in the flower garden: an exploration of plagiarism in graduate students' research proposals and its connection to enculturation, ESL, and contextual factors', *International Journal for Educational Integrity*, 6(1): 13–28.

Holbrook, A., Bourke, S., Lovat, T. and Dally, K. (2004) 'Qualities and characteristics in the written reports of doctoral thesis examiners', *Australian Journal of Educational & Developmental Psychology*, 4: 126–45.

Hyland, K. (1996) 'Writing without conviction? Hedging in science research articles', *Applied Linguistics*, 17(4): 433–53.

Hyland, K. (2001a) 'Bringing in the reader: addressee features in academic articles', *Written Communication*, 18(4): 549–74.

Hyland, K. (2001b) 'Humble servants of the discipline? Self-mention in research articles', *English for Specific Purposes*, 20: 207–226.

Hyland, K. (2002a) 'Authority and invisibility: authorial identity in academic writing', *Journal of Pragmatics*, 34: 1091–112.

Hyland, K. (2002b) 'Directives: argument and engagement in academic writing', *Applied Linguistics*, 23(2): 215–39.

Hyland, L. and Tse, P. (2004) 'Metadiscourse in academic writing: a reappraisal', *Applied Linguistics*, 25(2): 156–77.

'Improving your sentence structure'. Writing Services, The Learning Commons, University of Guelph. http://www.lib.uoguelph.ca/assistance/writing_services/components/documents/sentence.pdf (accessed 12 October 2010).

Jordan, R.R. (1980) *Academic Writing Course*. London: Collins.

Kane, T.S. (1988) *The New Oxford Guide to Writing*. Oxford: Oxford University Press.

Kaufer, D., Geisler, C. and Neuwirth, C. (1989) *Arguing from Sources: Exploring Issues through Reading and Writing.* New York: Harcourt Brace Jovanovich.

Mainhard, T., van der Rijst, R., van Tartwijk, J. and Wubbels, T. (2009) 'A model for the supervisor–doctoral student relationship', *Higher Education,* 58(3): 359–73.

McCloskey, D. (1985) 'Economical writing', *Economic Inquiry,* 23: 2. (Extracted from *PCI Fulltext,* published by ProQuest Information and Learning Company, 2002. pp. 187–221.)

Murray, R. (2003) *How to Survive your Viva.* Buckingham: Open University Press.

Oliver, P. (2004) *Writing your Thesis.* London: Sage Publications.

Orwell, G. (1946) 'Politics and the English language'. http://www.orwell.ru/library/essays/politics/english/e_polit (accessed 19 December 2010).

Perry, C.P. (1998) 'A structured approach to presenting PhD theses', thesis resource paper. http://www.scu.edu.au/schools/gcm/ar/art/cperry.html (accessed 22 November 2010).

Phillips, E. and Pugh, D.S. (1994) *How to Get a PhD: A Handbook for Students and their Supervisors.* 2nd edn. Buckingham: Open University Press.

Popken, R.L. (1987) 'Academic writing', *Written Communication,* 4(2): 209–28.

Preece, R. (1994) *Starting Research: An Introduction to Academic Research and Dissertation Writing.* London: Pinter.

Sadler, D.R. (1999) *Managing your Academic Career: Strategies for Success.* Sydney: Allen and Unwin.

Sadler, D.R. (2006) *Up the Publication Road.* 3rd edn. Milperra, NSW: HERDSA.

Shephard, K. (2005) *Presenting at Conferences, Seminars and Meetings.* London: Sage Publications.

Sprague, J. and Stuart, D. (2008) *The Speaker's Compact Handbook.* 2nd edn. Belmont, CA: Wadsworth.

Strunk, W. Jr and White, E.B. (2000) *The Elements of Style.* 4th edn. Boston, MA: Allyn and Bacon.

Swales, J. and Feak, C. (2004) *Academic Writing for Graduate Students: Essential Tasks and Skills.* 2nd edn. Ann Arbor, MI: University of Michigan Press.

Swales, J.M. (1990) *Genre Analysis. English in Academic and Reserach Settings.* Cambridge: Cambridge University Press.

'What is an academic essay?' Sussex Centre for Language Studies.

Taylor, D. (undated) *'The literature review: A few tips on conducting it',* Health Sciences Writing Centre, University of Toronto. http://www.writing.utoronto.ca/advice/specific-types-of-writing/literature-review (accessed 15 March 2010).

Tufte, E. (2003) 'PowerPoint is evil. Power corrupts. PowerPoint corrupts absolutely', *Wired Magazine,* Issue 11.09. September. http://www.wired.com/wired/archive/11.09/ppt2.html (accessed 31 December 2010).

Van Aalst, J. (2010) 'Using Google Scholar to estimate the impact of journal articles in education', *Educational Researcher,* 39(5): 387–400.

Wallace, M. and Wray, A. (2006) *Critical Reading and Writing for Postgraduates.* London: Sage Publications.

Watts, M. (2003) 'The holy grail: in pursuit of the dissertation proposal', dissertation proposal workshop: 'Process and parameters'. Institute of International Studies, UC Berkeley. http://globetrotter.berkeley.edu/DissPropWorkshop/process/ (accessed 3 January 2011).

Webster, J. and Watson, R.T. (2002) 'Analyzing the past to prepare for the future: writing a literature review', *MIS Quarterly,* 26(2): xiii–xxiii.

Weston, A. (2009) *A Rulebook for Arguments.* 4th edn. Indianapolis, IN: Hackett.

Woolsey, J.D. (1989) 'Combating poster fatigue: how to use visual grammar and analysis to effect better visual communication', *Trends in Neurosciences,* 12(9): 325–32.

Index